JEWELRY
GEM CUTTING
AND METALCRAFT

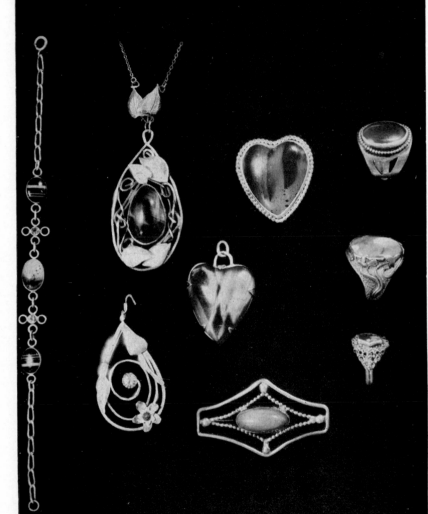

JEWELRY
GEM CUTTING
AND METALCRAFT

BY WILLIAM T. BAXTER, M.A.

INSTRUCTOR, JEWELRY AND GEM CUTTING
WOODROW WILSON HIGH SCHOOL, WASHINGTON, D. C.

THIRD EDITION, REVISED AND ENLARGED

McGRAW-HILL BOOK COMPANY, INC.

New York   London   Toronto

PREFACE

During the past decade there has been an ever-increasing interest in both gem cutting and jewelry making.

This is evidenced by the sale of books devoted to gem cutting and jewelry making; the increasing number of home craftsmen interested in gem cutting and jewelry making; the introduction of jewelry making and gem cutting in industrial arts courses in high schools and colleges and in evening classes for adults; the manufacture of equipment designed for the craftsman; the formation, on an amateur basis, of many lapidary societies in all parts of the country; and the overnight success of the *Lapidary Journal*, a national magazine started in 1947 "for the gem cutter, collector and jewelry craftsman."

The author, out of sheer curiosity, without having seen anyone cut a gem stone, cut his first cabochon gem stone in 1935, using meager equipment, all of which was improvised. He was assisted by several of his high school students. In a few weeks students— both boys and girls—in the author's jewelry-making classes were cutting and polishing their own stones.

Jewelry, Gem Cutting and Metalcraft was first published in 1938. The first edition had four printings. The second edition was published in 1942. It had 12 printings.

This third edition contains a great deal of new material. Much of it has never before appeared in book form. The section on gem cutting has been completely rewritten and brought up to date. Also included in this edition is a chapter on facet cutting of gem stones, using modern equipment and methods.

The section devoted to jewelry making has been completely rewritten and enlarged, with new drawings and many new illustrations of handmade jewelry. There is a chapter on centrifugal casting of jewelry, using the "lost wax" method. Students in the author's high school classes have for several years used this method in making many of the mountings for stones they have cut and polished. The chapter on Agate-handled Tableware contains complete instructions for making forks, spoons, letter openers, and other objects made of sterling with agate handles.

Photographs of a number of pieces of jewelry described have appeared in various national magazines illustrating articles written by the author.

A list of firms dealing in various equipment and supplies needed in the different types of work is given on pages 322 to 325 to help those who do not know where to secure their equipment and materials. A list of books and magazines that should be of interest will be found on pages 326 to 328.

WILLIAM T. BAXTER

ACKNOWLEDGMENTS

I should like to express my gratitude and appreciation to all of those who have helped in the preparation of this volume:

To the M. D. R. Manufacturing Company of Los Angeles, for the material on Facet-cut Gems; to Raymond M. Addison of San Jose, Calif., for Cameo and Intaglio Stone Carving; to Dr. Henry C. Dake, editor of the *Mineralogist*, for the section on Identification of Gem Stones and Gem Minerals; to George T. Davey of Van Nuys, Calif., for information on cutting cabochons from synthetic corundum and spinel; and to the following persons and firms for technical information and other assistance:

Kerr Manufacturing Co., Detroit, Mich.; Torit Manufacturing Co., St. Paul, Minn.; Alexander Saunders & Co., New York City; Handy & Harman, New York City; Wildberg Bros. Smelting & Refining Co., Los Angeles, Calif.; John M. Grieger, Pasadena, Calif.; Vaden Covington, Redlands, Calif.; J. W. Anderson, Baltimore, Md.; National Welding & Equipment Co., San Francisco, Calif.; Linde Air Products Co., New York City; The Carborundum Company, Niagara Falls, N. Y.; Norton Company, Worcester, Mass.; National Bureau of Standards, Washington, D. C.; The Copper and Brass Research Association, New York City; Lelande Quick, and the *Lapidary Journal*, Hollywood, Calif.; Dr. Henry C. Dake, Portland, Ore.; and R. W. Mitchell, T. L. Daniel, C. B. Rosenberg, Dr. R. W. MacCorkell, and A. B. Meiklejohn, all of Los Angeles.

My appreciation is also extended to the students, past and present, of the jewelry and gem-cutting classes of Woodrow Wilson High

School, Washington, D. C., for the privilege of photographing their work. I am especially grateful to Edward R. Bush, Bethesda, Md., a former student and personal friend, for the privilege of photographing his handmade jewelry and for assistance in experiments with the centrifugal casting of jewelry.

CONTENTS

synthetic boules; Drilling; How to cut a sphere; Making a doublet;
Horizontal laps; Inlaid paperweights; Cameo and intaglio stone carving; Facet-cut gems; Cutting and polishing titania; Care of equipment; Optical properties of gems.

Methods of testing gems; Physical properties; Color; Hardness;
Specific gravity; Specific-gravity fluids; Examining for flaws and inclusions; Ultraviolet light; Luster, chatoyancy, asterism, fracture, and
cleavage; Optical methods; Reflection test; Use of dichroscope;
Polariscope; Refractometer; Polarizing microscope; Synthetic gems
and altered gems; Agate coloring; Qualities enhancing values in gems.

FOREWORD

The foreword written for the first edition of this book called attention to the fact that it is a volume written by a true craftsman concerning a craft which he loves, by a teacher concerning his own work in which he has been successful.

It is interesting to know that the book has performed a real service, a service to other teachers in other schools whose interest has been excited by the author's practical and informing exposition and by his investigations into the whole field of jewelry making, gem cutting, and metalcraft as a hobby.

In the schools in the District of Columbia which have classes in these crafts, we have observed with great satisfaction the happy and concentrated enthusiasm of our students. We rejoice with the author of this book that it has played so significant a part in the development of these courses in our schools.

NORMAN J. NELSON
First Assistant Superintendent
Senior High Schools, Divisions 1–9

Washington, D. C.

INTRODUCTION

If further proof is needed that amateur gem cutting and jewelry making has increased in recent years to the point where it has now become America's third largest hobby, it can be found in the fact that *Jewelry, Gem Cutting and Metalcraft*, of which this is the third edition, is now in its seventeenth printing. This is phenomenal for a craft book, and it happens because Mr. Baxter's book has filled a great need in the meager literature on a "lost art."

For the lapidary art (gem cutting) was man's *first* art; his first form of self-expression, before he ever had a written language or wrote a song; before he invented his first crude musical instrument or painted his first pictures on the cave walls of France. With the discovery of faceting in the sixteenth century, gem cutting became a craft whose secrets were closely guarded in guilds until very recent times. As recently as 20 years ago all the available literature in the world on the art of gem cutting could have been placed in one average-sized cigar box. With the rise of the "rock hounds" in America, those amateur geologists and mineralogists who collect rocks on week ends, there arose a desire to process some of their finds into useful and beautiful gems. The natural desire to set them in jewelry for personal adornment followed. While the literature on the subject is now extensive, it is Mr. Baxter's book that has been a bible to those seeking knowledge, because it was, for a long time, the only book combining instructions on gem grinding and gem setting.

While the hobby, or art form, is increasing rapidly all over the land, it is difficult for people on the Atlantic seaboard to believe the profound influence gem cutting has in the lives of people on the West Coast. For in one California county alone (Los Angeles) more than 30,000 persons own some form of lapidary equipment. In July, 1948, a showing of gems cut by amateurs drew more than 36,000 attendance in 3 days at Long Beach, Calif. It is safe to say that fully half of the great number of lapidaries in Los Angeles County either own or have read Mr. Baxter's book and have been helped by it.

The great reason for the growth of the gem-cutting hobby is that it presents to the American people, with a lot of leisure time because of the short work week, the opportunity to express their native Yankee ingenuity by doing something with their hands. This is as true of women as it is of men. It makes people happy, for it knows no season, is not particularly expensive (unless one chooses to make it so), is not difficult, and gives unlimited scope for the use of imagination.

Many schools in nearly every state are now teaching gem cutting and silver craft, and young people are taking their enthusiasm home to infect the rest of the family with interest in an art form that can be enjoyed by all. Mr. Baxter was one of the very first to teach these things in a public school, and his book comes out of his wide experience and contact with amateurs all over the nation. He writes from practical experience and not from theory.

This new edition of *Jewelry, Gem Cutting and Metalcraft* is completely revised, contains much new information, and will no doubt become the accepted text in craft courses and a guide to the beginner everywhere.

LELANDE QUICK
Editor of the *Lapidary Journal*

Part 1
METALCRAFT

T HERE ARE a number of metals and alloys that are suitable for the home craftsman or the student to use in making ornamental and useful projects. Copper is, however, used more than any other material.

COPPER

Copper was known to the Greeks as "chalkos" and to the Romans as "cyprium aes," later "cuprum," the names being derived from the island of Cyprus in the Mediterranean, which had a natural wealth of copper. Copper was one of the first metals of which mankind made use. When it was first produced is not definitely known, although many of the ancient peoples used it.

The prehistoric Egyptians knew how to hammer native copper into sheets, from which they made harpoons, chisels, and adzes. The Chaldeans as early as 4500 B.C. were artisans with the metal. By 2750 B.C. the coppersmiths were able to hammer and form drainpipes of copper. During the Dark Ages the copper, brass, and bronze industries, which were well established in Roman times, passed into eclipse, although they were revived about A.D. 900.

When America was discovered, the art of working copper and brass was well understood. The first rolling mill in the United States was at Waterbury, Conn., in 1802, and it was used to roll sheets for the making of metal buttons, which were popular among civilians as well as military men. This mill was driven by horsepower. In 1808 a mill was built at Attleboro, where water power took the place of horsepower. The copper used in these early mills was imported or obtained by the purchase and melting of copper articles which the colonists had brought over with them. With the development of copper mines in the Lake Superior district, an adequate supply of raw copper became available. Although the production of copper in the United States prior to 1850 was very small, the production since then has amounted to about half the world's output.

Copper is distinguished by its red color. It melts at 1981°F. and may be worked into many shapes. It is especially useful to the craftsman because it is tough and malleable and will take a good polish.

Copper is usually supplied in sheets 30 by 60 inches, 30 by 96 inches, or 36 by 96 inches, although smaller pieces may be obtained from dealers. Its thickness may be measured by either of two gauges, the English Stubs gauge, used by plumbers and copper-smiths, or the American Brown and Sharpe gauge, used by silver-smiths and art metalworkers. Copper is also designated by weight, in ounces per square foot. For example, a square foot of 20-gauge Brown and Sharpe copper weighs approximately 24 ounces and is known as 24-ounce copper; 18-gauge Brown and Sharpe weighs approximately 32 ounces to the square foot.

Copper sheets may be purchased either hot-rolled or cold-rolled. The cold-rolled copper that has been annealed is much smoother and works better.

BRASS

Brass, an alloy of copper and zinc, is one of the most useful alloys in industry. The copper content varies according to the intended use of the alloy. Brass is somewhat harder for the craftsman to work than copper, as it is less malleable and splits easily.

NICKEL SILVER

Nickel silver (German silver) is an alloy containing approximately 60 per cent copper and 20 per cent each of zinc and nickel. It is used extensively in industry as a base metal for silver plating.

MONEL METAL

Monel metal is a technically controlled alloy of two-thirds nickel and one-third copper. It originally was melted and refined from natural ore mined in Canada, which consisted of 60 to 70 per cent nickel, $1\frac{1}{2}$ per cent iron, and the remainder copper.

Monel metal is silver-white in color and takes a high polish. It can be used by the craftsman in some forms of art metal and jewelry projects. Because of its noncorrosive qualities, it is used extensively in marine construction. It is also used for making kitchen sinks, drainboards, and table tops.

PEWTER

Pewter is an alloy of tin and lead, usually about 4 parts tin to 1 part lead. It is very soft and can be readily hammered into shallow trays and plates. Articles made of pewter are usually plain, without decoration. Pewter should not be heated to anneal, because of its low melting point. As it is soft, it should need no annealing.

SOFT SOLDERING

Soft soldering is the joining together of pieces of metal by means of another metal or alloy of lower melting point.

It is usually done with a soldering copper, also known as a soldering iron, of which there are two general types. One type is heated in a gas flame or with charcoal. The other type is heated electrically, like an electric iron, by means of resistance wire.

The most common type of soft solder consists of half lead and half tin, usually called half-and-half solder. It melts at a temperature of about 375°F. Soft solder may be purchased in bar, ribbon, or wire form. The wire and ribbon forms may be obtained with a flux, either rosin, acid, or paste inside the wire.

Fig. 1.—Furnaces mounted on brick-top table. Solid flame burner; soldering copper furnace; melting furnace; enameling furnace.

Several things are necessary in order to solder successfully.

1. The work to be soldered must be clean.

2. The soldering copper must be of correct temperature, the faces tinned, and it must be large enough to heat the work properly.

3. A flux must be used to help clean the parts and to prevent the work from oxidizing when heat is applied.

4. Both solder and the place of its application must be heated to the melting point of the solder.

In preparing work to be soldered, make sure that it is clean. Scrape or file until bright, if any oxide is present.

Tinning Soldering Copper. Heat the soldering copper until it will melt the solder. File the faces, and tin each. The tinning is done by placing some flux and solder on a piece of bright tin or copper and rubbing the hot soldering copper over the solder until the solder melts and coats (tins) the face of the copper.

Another method is to use rosin and solder on a brick. Make a depression in a brick, and in the hole place some rosin and a few pieces of solder. The point of the hot copper is placed on the solder and rosin and rubbed until the solder melts and coats the faces of the copper. Wipe the point clean with a cloth.

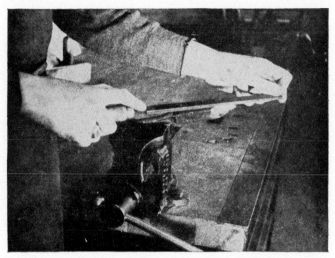

Fig. 2.—Filing a soldering copper.

Either sal ammoniac or soldering salts, dissolved in water in a small jar, makes a good solution in which to clean the soldering copper. Dip the tip of the hot copper, after filing, in this solution, and it will become bright and clean and will tin very easily. This solution will also clean a tinned copper that has become dirty through use, if the point is dipped, while hot, in the solution. Once a soldering copper has been tinned properly, it will seldom need retinning unless it is overheated.

Fluxes. There are several different kinds of fluxes that may be used in soft soldering.

For brass and copper use any of the following: rosin, soldering paste, chloride of zinc, or soldering salts.

On galvanized iron and zinc use raw muriatic acid, chloride of zinc, or soldering salts.

For black iron use chloride of zinc or soldering salts.

For soldering tin plate use rosin or soldering paste.

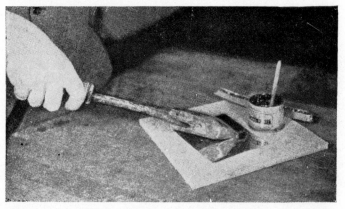

Fig. 3.—Tinning a soldering copper.

Soldering salts may be purchased in pound tins and a solution made by dissolving a small amount in water. Soldering flux, liquid or paste, may be purchased at almost any place solder is sold.

Chloride of zinc is prepared by adding small pieces of zinc to muriatic (hydrochloric) acid, which has been placed in a glass jar, until the acid no longer reacts with the zinc. This operation should be done out of doors. Add an equal amount of water to this solution before using.

Tinning the Work. After cleaning the piece to be soldered, rub some flux over the spot or seam, place a tinned face of the hot soldering copper on the work, and hold it there until the spot becomes hot. Melt a little solder on the work, and rub the copper back and forth, so as to tin the spot. More solder may then be used. Solder will not stick properly unless the work is tinned.

Solder will not stick properly to cold metal. When the work gets hot enough to melt the solder, the solder will stick. A small soldering copper cannot be used to advantage on heavy work, as it cannot heat the work properly.

Electric soldering coppers may be purchased for use where electricity, but no gas, is available. They need not be quite so large as the other type, for in using them the heat is being continuously applied.

Sweating. Sometimes it is necessary to solder one object to another and not have any solder show around the edges. In this case apply a thin coat of solder to the underside of the smaller piece, filing evenly if necessary. Apply flux to the spot on the larger piece where the ornament is to be soldered, and put the ornament in place. Wipe off all excess solder from the faces of the soldering copper, and hold the copper on top of the ornament until the solder underneath melts and joins the two pieces. This type of soldering is known as sweating.

Another method is to heat both pieces over a gas flame or with a blowpipe until the solder flows. In using the flame of the blowpipe, take care not to overheat the solder, for if heated too much it will not hold properly.

Small bits of solder may be picked up with the hot copper and transferred to the work being soldered, unless the solder is of the flux-cored type, in which case it is best to feed the solder to the work alongside the hot copper so as not to lose the flux.

Pewter Solder. Pewter, because of its low melting point, requires a special low-melting solder. Flux for pewter is prepared by mixing a few drops of hydrochloric acid in an ounce of glycerine.

ETCHING

Etching requires few tools and is an easy means of ornamenting objects made from sheet copper, brass, or silver. The object is made and polished, after which the surface is thoroughly cleaned. The design to be etched on the object is drawn full size upon paper and

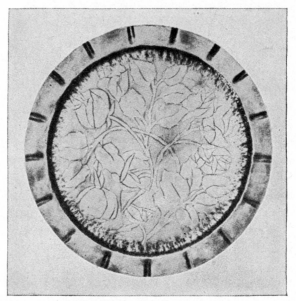

Fig. 4.—Etched copper tray.

is transferred to the surface of the project by using a piece of carbon paper.

The etched design is usually left raised, or higher than the sur-rounding metal, although it may be eaten into the metal. If the design is to be left raised, cover the design with a coat of asphaltum varnish, using an artist's brush to paint on the varnish. The lines in the design are left free of varnish. Be sure to cover with varnish the back of the project, as well as any other surfaces that are not to be eaten away. If the varnish is too thick, thin with turpentine. The varnish should be allowed to dry several hours, preferably overnight, before placing the object in the etching solution.

Prepare the etching solution by mixing 1 part nitric acid with 2 parts water in a glass or earthen vessel, *adding the acid to the water*. An old battery case makes an excellent container for the solution if small objects are to be etched. Place the object in the

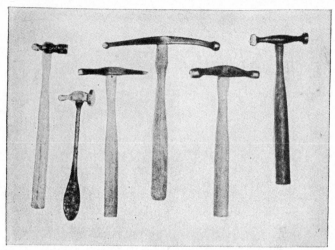

Fig. 5.—Hammers used in art metalwork. Ball peen, French chasing hammer, and raising and planishing hammers.

solution and watch closely for a few minutes. The acid should begin to eat away the metal almost immediately, the reaction forming tiny bubbles. If the reaction is too fast, the solution must be diluted with water, for the acid will eat under the edge of the asphaltum and possibly cause it to peel. A solution, especially after using, may cease to eat the metal. in which case add more acid, stirring thoroughly.

The length of time required for the etching process varies, depending upon the strength of the diluted acid and the depth of etching desired. It usually takes 45 minutes to more than an hour. The object may be taken from the solution at intervals for inspection. After the solution has eaten to the desired depth, remove the object, and wash with water. The asphaltum varnish is removed by rubbing with a cloth dampened with gasoline or turpentine. In etching the inside of a tray or bowl, the acid may be placed in the bowl.

ANNEALING

Copper and brass when subjected to hammer blows become hard and must be annealed (softened). Heat the metal over an open flame or with a torch, until it is a dull red color. Copper, like silver, may be cooled by plunging into water without affecting the metal. Brass, however, should be cooled slowly. Frequent annealings are necessary to keep the metal soft.

PICKLING

When copper or brass is heated to soften, an oxide scale forms on the surface which must be removed. Mix 1 part sulphuric acid with 10 parts water, *adding the acid to the water*. Place the solution in a large stone jar, and drop the metal into the solution while the metal is warm. If the reaction is too slow, add more acid. Use copper or brass wire or copper tongs to remove the metal. Never use an iron object, as the reaction of the iron in the acid will cause discoloring of the copper. On large pieces of work, to scour the metal with the pickle solution, use a swab made by tying a cloth on a stick. Be careful not to get the solution on your clothing. After an article is pickled, it should be washed in water.

Sparex No. 2, a scientifically developed powder for pickling non-ferrous metals, may be used. Mix 2½ pounds of the powder with 7 pints of water. It is fully active at 170°F. It has no disagreeable or corrosive fumes.

POLISHING

File marks and scratches are best removed by using fine abrasive cloth and steel wool and then buffing the surface.

The buffing is done on a felt or muslin buff attached to the shaft of a motor or mounted upon a special arbor powered with a motor, using a V belt. Tripoli in cake form is a good abrasive to use on the

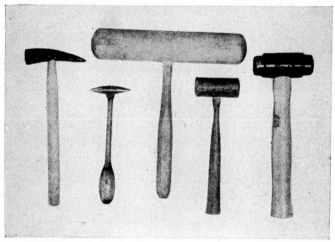

Fig. 6.—Horn mallet. Special-made spotting hammer. Bowl mallet made from wood. Rawhide mallet and rawhide end mallet.

buff. Fine pumice, dampened with oil and used on a walrus-hide buff, is widely employed in the commercial field for removing scratches prior to the final polishing.

Hold the work so that the buffing is done on the lower part of the wheel, to prevent the abrasive from being thrown on you. Grasp firmly, yet in such a manner that if the metal catches on the buff and is pulled from your hand your fingers will not be injured.

In buffing a flat piece of metal, place a piece of wood on the back to keep the metal from bending. After the buffing is completed, remove the tripoli by washing with soap and water.

Jewelers' rouge in stick form is excellent for the final buffing. It is a finer grit abrasive than the tripoli and is used for the buffing of silver. Use different buffs for each agent.

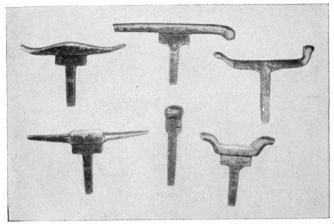

Fig. 7.—Metal stakes used in bending, forming, raising, and planishing.

COLORING

A good solution for coloring copper is made by dissolving a lump of potassium sulphide (liver of sulphur) about the size of a walnut in a gallon of water. Best results are obtained by applying the solution while it is hot. Small objects may be placed in the solution and the solution heated. A brush or cloth may be used to apply it to large surfaces. The stronger the solution, the darker will be the color obtained.

When copper or brass is heated, different colors appear on the surface. The first colors disappear, but the dark red and purple will remain if the metal is not overheated and if the surface is covered with wax or lacquer.

Copper surfaces will, when exposed to the air, oxidize to a certain extent. The coloring caused by oxidation is preferred by many workers to the artificial coloring.

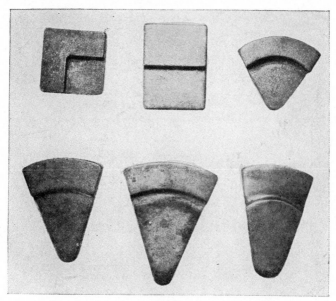

Fig. 8.—Metal plate- and tray-forming stakes.

Brass may be given a dark antique finish by applying butter of antimony to the surface and allowing it to dry. The object, after being colored, may be left as it comes from the solution, or it may be given light areas by rubbing the surface with a paste made of fine pumice and water. Kitchen cleanser may be substituted for the pumice. Clear lacquer may be brushed or sprayed on the surface to protect it against further oxidation. Wax rubbed on while the metal is slightly warm is also used for preserving the color.

JEWELERS' SAW FRAMES AND BLADES

Jewelers' saw frames may be obtained in a number of depths. The narrow-depth frame is excellent for small work, but if a frame that can be used for both small and large work is wanted, one with a depth of at least 4 or 5 inches is best.

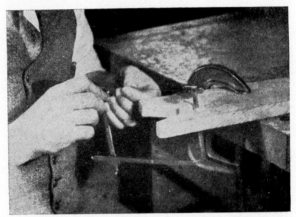

Fig. 9.—Inserting blade in jewelers' saw frame.

Jewelers' saw blades are available in a number of sizes; the higher the number, the coarser the blade. For most work the No. 0 and finer blades are used. For silver and thin copper and brass work the No. 3/0 and No. 4/0 blades are excellent.

The blade is inserted so that it will cut on the downward stroke of the saw, that is, the teeth point toward the handle of the saw. The saw blade will not cut unless it is held taut. To ensure tautness, fasten one end of the blade in the saw frame, and force the other end of the saw frame in before fastening that end of the blade (Fig. 9). It is absolutely necessary that the blade be stretched tight.

Sawing is usually done over a notched board (Fig. 10). A V-shaped notch cut into a small board clamped to a table top, works well. Place the piece to be sawed on the board over the notch. Use the fingers of the left hand to hold down the work. Grasp the handle of the saw in the right hand, holding it lightly, and with a little practice you will be able to follow outlines quite easily.

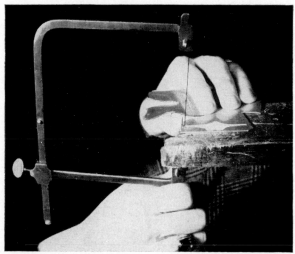

Fig. 10.—Using a jewelers' saw to cut ring blank from sheet metal.

If designs are to be sawed into the metal, it is necessary first to drill small holes in the waste material. Then fasten the blade in one end of the frame, run it through the hole, and make it fast in the other end. Sawing is then done in the usual manner.

Very slight pressure is needed on the blade to make it cut into the metal. In order to make sharp turns do not apply any pressure on the blade, but while continuing the up-and-down movement gradually turn the handle of the frame.

Paraffin, beeswax, or soap rubbed on the saw blade at frequent intervals will aid in the sawing and reduce the number of broken blades.

with a clamp at the other. One piece of wood must be exactly the thickness of the match box. The metal is bent over and down the side of this piece of wood. It is important that the metal be placed between the two pieces so that the bend will be at a right angle to the edge of the metal. Use a try square to measure the angles, mark the lines with a pencil where the bends are to be made, and place a line even with the edge of the board when a bend is made.

The boxes may be ornamented in a number of ways. Initials and various designs may be sawed into the metal with a jewelers' saw before the metal is bent, or they may be etched into the metal. Indian symbols, initials, monograms, animals, and various other ornaments may be sawed from 18-gauge or heavier brass and soldered in place. One's ingenuity alone limits the various ornaments that may be applied. For instance, one student, in order to have something individualistic, made a match box holder and ornamented it with a pipe, cut from 16-gauge brass. The design showed smoke curled from the bowl of the pipe in such a manner as to form the owner's initials.

Ornaments look better if the edges are rounded with a file and then buffed before they are soldered to the surface. The ornaments are best soft-soldered in place by sweating. If any of the solder flows out from under the ornament onto the surface, remove it by careful scraping, and then buff the surface.

BOOK ENDS

Book ends may be made from heavy sheet copper or brass, or combinations of the two, and decorated in a number of ways.

Figure 13 shows four book ends that were made by girl students, who used the jewelers' saw as the principal tool. Three of the book ends are examples of pierced sawing, with the outer rims hammered after sawing. Instead of using a ball peen hammer to planish the rims, the hammered effect in such projects may be obtained by using one of the dapping dies (Fig. 14). A medium-weight hammer is used to hit the punch, which is held in position on the metal. The metal is placed over an anvil or other metal surface during the hammering. By using the punch instead of a ball peen hammer, the

Fig. 13.—Book ends.

spots can be placed where desired without disturbing the edge of the rim.

To make the book end using the anchor for decoration, first cut out the book end to shape from sheet copper, planish with a ball peen hammer, and bend to shape. The anchor is made from heavy sheet brass. Draw the anchor design upon paper, paste on the metal, and then saw it out, after which file and buff the edges. Then rivet in place, using $\frac{1}{8}$-inch-diameter roundheaded copper rivets.

After the holes are drilled through the book end for the rivets, use a $\frac{3}{16}$-inch drill to countersink them on the reverse side. Then insert the rivet and cut off so that it barely protrudes. Place the head of the rivet in a rivet set, the correct-sized hole of a dapping die (Fig. 14), or on a lead block, and upset the end of the rivet with

Fig. 14.—Dapping dies and punches.

a small ball peen hammer. If the rivet is not left too long, it will fill the countersunk hole, as the end is hammered, and the book end will be smooth on the inside.

A right-angled bend, in forming the base, may be obtained by clamping the metal to the edge of a table, using a piece of wood on top of the book end, and bending over the portion that forms the base by hammering with a wood or rawhide mallet. A sharper bend may then be made by hammering on the edge of an anvil or other convenient piece of iron.

LETTER HOLDERS

Letter holders are made somewhat like book ends, except that they are usually made of thinner material, 20 gauge being ample in thickness.

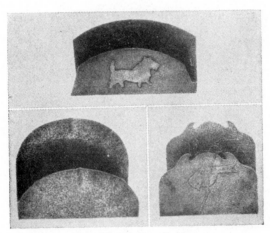

Fig. 15.—Letter holders.

They may be made in a number of sizes and decorated in various ways. The three shown in Fig. 15 make use of three methods of ornamenting. One shows a design cut from sheet brass and soft-soldered in place. Another is simply hammered with a ball peen hammer, after which the edges are fluted at intervals by beating the metal down into a notched block. The third has an etched design. Designs may also be sawed into the metal.

The angles are bent in somewhat the same manner as the base of the book end, that is, over the edge of a table.

DESK CALENDAR

The desk calendar offers many possiblities of ornamentation, as any of the methods already described may be used. The calendar leaves are ordinarily obtained from a small calendar and are used as the central figure in the frame.

Fig. 16.—Desk Calendar.

The calendar leaves may be held in place by drilling small holes through the metal and inserting split rivets of the type used in holding paper in folders or by using a thin strip of metal, as shown in Fig. 16. Holes must necessarily be drilled through the metal at the correct places.

One end of a piece of copper strip is soft-soldered to the back of the calendar near the top and is bent so that it will hold the stand at the desired angle.

PICTURE FRAME

Picture frames may be made in the same general way as a desk calendar, with a piece of metal soldered on the back to give the proper angle, or they may be made from one piece of metal, with one end bent at an angle to form the base, as shown in Fig. 17.

The opening for the picture or photograph is sawed out, and channels are formed from thin metal and soft-soldered in place at

Fig. 17.—Picture frame.

the bottom and along the sides of the opening to hold the glass and the picture. Designs may be sawed or etched into the metal, or it may be planished with a ball peen hammer.

WHISK BROOM HOLDER

The whisk broom holder consists of two pieces, the back and the band, or strap. The back may be made of either copper or wood.

If it is made of wood, the band should be tacked in place, using escutcheon pins; if it is made of copper, the band may be soldered or riveted in place, using roundheaded rivets.

Fig. 18.—Whisk broom holder.

It is necessary to have the whisk broom at hand before starting work, for the band must be shaped and bent so that the broom will not slip through it yet will fit loosely enough so that it can be pulled out from the bottom.

TRAY MAKING

The making of a tray necessitates using more tools than and somewhat different processes from those used in the making of the objects already described.

The depression forming the tray is usually made by beating down, that is, stretching, the metal with a hammer. Hold the metal

Fig. 19.—Pen trays.

Fig. 20.—Ash trays.

on the edge of the end grain of a block of wood or upon a specially cut wood block (Fig. 21), and beat down the metal following the design which has been previously drawn upon the metal. Strike the metal along the edge of the block, using a light stroke.

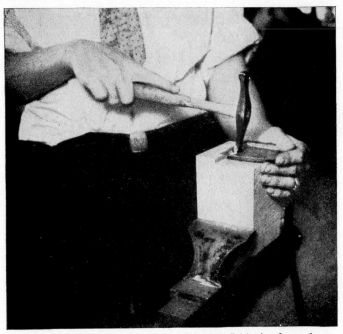

Fig. 21.—Raising a tray on end grain of block of wood.

After going around the design once, place the metal face down on a table top or other piece of wood, and straighten out the wrinkles in the rim. Then proceed with the hammering on the block of wood.

If the metal ceases to stretch after hammering, anneal by heating to a red heat, and proceed with the hammering. With light hammer blows and frequent annealing, the metal can be stretched to the desired depth.

In forming the tray the rim will pull in, as shown in Fig. 20. If this is uniform, it may be left, if desired, or after the hammering is finished the edges may be cut straight with a pair of snips. Then file and buff them. If the edges are to be cut straight, extra width must be allowed in the beginning, so as not to make the rim too narrow.

Instead of using wood blocks to form the tray, metal plate- and tray-forming stakes may be used. Or the tray may be formed on the wood block and finishing touches given on the metal stake.

The tabs, shown on the corners of two of the trays (Fig. 20), are cut from sheet material, shaped and soft-soldered in place by sweating. The match box holder in the center of the tray was made from one piece of metal bent into a U-shape and then soft-soldered in place. A piece of metal bent so that it will go inside the cover of a match box and soldered in place will force the box open.

MAKING A BOWL

The depression forming the bottom of the bowl is usually made first. It is made in the same manner as a tray.

If the bowl is to be very deep, it is best after beating down the bottom, to flute the sides at regular intervals in order to gain depth and help in the raising. Place the circular piece of metal over a notched block and hammer the metal down into the notch. This may be done with a wood mallet with the end shaped into a V or else by placing a length of round rod over the notch and striking the rod with a hammer. Then place the metal over a stake, and hammer out the flutes with a wood or a rawhide mallet. If the bowl is not of the required depth after the hammering on the stake, the process may be repeated. All hammering on the bowl should be done in circles, concentric with the base.

Instead of fluting to gain depth, the metal may be hammered on a sandbag with a wood mallet which has been rounded on the ends.

Sandbags may be purchased, or one may be made from heavy canvas. Partially fill the bag with sand. The hammering is done on the inside of the bowl, and the sand in the bag should be shifted

Fig. 22.—Fluted copper bowl.

Fig. 23.—Shaping a bowl upon a metal stake.

around so that there is a depression under the metal that is being hammered.

Shallow bowls may be raised without fluting by hammering on the sandbag or upon a metal stake.

Fig. 24.—Fluting a bowl.

Another method that is quite satisfactory on small bowls is to hammer over a depression made in the end grain of a piece of wood or in a block cut from a well-seasoned log.

After a bowl is raised to the desired shape and depth, the rim must be made the same height all around. This is done by first marking all around with a scriber and either filing or cutting off the uneven portion.

Instead of leaving the bowl plain, scallops may be cut at regular intervals, and, if desired, the bowl may be fluted. Figure 24 shows a bowl being fluted. A piece of wood is cut the same approximate curvature as that of the bowl, and a groove is cut and filed in the curve. The block of wood is then put in a vise, the bowl is placed over the block, and a rod is placed on the metal and hit with a mallet. It generally takes two people to do the fluting, one to hold the bowl in place on the block, and the other to hold the rod and do the hammering.

The rim of the bowl, between the flutes, may be flared out by hammering with a mallet while the rim is held against a block of wood that has been cut or filed to the desired shape.

TEA BELLS

Tea bells of various tones may be made of copper or brass by first raising the metal to the desired shape and then hammering with a ball peen hammer.

Fig. 25.—Tea bell raised from copper disk.

The bell shown in Fig. 25 was made of 20-gauge sheet copper cut into a 3½-inch disk. The handle was cut from brass.

The raising is done by hammering over a depression made in the end grain of a piece of wood or upon a sandbag. Frequent annealing and light hammer blows allow the metal to stretch.

Fig. 26.—Raising a tea bell over hole in block of wood.

The handle should have a piece left at the bottom that protrudes, through a slot, into the bell. A hole is bored through this projection through which the clapper is attached by means of a wire or chain. Make the piece on the handle that protrudes into the bell about ⅜-inch wide, and bore the hole in the center. Then saw a slit on each side of the hole to divide the piece into three divisions. In fastening the handle to the bell, bend one of the outer divisions one way and

A B C D E F G H I
J K L M N O P Q R
S T U V W X Y Z

Fig. 27.—Cooper black.

A B C D E F G H I
J K L M N O P Q R
S T U V W X Y Z

Fig. 28.—Cheltenham bold italic.

A B C D E F G H I
J K L M N O P Q
R S T U V W X Y Z

Fig. 29.—Old English.

the other the other way, leaving the portion with the hole protruding straight downward. Then soft-solder the two bent pieces to the bell, thus fastening the handle to the bell.

Bore a hole into the clapper, which is shaped from a piece of iron rod, and insert a small wire shaped like a cotter pin in the hole and soft-solder in place. Then connect the clapper to the handle with a chain made of copper wire.

The bell should be hammered with a ball peen hammer upon a metal stake before the handle is soldered in place. If the bell has lost its tone after the handle is soldered, hammer again with a ball peen hammer.

Many different designs may be worked out for the handle.

ALPHABETS

One of the most popular types of ornamentation utilizes letters sawed from copper, brass, or silver. It is first necessary to draw the letter, paste it on the metal, and then saw it out.

In outlining the letter allow for irregularities in the sawing. In other words, make it a little larger and wider than necessary in order to allow for the filing. Letters, as a rule, look better if they are made somewhat heavier than ordinary type letters. They also look better, in most instances, if the edges of the letters are rounded. The alphabets given in Figs. 27, 28, and 29 are three of those most frequently used. Many variations are possible, especially with the Old English letters.

Part 2
JEWELRY MAKING

AFTER PRIMITIVE man had satisfied his greatest need—food—his thoughts undoubtedly turned to ornaments, the claws and tusks of wild animals hung about his body. They were worn for two reasons: first, to show his prowess as a hunter, and second, because of a superstition that they would help him in combat against wild animals.

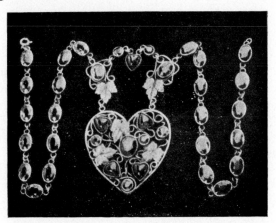

Fig. 30.—Necklace made by Edward Bush, seventeen-year-old high-school student.

Ornaments for personal adornment were in use long before clothing. They were of the type that adorned the neck, ankles, arms, and fingers. As man began to wear clothing, other types of ornaments such as pins and brooches came into use. Among primitive people the men wore most of the ornaments, as is true today among uncivilized people.

A study of history down through the ages show that, as man became acquainted with new materials and their uses, he immediately used that knowledge in fashioning his ornaments. The greatest advance was made in the Bronze Age, when man fashioned bronze into various forms of ornaments by hammering, riveting, and casting. Much of the jewelry worn in ancient eras was cumbersome. At one period some of the finger rings weighed as much as half a pound each, and the band was so wide that the joint of the finger was covered. When rings with stone sets first made their appearance in Rome, it was the custom to wear them on every finger and to change them with the seasons.

TOOLS AND EQUIPMENT

The making of simple jewelry does not require experience, nor does it require an expensive layout of tools and equipment.

Many of the tools needed for jewelry work are already at hand in almost any school or craftsman's shop. The essential ones are as follows:

Blowpipe. For hard soldering, a gas blowpipe or an alcohol, gasoline, Prest-O-Lite, or acetylene torch is needed.

Soldering Block. Charcoal blocks are very good to place the work upon while it is being heated to hard-solder, as the charcoal glows and reflects the heat back onto the work. An asbestos block or a magnesium block with asbestos fiber is also good.

Pliers. An assortment of pliers for various types of work usually includes a flat-nosed plier with squared ends; a round-nosed plier, the jaws of which are wholly round and taper toward the tips; a half-round-nosed plier, one jaw of which is rounded and has a convex surface, while the other is flat; a chain-nosed plier, the jaws of which have flat gripping surfaces that taper to narrow tips and the backs or outer surfaces of which are rounded. Most jewelry pliers are available in 4-, 4½-, and 5-inch lengths. End- or side-cutting nippers are almost indispensable.

Pliers with smooth-gripping surfaces are ideal for jewelry work, because the serrations on most pliers, although ideal for gripping a surface, will mar silver and gold. If your pliers have serrations, grind the jaws smooth and polish the surfaces with an abrasive cloth or an oilstone. It is much easier to prevent scratches on silver and gold than it is to remove the scratches after they have been made.

Saw Frame. A frame is essential for holding the jewelers' saw blades used in sawing out designs, ring blanks, and other forms. These frames are available in 3-, 4-, 5-, 6-, and 8-inch depths. For all-around jewelry work the 5-inch-depth frame is preferable.

Fig. 31.—Jewelers' saw frame.

Jewelers' Saw Blades. Jewelers' saw blades are 5 inches in length and are available in a number of sizes ranging from No. 8/0, the smallest, to No. 14, the largest. No. 0 or No. 2/0 blades are good for sawing 18- and 20-gauge silver. Smaller sized blades are used on thinner metal. See pages 16 and 17 for instructions on the use of a jewelers' saw.

Ring Mandrel. A ring mandrel (Fig. 32) is used in shaping and forming a ring blank. It is usually 12 or 14 inches in length, made of steel, and circular in the cross section and tapers from 1 to ½ inch. A ring mandrel can easily be made on a machinist's lathe. It may be purchased plain or graduated to the scale of United States standard ring sizes. The plain mandrel is available either hardened or not hardened. The graduated mandrel is hardened.

Fig. 32.—Ring mandrel. Used in shaping a ring blank.

Ring Gauge. A ring gauge, or ring stick (Fig. 33), is used for measuring the size of rings. It cannot be used to form a ring as it is hollow and usually made of thin material.

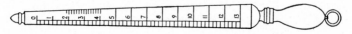

Fig. 33.—Ring stick. Used in finding the size of a ring.

Another use of the ring gauge is the determination, by the use of the scale on the gauge, of the length of a ring blank before the blank is formed into a ring. Measure from the metal tip of the gauge to the desired ring size on the small scale. The scale is shown in Fig. 36.

Burnisher. Oval steel burnishers with wood handles (Fig. 34) are used for turning, or burnishing, the top edge of the bezel over the stone to hold the stone in place. This is done after all soldering is completed and the mounting polished. A burnisher may have either a straight or a curved blade.

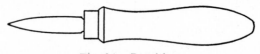

Fig. 34.—Burnisher.

Ring Sizes. Ring sizes (Fig. 35) consist of a number of metal rings, each marked with a standard ring size, which are slipped on the finger to determine the size of the ring desired.

Fig. 35.—Ring sizes are used in measuring the finger to determine the size of ring.

The finger size can also be determined by the use of the scale shown in Fig. 36. Cut a strip of paper that will go just around the largest part of the finger, and then measure this strip of paper on the scale to determine the ring size.

Fig. 36.—Actual size scale showing the length of blank required for various ring sizes.

Hammers and Mallets. Hammers that are useful in jewelry making include small ball peen hammers and the French chasing hammer. Small-sized wooden mallets are useful in many ways. Other mallets that are often found convenient are those which are made of rawhide or which have rawhide or fiber tips.

Files. Files are a necessity. An assortment should include at least one flat file, one half-round smooth file of 5 or 6 inches length, and a number of needle files.

Needle files are approximately 5½ inches in length, have a round handle, and are available in a number of shapes, such as round, half-round, flat, flat-tapered, square, knife, three-square, crossing, and slitting. The half-round, flat-tapered, knife, round, and square files are used more than any of the others. Needle files may be purchased singly or in a set that consists of a dozen assorted files.

Wire Gauge. The gauge size, or thickness, of wire and sheet metal can be determined by using a wire and sheet-metal gauge (Fig. 37).

Fig. 37.—Wire and sheet-metal gauge. (*Courtesy of Brown & Sharpe Manufacturing Company, Providence, R. I.*)

The gauge sizes are stamped on one side and their decimal equivalents on the reverse side. In gauging the size of wire, slip the wire into the slot, just as with sheet metal.

Drills. Twist drills, of the smaller sizes, are needed in making many pieces of jewelry. These drills may be purchased in fractions of an inch, such as $\frac{3}{32}$ inch, or by number. Numbered drills run from 1 to 80.

Before staring to drill a hole in a piece of metal, make a prick mark with a center punch.

Other Tools. Additional tools that are useful and sometimes essential include tweezers, a pin or hand vise, snips, a bench vise, dapping punches, chasing tools, engraving tools, drawplates, and drawtongs.

The silver jewelry shown in the accompanying illustrations was made by students, unless otherwise credited. A minimum number of tools were used. Some of the pieces were made at home by

No. by gauge	Decimals of 1 inch	No. by gauge	Decimals of 1 inch	No. by gauge	Decimals of 1 inch	No. by gauge	Decimals of 1 inch
1	0.2280	21	0.1590	41	0.0960	61	0.0390
2	0.2210	22	0.1570	42	0.0935	62	0.0380
3	0.2130	23	0.1540	43	0.0890	63	0.0370
4	0.2090	24	0.1520	44	0.0860	64	0.0360
5	0.2055	25	0.1495	45	0.0820	65	0.0350
6	0.2040	26	0.1470	46	0.0810	66	0.0330
7	0.2010	27	0.1440	47	0.0785	67	0.0320
8	0.1990	28	0.1405	48	0.0760	68	0.0310
9	0.1960	29	0.1360	49	0.0730	69	0.0292
10	0.1935	30	0.1285	50	0.0700	70	0.0280
11	0.1910	31	0.1200	51	0.0670	71	0.0260
12	0.1890	32	0.1160	52	0.0635	72	0.0250
13	0.1850	33	0.1130	53	0.0595	73	0.0240
14	0.1820	34	0.1110	54	0.0550	74	0.0225
15	0.1800	35	0.1100	55	0.0520	75	0.0210
16	0.1770	36	0.1065	56	0.0465	76	0.0200
17	0.1730	37	0.1040	57	0.0430	77	0.0180
18	0.1695	38	0.1015	58	0.0420	78	0.0160
19	0.1660	39	0.0995	59	0.0410	79	0.0145
20	0.1610	40	0.0980	60	0.0400	80	0.0135

Fig. 38.—Numbered drill sizes.

students using only a few files, a hammer, a ring mandrel, and in some instances an alcohol blowtorch.

Most of the articles illustrated were made from sterling silver. A few were made of gold. Gold is worked in almost the same manner as silver, except that gold solder must be used. Otherwise a white streak will appear on all joints.

HARD SOLDERING

In jewelry making one must master the art of hard soldering, which is done at temperatures ranging from 1250 to 1450°F. for silver and even higher for some golds and platinum.

Hard soldering is usually done with a gas torch. It cannot be done with a soldering copper, as soft (tin-lead) soldering is done.

Hard soldering is not difficult to learn. The joint to be soldered must fit snug as hard solder does not bridge a gap. The joint must be clean, the proper flux used, and the joint heated to the melting point of the solder. A very small piece of hard solder is needed to solder a joint.

Silver solder is an alloy of silver and copper with a small amount of zinc or other metals added to make it flow easily. Because of the neat, strong joint it makes, silver soldering is used widely in commercial work of many kinds. The silver solder used in jewelry making is of high silver content.

CAUTION: Do not attempt to hard-solder a joint if soft solder is present on the piece being soldered. Under the high temperature required for hard soldering, the soft solder will react with the silver and ruin the work.

METHODS OF HEATING

Melting hard (silver or gold) solder requires intense heat. There must be enough heat not only to melt the solder but also to bring the temperature of the joint being soldered up to the melting point of the solder; thus the solder will flow properly.

Heat for hard soldering can be supplied with torches that burn a mixture of oxygen and acetylene, city gas mixed with oxygen or compressed air, or acetylene mixed with oxygen drawn from the surrounding air.

The oxyacetylene flame burns at about 6000°F. and if employed for silver work must be used with extreme caution to prevent melting the work. Torches that burn oxygen and gas have a flame temperature of around 4900°F. Torches that burn either city gas or acetylene with compressed air give flame temperatures up to 3300°F. The Prest-O-Lite torch, burning acetylene without compressed air or cylinder oxygen, produces a 2800°F. flame.

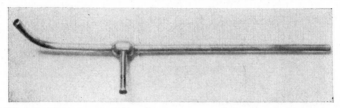

Fig. 39.—Blowpipe suitable for hard soldering where artificial gas is available.

Selection of the torch for hard soldering depends upon several factors: the amount of soldering to be done, kind of work, gas supply, and number of persons using equipment at the same time.

Gas and Air. Where city (manufactured) gas is available and where most of the soldering is on small pieces, the combined mouth blowpipe is satisfactory. This type of torch does not work on natural gases as the B.t.u. content is much higher; therefore more air is required than one can furnish by blowing. Natural gas is slower burning and requires a torch with a special tip.

The combined mouth blowpipe is connected with a rubber tube to a gas outlet. The torch is lighted, the amount of gas flowing through the blowpipe is regulated, and then by blowing through the end of the blowpipe a high heat is obtained. This type of torch may be used at home by connecting to any convenient gas outlet or to the kitchen gas stove, after removing the burner which usually slips over the gas stopcock.

When a number of blowpipes, such as the National 3-A (Fig. 40), Hi-Heat, automaton, or similar torches, are being used in a craft- or schoolshop, it is advisable to install an air compressor

Fig. 40.—National 3-A blowpipe. This type of blowpipe uses any type gas and compressed air. (*Courtesy National Welding and Equipment Co., San Francisco, Calif.*)

and storage tank equipped with pressure switch. If a storage tank is used, it is necessary to install a regulating valve in the air line leading to the torches to control the air pressure. From 2 to 10 pounds air pressure will operate a blowpipe satisfactorily, depending upon the size of the torch tip.

Fig. 41.—Vernon rotary air compressor. (*Courtesy Lee S. Smith & Son Mfg. Co., Pittsburgh, Pa.*)

Other means of supplying air for a blowpipe are the foot bellows or a rotary blower (Fig. 41). The small rotary blower may be belt-driven, or it may be connected directly to a ¼-hp or larger motor.

Many craftsmen improvise a blower from an old vacuum-cleaner motor (Fig. 42) or from a spray-gun outfit such as is used for painting.

If natural gas is to be used, be sure when you purchase your torch that it is the type for natural gas; the torch made for city

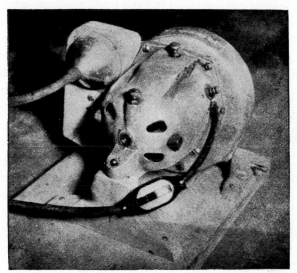

Fig. 42.—Blower made from vacuum-cleaner motor.

(manufactured) gas will not work satisfactorily on most natural gases. Torches made for natural gas will, however, work satisfactorily on either natural or manufactured gas.

Gas and Oxygen. Instead of using compressed air and gas, oxygen may be substituted for the air. Oxygen is obtainable in cylinders, and by using a reducing valve the proper amount may be fed to the torch with the gas. From 2 to 10 pounds pressure of oxygen in the hose leading to the torch is sufficient. Connect the oxygen hose to the hose connection on the torch marked "air" if using one of the standard torches with an oxygen tip.

Silver Solder. Silver solder is available in sheet, wire, strip, and granulated form. It is sold by the ounce (troy). Two general types are available for jewelry work, "Easy-" and "hard-flowing." The easy-flowing is preferable for most jewelry work as it melts at a lower temperature.

Fig. 44.—Self-pressurizing canned gas blowtorch. (*Courtesy Prepo Corporation, Edgerton, Wis.*)

Fig. 44A.—Automatic-type alcohol torch.

Silver solders suitable for most jewelry work have a melting point of 1325 to 1425°F. They are silver-white in color and a close match for sterling silver, as their silver content is high.

The author has found that 28-gauge "easy" silver solder in strips $\frac{1}{16}$ inch wide is excellent for both student- and home-workshop use. It is thin and narrow and can be easily cut into small pieces. Many supply houses dealing in jewelry findings handle silver solder that has been cut into small pieces and packaged in glass vials.

If your silver solder oxidizes through exposure to air before you use it, rub it with fine steel wool until it is bright.

In soldering a joint use a very small piece of silver solder. It is easier, if necessary, to add more solder than it is to remove the excess. Most beginners are likely to use too much.

Making Silver Solder. Small amounts of silver solder may be made by fusing small pieces of silver and brass on a soldering block, the proportions being about 4 parts silver to 1 part brass. If a melting furnace is available, a larger amount may be prepared. Place the silver in a crucible; put in a small amount of borax, and melt the silver. Then add brass filings, and stir with a carbon stirring rod. Pour the alloy from the crucible, and when cold make into granulated form by filing with a coarse file, or hammer or roll into the desired thickness.

Silver solder, however, is not expensive considering the small amount necessary for a joint, and it is best bought ready-made.

Gold Solder. Gold solder is made of fine (pure) gold alloyed in varying degrees to melt at different temperatures for the different karat golds. Gold solder is used the same way as silver solder with any good flux.

Gold solder is sold by the pennyweight (dwt.), which is 1/20 troy ounce, in thin sheet form. In purchasing gold solder specify the color wanted, yellow, green, white, pink, or red, and for what karat work (usually 10-, 12-, 14-, or 18-karat). Gold solders are of a lower karat than the work for which they are recommended.

Gold solders have melting points of 1225 to 1550°F., depending upon the composition of the solder. Solder for 10-karat yellow gold melts around 1225°F.; that for 14-karat yellow gold melts around 1290°F.; and that for 18-karat yellow gold melts around 1500°F. Solders for white and green golds melt at temperatures slightly higher than the solders for the yellow golds.

Platinum Solder. Platinum solders are available in a number of grades, each grade having a different melting point. They are sold by the pennyweight. Wildberg Bros. Smelting & Refining Co., for instance, makes 10 different platinum solders with approximate melting points ranging from 1633 to 2875°F. It reports its most popular solders to be No. 1300, medium hard, with melting point of approximately 1831°F.; No. 1400, hard, 2080°F.; and No. 1500, extra hard, 2227°F. Number 1100, soft, with melting point of 1633°F., and No. 1200, medium, with melting point of 1702°F., are used extensively in repair work.

For soldering hard (jewelers') palladium, which has a melting point of approximately 2970°F., No. 1200, medium, platinum solder is used extensively.

Soldering Blocks. Most hard soldering of jewelry is done upon a soldering block. These blocks are usually of asbestos, magnesium carbonate and asbestos, charcoal, or compressed carbon black. The charcoal block is excellent but soon burns up. Blocks of thick asbestos or magnesium carbonate and asbestos last longer than charcoal. Syn-Char soldering blocks, made of compressed carbon black, are used by many craftsmen instead of the charcoal blocks as they, too, last much longer.

Coarse silicon carbide grit, No. 10 or 12, is excellent for many soldering jobs. Place the grit in a metal pan and the object to be soldered in the grit. The grit is very useful in soldering ornaments onto rings since the ring can be placed in any convenient position.

Lump pumice, broken into small pieces, is also excellent for soldering. Use it in the same way as the coarse silicon carbide grit.

Preparing the Joint. Any joint to be hard-soldered must first be cleaned by scraping, filing, or pickling and then made to fit snug, for this type of solder will not bridge a gap. If there is any likelihood of the pieces moving while being soldered, bind them with black binding wire, which is available for this purpose. Do not use copper, brass, silver, or any bright wire for binding purposes as the solder will stick to them.

Whenever possible, solder without the use of binding wire, for sometimes the solder will flow alongside or over the wire. When this happens, remove the ridge of solder by filing.

Fig. 45.—Applying solder to a ring shank-bezel joint.

Fluxes. A flux must be used on the joint to prevent oxides from forming when the work is heated. Powdered borax or cone borax, dissolved to a saturated solution in warm water, is used by many craftsman. Borax, however, has one disadvantage: when heated it rises, which often causes the piece of solder, as well as leaves and other ornaments, to move.

In general, commercially prepared fluxes are better than common borax powder and are strongly recommended. These fluxes are available in both paste and liquid form.

Two of the well-known all-purpose paste fluxes are Rapid-Flo-Flux (Wildberg Bros. Smelting & Refining Co.) and Handy Flux (Handy & Harman). Both are available in various sized jars. They are fluid and active around 1100°F., which is 200 to 300° below the melting point of most silver solders, and keep their protective properties to around 1850°F. By watching the melting point of one of these fluxes, one knows the temperature of the joint being soldered and can better direct the torch flame on the work. Borax is fluid at 1400°F.

Mix small portions of the flux with water to obtain the desired consistency, and apply to the joint with a small artist's brush. Dip

Fig. 46.—Student silver-soldering a ring, using mouth blowpipe and artificial gas.

the solder in the flux before applying to the joint with brush, tweezers, or toothpick.

Liquid fluxes are available in various sized bottles and are applied to the joint with a small artist's brush. Almost all commercial fluxes contain a fluoride or other agent which helps clean the joint.

Applying the Heat. With the work on a soldering block, apply the heat gradually until the water in the flux has evaporated. If the heat is applied too strongly at first, the moisture in the flux will cause the flux to rise and thus to move the solder.

Keep the flame in motion at all times, and off the joint as much as possible. When the joint shows a dull red, indicating that the temperature is around 1200°F., concentrate the heat upon the joint. The solder will flow when the parts to be joined are heated to the melting point of the solder.

Use a soft, blue flame when soldering, as a small, needlelike flame is very hot and is likely to melt the joint, especially on bezels, small wires, and thin sections. Very little air is needed to produce the correct flame, especially if you are using manufactured gas. If too much air is mixed with the gas, it is difficult to heat the work to the flowing point of the solder. Practice and experience will show what type of flame is best.

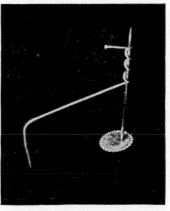

Fig. 47.—Method of holding scarf-pin stem in place on a charcoal block while it is being soldered.

On large pieces such as bracelets, it is well not only to place the work upon a soldering block but to use a block back of the work to reflect the heat, especially if one is using the combined mouth blowpipe. Soldering should not be done in a draft, as the air current will cool the work. A shield made from any convenient sheet metal, about 2 inches wide and 6 to 8 inches long, bent into a half circle and placed back of the work on the soldering block, protects the work from air currents.

In soldering a small piece to a large piece, apply more heat to the large piece, for the solder will flow and join the two pieces only when both pieces are of the correct temperature.

If possible do your soldering without too much light, for then you can watch the color of the work as it is being heated. The first visible red shows that the work is around 900°F. When the work is a dull red, the temperature is around 1200°F. A cherry red indicates that the work is 1400°F. Handy Flux is liquid at 1100°F. Borax is fluid at 1400°F. Most of the silver solders are fluid at 1325 to 1400°F.

Avoid overheating the work. Sterling silver should never be heated above 1500°F. Remember that sterling silver is molten at 1641°F. and fine silver at 1760°F. When sterling silver is heated above 1400°F., the surface is likely to have a rough texture, or crack, or a fire coat. Avoid heating the work beyond the flowing point of the solder.

Fire coat. Overheating or repeated annealings of sterling silver often form red oxides of copper in the metal, which show up as dark clouds after the pickling and when the piece is being polished. Remove the dark spots by dipping in a cold solution of 50 per cent nitric acid and 50 per cent water in a porcelain beaker. (In mixing *add the acid to the water.*) The dark spots will soon turn black and the unfired portions a light gray. Remove the work from the acid solution in a few minutes as this strong a solution will completely dissolve the silver if it is left in for a long time. The silver should now be clean and white after it is polished. If not, repeat the process.

Protection against Fire. Sterling silver can be protected against fire burns by painting the piece with, or dipping it in, a solution made of 2 parts boric acid and 1 part borax dissolved in water. In many commercial establishments large silver pieces, before being soldered, are dipped into this solution, which is kept hot.

Balling of Solder. If the solder rolls into a ball when it melts and refuses to flow readily, this is probably because the work has not been heated enough or because the solder or joint was not covered with flux. Keep the flame upon the work as much as possible, instead of upon the solder; otherwise, the solder will melt and ball and will not flow readily when the work reaches the melting point of the solder.

Pits and pinholes in the finished joint may be caused by dirt, oil, or improper fluxing, or by too much or not enough heat, or by heat applied too strongly at the joint without preheating the work.

Soldering Ornaments. Small ornaments, shot, twisted wire, leaves, and other decorations, can be soldered onto large pieces easily by the use of solder filings, known also as granulated silver solder. If granulated solder is not available, use tiny pieces of cut solder.

Make sure, by pickling, that both the work and the ornament to be soldered in place are clean. Using one of the commercial fluxes, such as Handy Flux or Rapid-Flo-Flux, paint with an artist's brush the place where the ornament is to be soldered, and heat the piece until the flux melts or glazes. Paint the flux on the underside of the ornament, and sprinkle a few grains of the solder onto the wet underside of the ornament, or place a tiny piece of cut solder in place if granulated solder is not available. Using tweezers, set the ornament in place, and apply heat until the solder melts, being careful to keep the flame off the ornament.

Silver-brazing alloys, made by grinding the solder to a powder and mixing it with flux and a special cleaning agent, are excellent for soldering ornaments in place. These alloys are available from Grieger's and other dealers. Use a type that has a melting point lower than the solder used in making the article.

Some craftsmen wet the tip of the tang end of a small discarded file or pointed iron wire and dip it into a mixture of solder filings and flux; they then touch it to the joint or piece to be soldered when it becomes red hot. Flux must be applied to the joint, before the heat is applied, to prevent oxidation.

Large joints can sometimes be hard-soldered by applying flux to the joint and heating to a point that will melt the solder. A thin strip, or wire, of solder is then dipped in the flux and touched to the joint. This method is used extensively in work on long seams and joints.

Protecting Soldered Joints. When more than one joint is to be soldered, coat previously made joints with borax or other flux. If there is danger of the joints opening, a solder of lower melting point may be used, or the soldered joints may be coated with a paste made of yellow ocher and water, whiting and water, or jewelers' rouge and water. Clay and water may be used if nothing else is available. After the soldering is completed, the coating may be removed by soaking the article in water and scrubbing with an old toothbrush.

All the silver jewelry shown in the illustrations in this book was made with one grade of solder, "easy," and very little difficulty was encountered. Yellow ocher was used on some pieces by beginners. Advanced students, as a rule, depend upon the flux to protect previously soldered joints, seldom using either binding wire or yellow ocher if this can be avoided. Cautious application of heat in evaporating the water from the flux, so as not to disturb the solder or the joint, is essential.

Use of Investments. In soldering a large or complicated piece of work made of gold or silver, it is often wise to protect previously soldered joints. These may be protected with yellow ocher, as already described, or with investments used by dentists. These materials called bridge investments, consist essentially of finely shredded asbestos and plaster of Paris. Soldered joints protected by investments will not separate during the soldering of other parts.

An investment can be made quite easily by mixing 1 part finely powdered or shredded asbestos with 2 parts plaster of Paris. The material is then mixed with water and handled like plaster of Paris.

It will set in about 5 minutes and can then be heated by the blow-pipe without cracking and with little shrinkage. Plaster of Paris alone would tend to fracture under high heat. In applying the investment to the part of the work to be protected, mix the investment material with water to obtain a fairly thick mass, and apply, leaving exposed the parts to be soldered. After the investment has set for 5 minutes, trim off the excess with a knife before heating. Do not leave a huge bulk of investment attached to the work, as this will absorb heat and make the soldering operation harder. Only a thin layer of investment is needed to prevent any part of the work from "burning up" or separating. The large and complicated gold bridges made by dentists are assembled by the use of investments.

Pickling. Glazed borax, as well as oxides left on the article after the joint is soldered, may be removed in a pickling bath made up of 1 part sulphuric acid and about 10 parts water. *Add the acid to the water.*

The solution is more effective when used hot and should be heated in a copper pickling pan. When not in use, it should be kept in a glass or earthen jar.

Remove all iron binding wire, and place the soldered article in the heated pickling bath. Use copper or brass tweezers or tongs to remove the work from the bath. If copper or brass tweezers are not available, copper or silver wire may be used. Never use iron wire or any other iron object to retrieve the work as the reaction of the iron in the solution will discolor silver.

Sparex No. 2, a dry granulated powder specially developed for pickling and cleaning nonferrous metals, may be substituted for the sulphuric acid, which must be used with caution. Sparex No. 2 is safe to use, easy to handle, noninflammable, and nonexplosive, and it may be stored safely in any dry place.

This dry granular compound when dissolved in water (2½ pounds to 7 pints of water) makes a highly effective pickling solution which has no corrosive, obnoxious, or poisonous fumes. Sparex

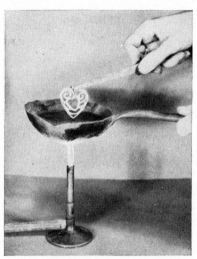

Fig. 48.—Pickling a pendant.

No. 2 may be used at room temperature, but it is most effective when heated to 170°F. Sparex No. 2 is available in 2½-pound cans and larger sized drums.

After pickling, rinse the pickled object in water. If it is inconvenient to heat the acid solution, the article to be pickled may be heated and lowered into the cold pickling solution by means of copper tongs or a copper or silver wire.

CHAINMAKING

Before attempting to silver-solder a ring or other piece of jewelry, one should practice first upon copper, which is inexpensive, in order to become acquainted with the torch, flux, and the melting point of the solder. Copper works much the same as sterling silver, except that it has a higher melting point, 1981°F. Sterling silver melts at 1640°F. A useful beginning exercise in hard soldering is the making of a chain.

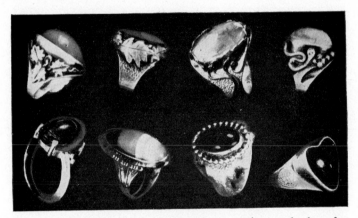

Fig. 49.—Sheet-silver rings using leaves, wire, and shot for decoration.

Wrap a short length of 18- or 20-gauge round annealed copper wire around a small round mandrel. A convenient-sized mandrel is $\frac{3}{16}$ or $\frac{1}{4}$ inch diameter. Remove the coil of wire from the mandrel, and saw or cut into links. Small wire can be easily cut with end nippers, but it is better to saw a coil of heavy wire into links with a jewelers' saw, as there is less filing to be done after sawing.

Solder a number of links into single units. Then connect two such soldered units with a third unit, making a unit of three. When two units of three links each have been made, join these with another link, thus making seven connected links. Repeat until the desired length is obtained.

Links of various shapes can be made on mandrels of the desired shape cut from metal or wood. A round link can be made into an oval link by placing the link on the jaws of a pair of round-nosed or chain pliers and pulling the handles apart. After all soldering is completed, links can be twisted by using two pairs of pliers. Hold one pair of pliers stationary, and twist the link about 90° with the other pair.

Fig. 50.—Wire shank rings.

RING MAKING

Finger-ring making, the most popular form of jewelry work for students, may be divided into eight operations: (1) designing, (2) bezel making, (3) shank making, (4) assembling shank and bezel, (5) ornamenting, (6) polishing, (7) oxidizing, and (8) setting the stone.

Rings may be made from wire, from wire and sheet silver, or from sheet silver only.

Designing. The designing of a ring must necessarily be based upon the stone or other ornament that is to be used on the ring. Different kinds and shapes of stones require different mountings. Faceted and cabochon stones generally require different methods of ornamentation as well as of mounting. In designing a ring, one is limited only by his ability to execute his designs and by the material at hand.

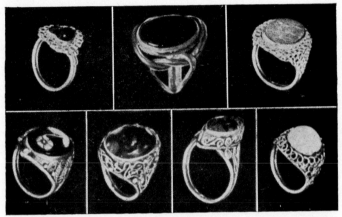

Fig. 51.—Rings ornamented with twisted wires and small balls of silver, termed "shot."

Before starting work on the actual making of a ring, it is well to prepare a number of sketches of different types of mountings with decoration or ornamentation for each and decide definitely which is to be used. Often it is advisable to make these sketches larger than the actual size of the ring.

Bezel Making. Although either sterling or fine silver may be used in making the bezel, it has been the experience of the author that fine silver is preferable for student work, as it is much softer and will bend to shape more readily. Regular bezel made of sterling, gold, or gold-filled may be purchased in strip form.

The bezel consists of two parts: an outer rim that is burnished over at the top to hold the stone in place and an inner part, or bearing, that supports the stone and keeps it from going on through the

outer rim. The outer rim is generally made of 26- or 28-gauge
Brown and Sharpe fine silver. It is made to the exact shape of the
stone, and the ends are silver soldered together. Fine silver may be
purchased in widths suitable for bezel making, usually either ⅛ or
³⁄₁₆ inch.

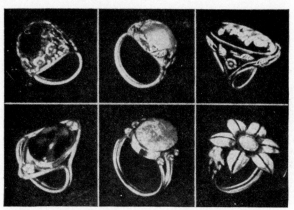

Fig. 52.—Rings using leaves and shot for decoration.

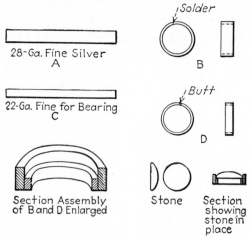

Fig. 53.—How the bezel is made.

If the outer rim of the bezel, when made, is too small, it may be stretched by slipping it over a round mandrel and hammering lightly. It may then be shaped to fit the stone. As the metal is quite soft and stretches easily, avoid heavy hammering.

The bearing may be made of small round sterling wire or of sterling or fine sheet silver cut into strips about $\frac{1}{16}$ inch wide. Fine silver $\frac{1}{16}$ inch wide may be purchased and then cut into the desired

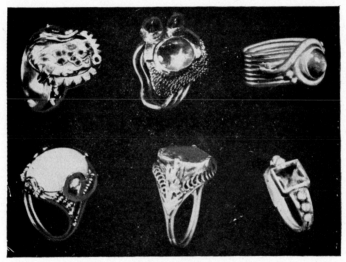

Fig. 54.—Rings.

lengths. Although any of several gauges of silver may be used for the bearing, the 24-gauge Brown and Sharpe works satisfactorily. The bearing is made so that it fits exactly the inside of the outer rim. Solder together the ends of the bearing before inserting the bearing in the outer rim. If too small, stretch by hammering on a ring or bezel mandrel.

After the two parts are assembled, place them upon the soldering block, and solder together.

Although fine silver has a melting point approximately 400°F. higher than that of solder, it will quickly melt if too much heat is applied or if a pointed flame is used.

Shank Making. Shanks for rings may be made either from round wire or from sheet silver. Sterling silver is used for shanks, as the

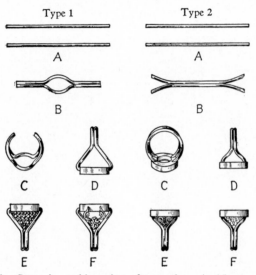

Fig. 55.—Steps in making rings from wire. *A*, 15-gauge round sterling wires. *B*, wires bent to fit bezel and soldered together. *C* and *D*, wires shaped and soldered to bezel. *E* and *F*, decoration applied to ring assembly.

fine silver is too soft. If the shank is to be made from round wire, use 14- or 15-gauge Brown and Sharpe. Wire shanks may be made in either of two styles, as shown in Fig. 55. Obtain two pieces of wire about 3 inches in length, and anneal by heating to a dull red. Pickle and then bend the wires to shape. If desired, bind with binding wire to keep them from moving while they are being soldered. Use several small pieces of solder instead of one large piece.

After the wires have been soldered together, bend them to shape, and solder to the bezel. The only difference in the two styles is that in type 1 the shank is made the size desired after it is soldered to the bezel and in type 2 it must be sized before it is soldered to the bezel.

Fig. 56.—Four types of ring construction showing the various parts and assembled rings.

Square or triangular wire may be used in making shanks. Shanks may also be made of sheet silver, 16- or 18-gauge Brown and Sharpe ordinarily being used. In this case the bezel may be soldered upon a thin sheet of sterling and the shank soldered in place after being cut to shape and sized.

Assembling Shank and Bezel. After the shank and bezel have been made, it is necessary to solder them together. Place the bezel, inverted, upon the soldering block, and put the shank in place.

If a wire shank, type 1, is used, the wires may be sprung apart just enough to insert the bezel, which usually will stay in place while

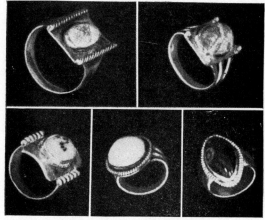

Fig. 57.—Rings made with sheet-silver shanks using twisted wire, shot, and beaded wire for ornamentation.

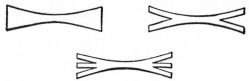

Fig. 58.—Shanks made from sheet silver.

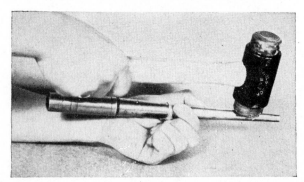

Fig. 59.—To remove a cabochon from a mounting, loosen the bezel around the stone with a penknife, place ring on mandrel, hold as shown, and strike end of mandrel a sharp blow.

being soldered. Both sides are soldered at the same time. If a wire shank, type 2, is used, it must be made of correct size and the end of each wire filed so that it fits against the bottom of the bezel. All joints may be soldered at the same time. No binding is necessary if the flame is cautiously applied so that the flux will not "rise" to disturb the assembly.

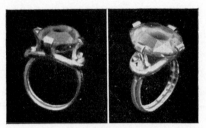

Fig. 60.—Faceted gem stone set in mounting made of gold wire.

Shanks made from sheet silver are shaped, sized, and placed upon the bezel or upon a thin sheet of sterling to which the bezel has been soldered, and both sides are soldered at the same time.

Ornamenting. The ornamentation that is to be applied to a ring depends to a large extent upon the kind and shape of stone, as well as upon the kind of mounting, that is being used. One's ingenuity is, however, a large factor, as many variations and adaptations are possible.

The ornamentation usually consists of the following or combinations of the following: bent and twisted wires, small balls of silver, called shot, leaves, beaded wire, special designs cut from sheet silver, and saw piercing.

Bent and Twisted Wires. Small wires, ranging in size from 20 to 30 gauge, may be twisted together and used for ornamentation. A good way to twist them is to tie the ends of two or more wires together, fasten on a hook, which is held in the chuck of the drill press, hold the free ends, and start the drill press. One can, however, twist them by hooking them onto any revolving arbor or by using a small hand drill.

The twist should be annealed before being used, and then pickled. In annealing the twist, roll it into a coil about 2 inches in diameter, and use a large flame of the torch with very little, if any, air.

Scrolls and various shapes may be made of the twists. The use of this type of decoration is shown in Fig. 51.

Instead of the wire being formed into scrolls, circles are sometimes made. If this type of decoration is to be used, the bezel may be mounted upon a piece of 22-gauge sheet silver. The circles are made by wrapping the twisted wire around a small drill, usually a No. 55 or a No. 60. The coil is cut into links, which are soldered on the sheet silver. The drill is then used to bore out the metal. Shot may be soldered onto the circles.

Wire bent into many shapes or designs may be used to great advantage for decorating rings. Shot may also be used on this kind of decoration. If desired, the shot may be filed partly away to produce a flat effect. In using wire or any ornamentation that is applied to the bezel, do not get it too near the top of the bezel, or difficulty will be encountered in setting the stone.

Shot. Small balls of silver, or shot, may be made by melting scraps of silver upon a soldering block. If, however, several balls of the same size are desired, equal lengths of wire may be cut and a ball made from each length.

To cut wires of equal length, wrap a piece of wire around a nail or other suitable mandrel, and then cut the coil into single units. Always use flux on the silver when melting to form the balls. The shot should be pickled before it is soldered onto the ring.

Shot may be soldered in clusters, placed at regular intervals, or used to fill in spaces that otherwise would appear open.

Leaves. You can shape leaves from sheet silver by first sawing to the desired shape, cutting in the veins with an engraving tool or other sharp instrument, and then doming or dapping. The dapping is usually done on the end grain of wood or upon a lead block, with dapping punches, which may be purchased or made from tool steel.

Fig. 61.—Leaf designs.

A large nail, the end of which has been ground to the desired shape and then polished, is excellent for emergency use when dapping punches are not available.

Commercial stamped leaves of various shapes and sizes are available for ornamenting.

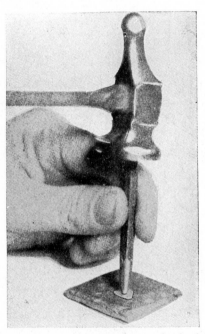

Fig. 62.—Making an ornament on the lead block.

If leaves instead of the bezel are to be used to hold the stone in place, make the bezel in the usual manner but very low, so that when the leaves are soldered in place they will project above the bezel. Solder each leaf on separately. After the ring has been cleaned, polished, and oxidized, the leaves are burnished over to hold the stone in place.

Beaded Wire. Beaded wire of various gauges may be obtained from supply houses in any length desired, or it may be purchased by the ounce from a silver dealer. It is available in round, half-round, and pearl bead. Often it is necessary to anneal beaded wire before bending it into shape to keep it from breaking.

Weight per foot, ounces		Brown and Sharpe gauge
0.073		18
0.096		16
0.124		15
0.168		14
0.218		13
0.254		12

Fig. 63.—Round-bead wire. (*Courtesy of Wildberg Bros. Smelting and Refining Co., Los Angeles.*)

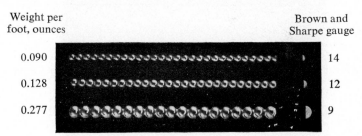

Weight per foot, ounces		Brown and Sharpe gauge
0.090		14
0.128		12
0.277		9

Fig. 64.—Half round-bead wire. (*Courtesy of Wildberg Bros. Smelting and Refining Co., Los Angeles.*)

Triangular Wire. Low-dome triangular wire is useful in jewelry making in a number of ways. The smaller sizes can be used in making ring shanks, as shown in the lower left ring in Fig. 49 and in the top center ring of Fig. 50, where two pieces of the wire were

Weight per
foot, ounces

Brown and
Sharpe gauge

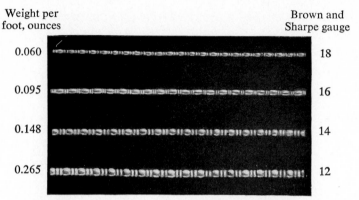

0.060	18
0.095	16
0.148	14
0.265	12

Fig. 65.—Pearl bead wire. (*Courtesy of Wildberg Bros. Smelting and Refining Co., Los Angeles.*)

Weight per
foot, ounces

Thousandths
of an inch

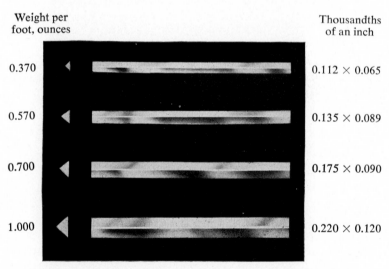

0.370	0.112 × 0.065
0.570	0.135 × 0.089
0.700	0.175 × 0.090
1.000	0.220 × 0.120

Fig. 66.—Low-dome triangular wire. (*Courtesy of Wildberg Bros. Smelting and Refining Co., Los Angeles.*)

used and the V formed between the two was filled in with a beaded wire. Bracelets may also be made of the various sizes of triangular wire, as shown in Fig. 83, where each of the bracelets shown at the left was made from two pieces of the smaller sized wire with bead or twisted wire for decoration.

Sheet-silver Ornaments. Initials, monograms, Indian symbols, and many other designs may be sawed from sheet silver and soldered in place as ring decorations. The ring is usually made the correct size and the ends of the blank are soldered together before the ornaments are added.

If the ornament needs to be curved to fit the ring, this may be done by making an impression in a wood or lead block with a ring mandrel and a wood mallet. The ornament is then put in this impression and the mandrel placed on top of it and again hit with the mallet. Be sure that the ornament is face down in the impression; otherwise the curve will be wrong.

Saw Piercing. Saw piercing is often used on rings made from sheet silver and must be done before the blank is bent to shape. The piercing is done with a fine jewelers' saw, as explained on page 17.

POLISHING

After all soldering is completed, the ring should be cleaned in a pickling bath to remove oxidation and glazed flux and then polished.

Rough spots may be removed with files and fine abrasive cloth or paper, or rubberized abrasive and polishing wheels and points may be used. Crocus cloth is excellent to give silver a smooth surface prior to the final polish.

Tripoli, a coarse-cutting compound, may be used on a muslin buff to eliminate deep scratches. Number OO steel wool may also be used to advantage. Rouge or other similar polishing compounds are generally used for the final polish. This is best done upon a muslin buff, which is mounted upon a polishing arbor or motor. Do not polish silver or gold upon a buff that is used for polishing brass or copper. Use separate buffs for each polishing compound used.

Fine pumice with a small amount of lubricating oil mixed into it is often used with walrus-hide buffs to smooth a silver surface before the final polishing. The pumice is generally placed on the piece being buffed and held against the buff.

Water-of-Ayr (Scotch) stone may be used to remove scratches and file marks in places impossible to reach with the buffing wheel. Fine abrasive cloth may be used to clean the inside of a ring. This may be used in the fingers or wrapped around a ring mandrel. Felt ring buffs, for use on a tapered screw arbor, are available for polishing the inside of a ring.

Rubberized Abrasives. Soft rubberized abrasive and polishing wheels and points find many uses in jewelry work. The small wheels, varying in diameter from $\frac{3}{8}$ to $\frac{7}{8}$ inch and in thickness from $\frac{1}{16}$ to $\frac{1}{4}$ inch, and the various-sized points may be used in a hand motor tool or flexible-shaft tool to smooth edges and surfaces prior to final buffing.

Blocks and sticks, made of the rubberized abrasive, are useful in removing scratches. Rubberized abrasive and polishing ring buffs are available for use with the tapered screw arbor. The abrasive ingredients are incorporated in a tough wear-resisting compound that covers the tapering wood mandrel. These ring buffs are available in medium and fine grit. Wheels up to 8 inches in diameter are available and find ready use in smoothing the surfaces of cast rings.

Rubberized abrasive and polishing wheels and points are available in several grits. The Cratex Manufacturing Company, San Francisco, Calif., makes them in four standard grits: (1) coarse, which cuts rapidly; (2) medium, for light grinding and general finishing; (3) fine, a needle-sharp, fine-grained abrasive that quickly produces a clean and polished surface; (4) extra fine, a superfine abrasive that will produce a high polish or special finish before polishing with muslin buff.

OXIDIZING

A silver ring when polished will appear very bright. It will gradually turn darker if left exposed to air, especially if any sulphur is present in the air. It may be readily darkened by dipping into a solution made by dissolving a lump of liver of sulphur in a small jar of water. Reaction is better if the solution is hot. Because of the objectionable odor of the liver of sulphur, a commercial oxidizing solution may be preferred. This is usually applied with a small brush to the ring while the ring is warm.

The oxidizing solution will discolor the entire ring. To remove part of the oxidization, a fine pumice powder or a kitchen cleanser mixed with water may be used. Rub it on with the fingers until the desired hue is obtained.

SETTING OF STONE

After the ring has been polished and oxidized, the stone is ready to be set. First taper the edge of the bezel with a file, and then place the stone in the bezel.

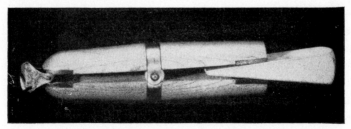

Fig. 67.—Ring clamp used for holding rings.

Hold the ring in a ring clamp, and with a burnisher gradually turn the top edge of the bezel over onto the stone. The bezel may then be smoothed, if necessary, with a jewelers' file. Polish with a hand buff, which is a piece of felt glued to a thin wood strip, using rouge as an abrasive.

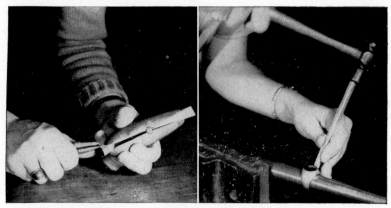

Fig. 68.—Setting a stone with a burnisher, left. Stones in heavy cast rings may be set with a hammer and flat nose tool.

The burnisher, or file, will not easily damage the majority of cabochon stones that are used, as the stones are harder than the file. The softer stones, however, such as turquoise, variscite, malachite, opal, and a few others, can be easily damaged.

SHEET-SILVER RINGS

To make a ring from sheet silver, it is necessary first to make a paper pattern. If a stone is to be used, the width of the paper should be somewhat wider than the length of the stone. The length of the piece of paper is determined by the size of the ring. It is well to make a number of patterns and then to select the best. After the pattern for the ring blank has been selected, the design of the ring should be sketched on the pattern, especially if the decoration is to be saw-pierced. One method of developing the paper pattern is shown in Fig. 69. Fold the paper lengthwise, then crosswise. Draw the outline on the folded paper, cut it out with scissors, and unfold.

Make the paper pattern the correct length for the ring size desired by measuring on a ring stick or upon the full-sized scale, as shown in Fig. 36. Add three times the thickness of the metal to the correct length to take care of filing and bending.

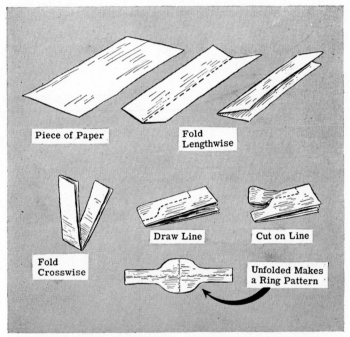

Fig. 69.—Making a paper pattern for a sheet-silver ring.

Glue the paper pattern to the sheet silver, 16-, 18-, or 20-gauge Brown and Sharpe, and, using a jewelers' saw, saw out the silver blank. If designs are to be sawed into the blank, drill small holes, insert the blade, and saw out the design. Fine saw blades (No. 2/0 or 3/0) are preferable, for they leave a smoother cut. Saw over a notched block or a piece of wood fastened to a table top (Fig. 10).

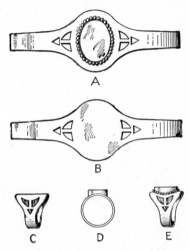

A

B

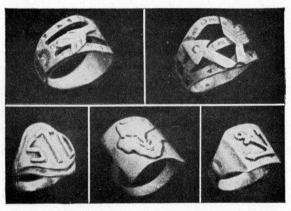

C   D   E

Fig. 70.—Steps in making a sheet-silver ring. *A*, paper pattern with design. *B*, blank sawed from sheet silver. *C*, blank sized and ends soldered together. *D*, bezel soldered in place. *E*, ornamentation soldered in place.

Fig. 71.—Rings made from sheet silver using simple designs.

The blade cuts on the downward stroke. The method of applying tension to the blade as it is being inserted in the saw frame is shown in Fig. 9. Paraffin, beeswax, or soap rubbed on the saw teeth, aids in the sawing.

After the blank is sawed out and pierced, if designs are to be sawed into the blank, bend it to shape around a ring mandrel, using a wood or rawhide mallet. Then size the blank, and solder the ends together.

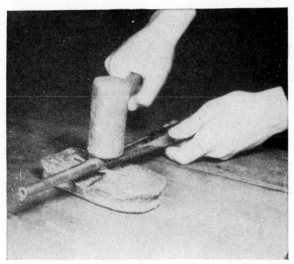

Fig. 72.—Use a mallet, ring mandrel, and lead or wood block to shape a sheet-silver ring blank.

Next make the bezel. Wider strips of silver than those utilized in making bezels for wire rings must be used, as the bezel must be cut away on the underside to fit the curved surface of the ring. Bezel material $\frac{3}{16}$ inch and in some cases $\frac{1}{4}$ inch wide is used. The bearing or support is about $\frac{3}{32}$ inch less in width.

To file the bezel to fit the ring, wrap one thickness of abrasive cloth around a ring mandrel, and cut out the metal on the underside of the bezel by drawing the bezel back and forth over the cloth. At some place along the mandrel is the exact curvature of the ring, and when this is found and the cutting done there, the bezel can be cut away to fit the ring exactly. In order to avoid a tapering cut, change

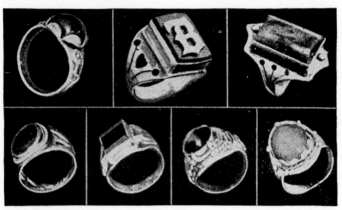

Fig. 73.—Sheet-silver rings with various kinds of ornamentation.

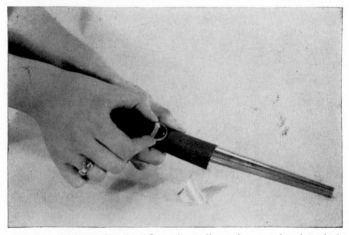

Fig. 74.—Filing a bezel to fit a sheet-silver ring on abrasive cloth wrapped around a ring mandrel.

the ends of the bezel frequently during filing. Avoid mashing the bezel out of shape while filing. If desired, the stone may be kept in the bezel during the filing operation.

To solder the bezel to the ring, coat the joint in the ring with flux, and place the ring so that the bezel will be on top. Hold the ring in position with small pieces of charcoal or asbestos blocks. Place the bezel in position, and coat the inside of the bezel as well as the joint of the bezel with a flux. Place several pieces of solder on the ring, inside the bezel, and apply heat gently until all water is evaporated. Heat should then be applied upon the side of the ring, below the bezel, from a rather large flame, until the ring is red-hot, at which time the flame may be directed upon the top of the ring and bezel.

If ornaments are to be added, solder them in place, and clean, polish, oxidize, and set the stone in the usual manner.

RINGS FROM WIRE

Using round, half-round, and square wire one can make a wide variety of finger rings that are inexpensive, costing only a few cents each.

Five different types of rings are shown in Fig. 75. These are made from round or round and square wire. The ring shown at the right is made from 16-gauge round wire and a small piece of sterling sheet. A chain, with oval links, is made of the wire, and the links are then soldered together to form the shank. The plate is then soldered to the shank.

The knot ring in Fig. 76 is very easy to make. Two 4-inch lengths of wire, usually 14- or 16-gauge, are used. Tie the knot in one piece of wire, but just before drawing the knot tight insert the other piece of wire through the knot and tie the knot in this piece. Draw both knots tight, and solder the wires together. Saw to the correct length, file the ends, bend to shape, and solder the ends together.

Another type of ring, not illustrated, is made by doubling a 7- or 8-inch length of wire, placing the ends in a vise, and using a nail in the loop end to twist the wire to the right. Repeat with another loop of wire, this time twisting to the left, making the exact number of twists to the inch as in the piece twisted to the right. The twisted

Fig. 75.—Rings made from round and square wire.

Fig. 76.—Knot ring made from round sterling wire.

wires, when placed alongside each other and soldered, will give a herringbone pattern. Saw to correct length, file ends, bend to shape, and solder ends together to make the ring.

Unique rings can be made from square wire, using 10-, 12-, or 14-gauge wire. A pleasing effect can be given the ring by twisting the square wire. This may be done all in one direction, or sections of the wire may be alternately twisted left and right. If desired, the twisted wire, *after being annealed,* may be run through a roller or hammered with a smooth-faced hammer upon a smooth surface. Another method is to file or grind on a rubber-bonded abrasive wheel the inside surface of the ring or both the inside and outside surfaces.

Snake rings, single- and double-headed, are made by soldering a short piece of heavy wire onto a length of 12- or 14-gauge wire. Shape the head by filing. The length of wire needed depends upon the size of the ring.

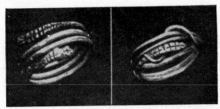

Fig. 77.—Snake rings made from round sterling wire.

BELT BUCKLE RING

Of the many rings already described and shown, the belt buckle ring is perhaps the most popular with high school students. Girls, instead of wearing it as a ring, often wear it as a scarf slide.

The belt buckle ring is a filing, bending, and fitting project, excellent for beginners, because it acquaints the worker with many tools and processes.

The ring may be made without soldering any of the joints holding the ring together by clamping the U-shaped strap underneath the band. However, silver soldering the parts together make a neater ring.

This ring is made by sawing the blank from 20-gauge or heavier sterling sheet silver with a jewelers' saw and filing it to shape. If a piece of silver 4¼ inches wide is used and the blanks sawed out as illustrated, there will be no waste and the cost of the blank will be very little. The width of the master blank used in marking out the blanks is approximately $\frac{3}{16}$ inch for the narrow part (the band) and $\frac{5}{16}$ or $\frac{3}{8}$ inch for the wide part, from which the buckle part is formed.

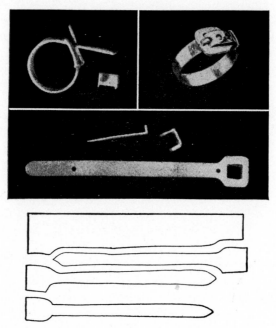

Fig. 78.—Belt buckle ring, showing method of assembling and how blanks are cut from a piece of sterling sheet.

File the narrow part of the blank until it is smooth, and then draw the outline for the square hole on the buckle part of the ring, making the width of the outlined hole slightly less than the width of the band, or narrow part of the ring. Drill a hole through the outlined square, and either saw to the drawn outline and finish by filing or use a small file and file to shape. Be sure the width of the square hole is such that the narrow part of the ring will just slip through; otherwise the finished ring will not be so neat-looking. File a taper on the underside of the front of the square hole and another taper on the top of the reverse side of the square hole.

File the buckle part to the desired shape. The tongue and the U-shaped strap are made from small pieces of sheet silver. The tongue can, however, be made of 16-gauge round wire, flattened slightly if desired.

If no soldering is being done, bore a $\frac{1}{16}$-inch hole near the square hole, as shown in the illustration. Bend the ring to shape, running the band through the square hole, and, after making it round and the desired size on the ring mandrel, mark the spot where the second hole, $\frac{1}{16}$ inch diameter, is to be drilled. If desired, three holes may be drilled instead of one. In assembling, make sure that the tongue goes between the buckle and the band, with the bent portion extending into the hole. The strap is bent to shape with flat-nosed pliers. The ends of the strap are bent under the band to hold the assembly in place.

If the parts are to be silver soldered together, omit drilling the small hole in the buckle. After filing the blank and smoothing all edges, run the shank through the square hole, place upon a ring mandrel, and form to the desired size. Cut off excess length of band, and then silver solder in place, at the same time soldering the front part of the buckle to the shank, or band. Make the U-shaped piece, the strap, fit snug, and solder the strap in place. Do not bend the ends of the strap under the band, as this is not necessary when soldering the parts together. File off the ends until they are even with the underside of the band. Place the ring upon a ring mandrel, and with a center punch make a small indentation where the hole is to be drilled for the buckle tongue. Holding the ring in a drill-press vise or wood clamp, drill the $\frac{1}{16}$-inch hole for the tongue. Place the bent portion of the tongue in the hole, and solder the tongue in place, being sure the tongue is soldered to the buckle as well as to the band.

BRACELETS

Bracelets may be made in a number of designs by using sterling sheet and wire, with or without gem stones, and they may be decorated in various ways.

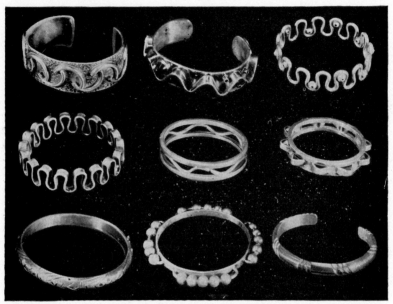

Fig. 79.—Bracelets made of sheet and wire.

Bracelets may be divided into three general types: (1) clamp-on, or open end; (2) slip-on, or bangle; (3) those with fasteners.

Attractive clamp-on bracelets, requiring no soldering, may be made from half-round sterling wire, $\frac{1}{4}$ or $\frac{5}{16}$ inch diameter. A $5\frac{1}{2}$-inch length makes an average-sized clamp-on bracelet. After rounding the ends and bending the blank to shape, the surface may be hammered lightly with a ball peen hammer, or one can cut decorative grooves into the blank (as shown at the lower right in Fig. 79) with a small round needle file.

Another clamp-on bracelet requiring no soldering may be made from heavy square wire, 8 gauge or heavier. The surface may be left smooth or may be hammered, or the wire may be twisted. For the twisted type use a 6½-inch length of wire, fasten one end in a vise, and with drawtongs grasp the free end; pull and slowly twist the wire.

If desired, a set of three square-wire bracelets may be made. Leave one plain, twist the other two blanks, twisting one blank to the right and the other to the left. After twisting, saw off the ends,

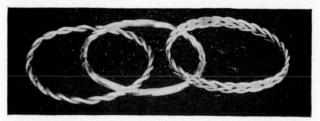

Fig. 80.—Bangle bracelets made of round and square wires

and bend to shape. It may be necessary to anneal the blank before bending to shape as the twisting hardens the silver. If desired, the inside of the twisted bracelet may be filed or ground smooth on a rubber-bonded abrasive wheel.

Unique bracelets may be made of square wire, in either the clamp-on or the slip-on type, by twisting one section to the right, the adjacent section to the left, and repeating until the length of the blank has been twisted. Vary the amount of twist and the length of each twisted section. The center bracelet (Fig. 80) was made in this manner.

A simple, popular slip-on or bangle bracelet is made by taking a 21-inch length of 12-gauge or heavier round wire, and doubling and twisting as in Fig. 80. After doubling the wire, fasten the free ends in a vise, insert a heavy nail or small metal rod in the loop, and twist. Before sawing to the desired length, 8 to 8½ inches for the average size, silver solder the wires together to keep them from moving while preparing the joint for soldering.

A herringbone pattern, shown at the right in Fig. 80, may be obtained by twisting one doubled wire, as described above, to the right and another to the left, making the same number of turns or twists per inch. Solder the ends of each twist, and saw off the loop

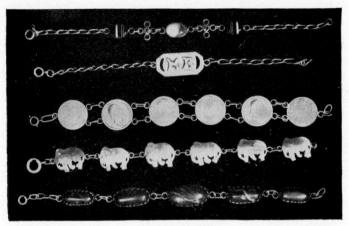

Fig. 81.—Bracelets.

and the free ends. Place the twisted wires alongside each other, and solder them together, placing tiny pieces of solder all along the joint. Saw to the desired length, file, and solder the ends together.

Five bracelets, made by different means are shown in Fig. 81. The one at the top makes use of three cabochons and two small faceted gem stones. The initial type bracelet is made by sawing the initials out of sheet silver and soldering them onto an appropriate piece of sterling sheet. The chains are handmade.

The coin bracelet, made of souvenir coins, is simple in design and quite popular. Six coins are generally used, although five are sufficient. Small silver medals and commemorative pieces are sometimes substituted for the coins. Two of the pieces in the coin bracelet shown are not coins but are commemorative pieces. In selecting pieces for a bracelet of this type, choose those with a high silver content. Coins from some countries have a low silver content and will, unfortunately, melt at about the same temperature as the silver solder, thus rendering them useless unless solder with a very low melting point is used. Coins that are unsuitable are generally yellow or brassy-looking.

Fig. 82.—Bracelet made from three heart-shaped stones.

Fig. 83.—Bracelets made from triangular wire.

The elephant bracelet is very similar in construction to the coin bracelet, except that the elephants are handmade from 20-gauge sheet silver. The blanks are first sawed out and the edges filed. Body lines and features are then cut with an engraving tool. The figures are made lifelike by being raised from the back. This is done by making a depression in a piece of wood or lead with a small ball peen hammer, placing the blank over the depression, holding the small hammer on the metal, and hitting lightly with another hammer. Solder small circles, made from 20-gauge wire, onto the elephants so that they may be connected with links. Solder the joint in each link.

Many other designs may be worked into bracelets of this type. For instance, Indian symbols such as thunderbirds, sun rays, arrowheads, or rattlesnake jaws, may be sawed to shape and soldered

Fig. 84.—Bracelets.

upon sheet-silver blanks, cut into various shapes, and then linked together. If desired, a small turquoise may be set in each of the symbols.

The bracelet with five stones in Fig. 81, is only one of many designs featuring gem stones that may be worked out. Three stones make a pleasing design if the central stone is larger than the other two, which are usually matched.

Either spring rings or sister hooks may be used to fasten the bracelet around the arm. They may be purchased from supply houses or jewelry stores. The spring ring is usually attached by opening the small loop with a pair of pliers, inserting the chain, and then closing the loop with the pliers. Do not solder since the heat will ruin the spring in the catch. Do not place the spring ring in the pickling solution as the acid may cause the spring to rust. Sister hooks may be fastened to the bracelet by making a link of round wire, inserting the link through the sister hook and the bracelet chain, and soldering the ends of the link together. If a small connecting link is used, protect the sister hook with yellow ocher mixed with water, which will keep the solder from flowing accidentally onto the sister hook and ruining it.

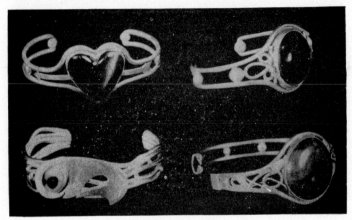

Fig. 85.—Bracelets.

Three bracelets of the clamp-on type, made from sheet silver, are shown in Fig. 84. Either 16- or 18-gauge sheet silver is generally used for this type of bracelet. A piece of material of the desired width, about $5\frac{1}{2}$ inches long, is needed. Many different designs may be engraved, etched, stamped, or soldered onto the band for ornamentation; or stones in combination with any of the above methods may be used.

Round wire, 10 or 12 gauge in diameter, is satisfactory to use in making the wire bracelets featuring a gem stone, as shown in Fig. 85. After selecting the stone and making the bezel, bend the

heavy wires to fit the bezel, and solder in place the ornaments holding the wires apart. Bend the blank to the approximate shape,
solder the bezel in position, and then solder in place the ornamentation that touches the bezel. If the bezel is soldered to the wires and
the wires are then bent to the desired shape, it is very likely that
the bezel will be pulled out of shape.

Fig. 86.—Bracelets.

Identification bracelets may be made of 12-gauge or heavier
round wire. Approximately 2 feet of wire is needed for the average
size bracelet. The plate may be made of 12-gauge or heavier sheet
silver. The average-sized plate is 2 inches long and ½ inch wide.

NECKLACES AND PENDANTS

The number of designs in which necklaces and pendants may be
made is limited only by the material at hand and one's own
ingenuity.

The necklace in Fig. 30 is made of garnets, both faceted and
cabochon, ornamented with leaves and twisted wire. The heavy wire

forming the outline of the heart was shaped and smaller wires carefully worked into the design so that they held the bezels of the four heart-shaped cabochons and the five faceted stones. The leaves were then soldered to the wires.

Fig. 87.—Pendants.

Fig. 88.—Drilled pendants are always popular.

To form the chain of faceted stones linked together, first the required number of bezels was made, with rings soldered on at each end. The bezels were then connected with links. In work of this type no stone is set until all soldering is completed and the mountings cleaned, polished, and oxidized.

Four different pendants are shown in Fig. 87. In No. 1 one oval and three round cabochons are used; No. 2 uses a single stone, a moss agate ground into a heart shape, with the same curvature on both sides. No bearing is needed in setting a stone of this type. A narrow band of silver is shaped to fit the stone, a ring soldered in place, the stone inserted, and the edges of the silver burnished over against the stone.

Fig. 89.—Pendants.

Similar pendants may be made by using heart-shaped cabochons that are flat on one side (Fig. 90). Use the conventional-style bezel.

A large amethyst, surrounded by garnets and leaves, is used in No. 4, Fig. 87. After the bezel for the large stone had been made in the usual manner, a wire was soldered on the outside of the bezel. Another wire was shaped so that the small bezel might be soldered onto it and onto the wire on the outside of the bezel. The leaves and shot were then soldered in the spaces between the small bezels.

Twisted wires and shot were used in decorating the pendant using four amethysts mounted upon sheet silver, as shown at lower right in Fig. 90.

Fig. 90.—Pendants.

Many simple designs may be sawed from sheet silver, such as the cross in No. 3, Fig. 87. A circle is soldered in place to hold the link through which the chain is run. A number of Indian symbols, sometimes set with small turquoise, may be used for pendants.

A chain 18 or 20 inches long is generally used for necklaces and pendants. This may be purchased with the catch already attached, from dealers, or the chain may be purchased by the foot and cut to the right length and the spring ring attached. Instead of a spring ring, a fastener made from a short piece of wire may be used. A ring

Fig. 91.—Pendants made of sheet silver and gold wire.

Fig. 92.—Pendants using twisted wire for decoration.
(*Courtesy of N. Mardirosian, New York City.*)

is usually soldered to the middle of the wire, and the chain attached to this ring. A large loop is needed on the other end of the chain, through which the wire, or bar, is inserted. If desired, a ball may be soldered on each end of the bar.

CUFF LINKS

Two methods of connecting the halves of a cuff link are shown in Fig. 93. A handmade chain is shown on the left. At the right a piece of square wire was soldered in place for the stem. A joint

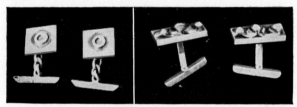

Fig. 93.—Cuff links.

was soldered to the cross piece, the stem filed and drilled to fit the joint and then riveted in place. If a stone is to be used, solder the bezel onto a piece of sheet silver. Several types of cuff-link backs are available from dealers.

EARRINGS

By the use of pierceless ear wires, many types of earrings may be made with both faceted and cabochon stones. The earrings shown

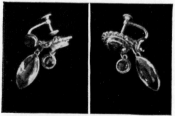

Fig. 94.—Earrings.

in Fig. 94 were made of amethysts. The bezels for the large round stones were soldered to sheet silver, decoration applied, and the ear wires soldered in place with pure tin, using soft solder flux.

The stones used in the earrings in Fig. 95 were also mounted upon sheet silver. The decoration is shot of uniform size soldered to the sheet silver. The connecting link is made of wire.

Unique earrings may be made by cutting and polishing two matched gem stones, in oval or teardrop shape, and cementing the ear wires in place.

Fig. 95.—Earrings. (*Courtesy of N. Mardirosian, New York City.*)

TIE CLIPS

Using hard or spring hard sheet silver, 18-gauge thickness, or heavy round wire, many types and designs of tie clips may be made with initials, wire, or gem stones for ornamentation.

The tie clips shown at the left in Fig. 96 were made from springy, hard sterling sheet. This type of sterling is made by reducing the thickness of the silver from 6 to 10 gauges without annealing. Hard or springy, hard silver must be specified when ordering.

Initials may be cut into one end of the blank, which is 5½ or 6 inches long and ⅜ to ½ inch wide, by using file, saw, and engraving tool. The decorative wires were hard-soldered onto the blank. If, in soldering, the blank should become annealed, hammer on a smooth surface to make the silver hard and springy. Bend the curve on the end of the clip so that it can easily be slipped over the tie, and bend the clip to shape around a steel rod. Finish the bend by tapping with a wood mallet or fiber-faced hammer, after removing the steel rod.

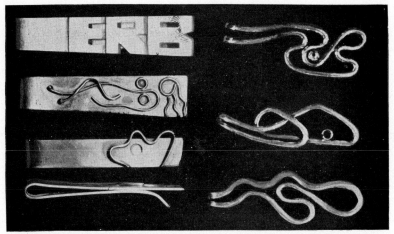

Fig. 96.—Tie clips made of spring sheet silver and wire.
(*Courtesy E. R. Bush, Bethesda, Md.*)

The clips shown at the right (Fig. 96) were made from 10-gauge round sterling wire. The length of wire depends upon the design, 10 or 12 inches generally being used. After all soldering is completed, hammer the part that goes under the tie to add stiffness, and then bend to shape.

KEY CHAIN

A key chain may be made of a sort length of chain, one end of which is soldered onto a metal plate and the other onto a short bar over which the key is placed on the chain.

Souvenir coins, monograms, gem stones set in bezels or drilled, or clevises or bails, riveted in place, may be used instead of the metal plate.

Fig. 97.—Key chains.

BROOCHES AND CLIPS

Brooches and clips may be made of sheet silver and wire and ornamented by any of the methods described under Ring Making. Bezels for the gem stones are made in the same manner as those for rings.

The bezels for the three small turquoises used in the handmade flowers (Fig. 99) were made by twisting three strands of 30-gauge wire and then running the twist through a flat rolling mill. If no rolling mill is available, hammer lightly. No bearing or inner ring is required to support the stone. If the stone is not high enough, a piece of cardboard may be placed underneath it. The bezel, being made of twisted wire, has a pleasing effect when burnished over against the stone.

The brooch shown at lower center (Fig. 99) was made by mounting the bezels upon thin sheet silver and sawing out the portion inside the bezel. Twisted wire and shot were then used to fill in between the small bezels.

Catches, both plain and safety, as well as joints, are obtainable on patches, which can be tinned with soft solder. They are sweated into place. A much better, stronger joint may be made by obtaining

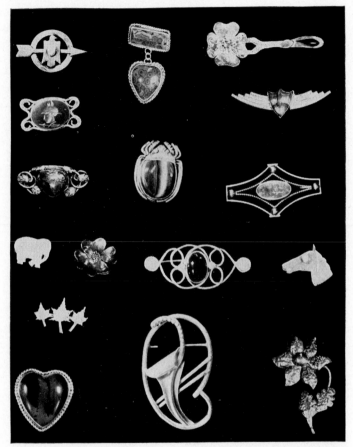

Fig. 98.—Pins made from sterling sheet and wire and inexpensive gem stones.

catches and joints made for hard soldering. The catch or joint is put in position, a piece of solder placed beside it, and the brooch heated until the solder flows, soldering the catch to the brooch.

Another method, preferred by many students, is to place a piece of solder covered with flux on the brooch at the spot where the catch or joint is to be attached and to heat the brooch until the solder melts. The base of the catch is then coated with flux and held upon the brooch, which is still hot, until the water has evaporated. The

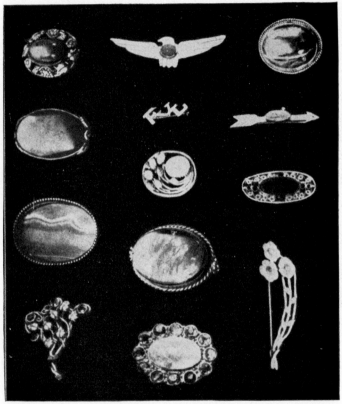

Fig. 99.—Brooches.

catch will usually stay in place when the brooch is again heated and the solder melted. Keep the flame off the catch; for if the catch is heated too much, the solder is likely to flow onto it, rendering it useless.

Both joint and catch are usually soldered above the center of the brooch, so that the brooch will hang better. The joint is soldered on the right-hand side, in relation to the wearer. The catch is soldered on with the opening toward the bottom of the brooch.

The pin stem is riveted to the joint by the use of a small nickel wire, called rivet wire, which is available in assorted sizes. Pin stems with the rivets in place may be obtained and are easier to use.

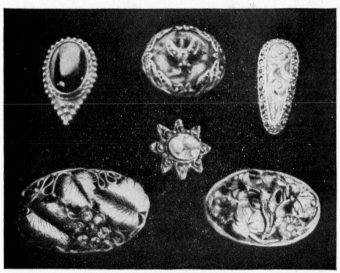

Fig. 100.—Brooches and clips. (*Courtesy of N. Mardirosian, New York City.*)

The design of the top center brooch (Fig. 100) is unusual in the handling of both leaves and ornament. The leaves are of twisted wire coiled into shape. The ornament, a bee, in the center of the carved carnelian stone is of sterling, with the body made of a tiger-eye gem stone. The bee is mounted upon a silver tube, which extends through a hole drilled in the carnelian, and is burnished over on the underside to hold the ornament in place.

Clips may be made with a solid back of sheet silver or with the conventional-style bezel, which is open on the back. The spring clips used on the back of dress clips must be taken apart before being soldered into place, in order to protect the spring.

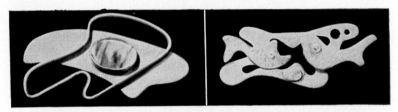

Fig. 101.—Pins.

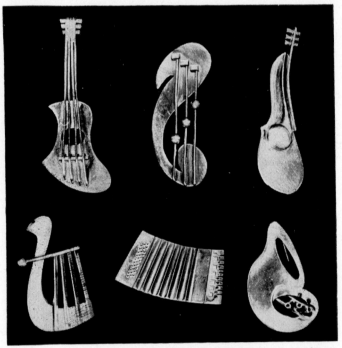

Fig. 102.—Lapel pins. (*Courtesy E. R. Bush, Bethesda, Md.*)

Various ornaments may be made that are to be sewed to the clothing, or they may be attached by using clutch backs. Initials and monograms may be cut out of sheet silver and attached with clutch backs, or small wires, which are to be pushed through the material and bent over on the underside, may be hard-soldered to the back of the initial.

BELT CHAINS AND WATCH FOBS

Belt chains may be constructed by making the belt loop out of sterling sheet and attaching the chain and the swivel. The belt loop, or slide, is made of one piece of silver, bent to shape and the end soldered. One end ordinarily projects, through which a hole is drilled to attach the chain.

Watch fobs are usually a sawing project, initials, monograms, gem stones, or other desired ornaments being soldered to the fobs.

BARRETTES

Barrettes of any shape may be made from 20-gauge sheet silver. Ornamentation may be of wire, designs may be sawed and filed in the blank, or a combination of the two may be used.

Fig. 103.—Barrettes made from sheet silver and wire.

Solder a piece of tubing on the back to form the hinge for the wire. If the correct size of tubing is not at hand, make it by pulling a piece of 26- or 28-gauge sheet metal, $\frac{1}{4}$ inch wide, through a drawplate. Make the catch from wire or sheet silver. Reduce a piece of heavy wire to the desired size by using a drawplate, so that the wire will be springy.

Fig. 104.—Belt buckles made of sterling sheet and wire.

INDIAN JEWELRY

When one thinks of Indian jewelry today, he almost invariably thinks of the Navajo Indians of the Southwest, who long ago became artisans in the use of silver, decorating most of their jewelry with turquoise.

Mexican pesos were used for many years by the Indians as the source of supply for silver, but today silver alloyed to .900 fine, known as coin silver, is generally used.

The nomadic Indian, herding sheep over the barren areas and moving from place to place, had to make use of simple tools to fashion his silver. These usually consisted of a hammer and a piece of iron upon which to hammer. For heat he used charcoal and a hand bellows. In soldering he used silver dust and alum moistened with saliva.

Genuine Navajo dies were fashioned by each silversmith from pieces of iron and, being soft, could not be used to stamp the imprints into the silver. Instead the dies were pressed into the silver while the silver was red-hot.

Turquoise, which from the dawn of civilization has always been held in high esteem, has long occupied an important place in the mythology and folklore of the Indians of the Southwest. Marvelous virtues have been attributed to it: "One who sees turquoise early in the morning will pass a fortunate day"; "The eye is strengthened by looking at a turquoise"; "The turquoise helps its owner to vic-

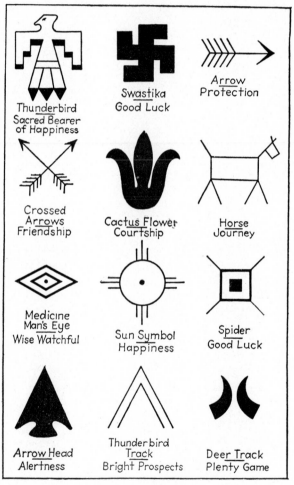

Fig. 105.—Indian symbols.

tory over his enemies, protects him against injury, and makes him liked by all men."

Much of the present-day Indian jewelry that is bought at trading posts and gift shops is made by Indians under the supervision of

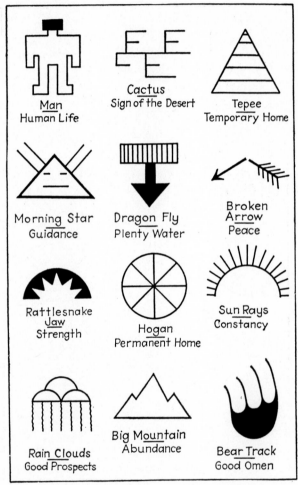

Fig. 105 (*Continued*).—Indian symbols.

the white man. It is stamped out on presses, with an Indian operating the press, and taken to an Indian silversmith, who solders on the
cups or bezels, which are often factory-made. The Indian is allowed very little scope for, or opportunity to use, his own ingenuity.

Indian-type jewelry is quite popular with high school students.
Many of the Indian symbols can be used for decoration. They can
be cut from sheet silver and soldered to rings, bracelets, and other
pieces of jewelry.

Steel dies of Navajo design, to be used in stamping Indian designs
into silver, may be purchased and used in ornamenting handmade
jewelry.

DISCARDED DENTAL INSTRUMENTS

Many of the instruments and tools used by dentists are useful in the
fashioning of handmade jewelry by the home craftsman. Dentists
generally discard scalers, burnishers, excavators, enamel cleavers,
and similar instruments, as they break or wear down through use
or frequent sharpenings. A discarded instrument can be readily
ground on a grinding wheel to a shape or point that will prove very
useful in jewelry making.

Since dental instruments are generally made of the finest type
of steel or one of the many chrome-steel alloys, even discarded
instruments will give long and useful service in jewelry making. A
broken scaler or chisel, for instance, can be sharpened to a point
and will make a hand punch or scratch awl. Burnishing down of
small bezels can also be accomplished by the use of many of the
dental instruments.

The hand electric motor tool or flexible-shaft motor tool will
serve admirably for holding small grinding wheels, mandrels, sandpaper disks, abrasive wheels, and polishing buffs.

After the assembling and soldering of a ring or ornament, there
are generally rough spots that should be ground away prior to

polishing; this can be easily accomplished with the above equipment. The abrasive disks will be found more serviceable than files in many instances. Polishing can also be carried out with the small felt buffs about the size of a five-cent piece, with cake rouge used

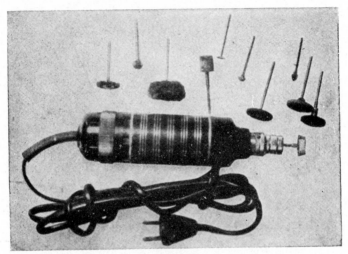

Fig. 106.—Hand motor tool and accessories.

as an abrasive. The claw type of rings are especially difficult to finish and polish by ordinary means but are a simple problem with the dental equipment.

RING CASTING IN SAND

A flask, some fine casting sand, glycerine, parting sand or powder, a crucible, a melting furnace, and models are the requirements for casting rings and other objects in silver or gold.

Making the Flask. Although the flask shown in Fig. 108 was made from two 1½-inch lengths of 3½-inch inside-diameter brass tubing, other sizes of tubing, or pipe, or wood frames could be used equally well. First cut off the tubing, or pipe, to the required lengths, and file smooth. Then, using a piece of copper, steel, or brass rod, shape the two eyes, or ears, and soft-solder them to one of the pieces of tubing. Next bore a $\frac{3}{16}$-inch hole in each ear, being sure that the hole just touches the piece of tubing. The half of the flask with the ears is known as the drag; the half with the pins is known as the cope.

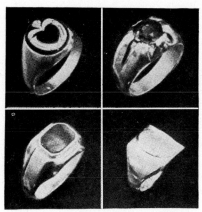

Fig. 107.—Rings cast from silver.

Fig. 108.—Drag ready to receive sand.

Put the two pieces of tubing in a vise, insert short pieces of $\frac{3}{16}$-inch rods through the holes in the ears, align, and soft-solder in place. If the rods fit too tightly in the holes, reduce their size with a file and smooth with abrasive cloth. Flasks for ring casting may, however, be purchased ready for use.

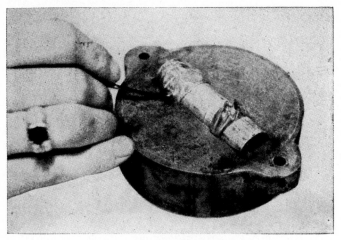

Fig. 109.—Repairing a mold.

Preparing the Sand. Fine casting sand is needed for silver casting. In preparing the sand for use, sift through a sieve made of screen wire. Then work in just enough glycerine to hold the sand together, mixing both thoroughly. After each use the sand should be sifted, and after repeated use, if the sand becomes dry, work in more glycerine. Satisfactory commercial sand for silver casting may be purchased, ready for use, in 5-pound cans.

Mandrels and Core Tube. Obtain a 3-inch length of copper or brass tubing that has an inside diameter equal to the size of the ring to be cast. Then, on a lathe, turn a wood dowel about 12 inches long, which will just slip inside the tubing.

Cut off two pieces of the dowel the exact length of the piece of tubing. Take one of these pieces, split it in half lengthwise, and mount it upon a 5- by 5-inch board, as shown in Fig. 108. Use the other short piece of dowel for the casting mandrel to hold the models, as shown in Figs. 109 and 111. Use the long piece of dowel to push the sand core out of the small tubing. Different-sized mandrels and core tubing must be used for each size of ring.

Models. Before a ring can be cast, a model, or pattern, is necessary. It may be made of wood, soft solder, or a plastic rod.

In the making of models avoid undercutting, for the sand will not leave the pattern properly unless the pattern has a gentle slope from the bottom toward the top or, in the case of a ring, from the inside toward the outside.

Sprue Pins. Tapering plugs, called sprue pins, are needed to make holes in the sand through which the molten metal can reach the mold. These holes are known as sprue holes. After making the pins from either wood or metal, bore small holes in the half mandrel to hold them in an upright position, as shown in Fig. 108.

Preparing the Mold. In preparing for a cast, place the tapering plugs, (sprue pins) in the half mandrel, dust both mandrel and plugs with the parting powder, and place the eye half of the flask, the drag, over the mandrel. Fill with sifted sand, packing lightly. Remove the pins, invert the flask, lift off the board, and you have what is shown in Fig. 110.

Place the model, or models if two rings are to be cast, on the round mandrel, dust with parting powder, and put the mandrel in the sand, pressing it down firmly so that the model will make an imprint in the sand. If any sand is disturbed, it may be repacked with a small spatula.

Dust the sand, mandrel, and patterns with parting powder. Place the pin half of the flask in position, and pack it with sifted sand. After this has been done, carefully pull the two halves of the flask apart, and remove the mandrels and patterns, as shown in Fig. 111. If any sand falls into the mold, it should be carefully removed.

Fig. 110.—Mandrel and sprue pins removed.

Fig. 111.—Mandrel and patterns removed.

Making the Core. Using the piece of tubing with the inside diameter the same as that of the model, pack it with casting sand, and push out with a dowel (Fig. 112). If it is correctly packed and if care is used in removing, the sand will come out in a cylinder, or core. Place this carefully in the pin half of the flask, and put the eye half of the flask in position.

Fig. 112.—Removing the sand core from tubing.

Fig. 113.—Crucible and flask after pouring.

Melting the Silver. Place some silver in a suitable crucible, and sprinkle a little powdered borax over the top of the silver. Place the crucible in the melting furnace, which is shown in Fig. 1. This type of furnace requires constant air pressure, which may be supplied by a rotary air blower or a compressor.

After the silver has melted, remove the crucible with a pair of tongs, and pour the molten metal into the holes left in the sand by the sprue pins. Allow the metal to cool for a few minutes, and then pull the flask apart. If the cast is satisfactory, the ring, when cool, may be sawed from the tapering piece of silver formed in the sprue hole. It may then be finished by filing, sanding with abrasive cloth, and, finally, buffing. If for any reason the cast is unsatisfactory, the silver may be remelted.

Metal Models. If a large number of casts are to be made from a model, it is advisable to prepare a metal model from the wood model, as the wood model is likely to break. The metal model is also superior in that it can be made to more exacting dimensions and will make a much cleaner cast that requires less filing.

To make the metal model, instead of pouring silver into the mold, pour molten brass. Then file and buff the brass model until it is smooth. As the cast-ring model will be a little smaller than the wood model, it will not fit the mandrel unless it is stretched or sawed through the shank. Sawing is preferable, for then the model will fit several sizes of mandrels.

The gap left between the sawed ends will not interfere with the casting. When the impression is made in the sand, this irregularity may be removed with a small spatula or by inserting a finished cast ring in the mold and gently pressing it into place.

CASTING FLAT OBJECTS

Small flat objects may be cast very easily. Make a pattern, and then place the pattern and the eye half of the flask on a board. Pack with sand, holding the sprue pin in place. Remove the pin, invert the flask, lift off the board, but leave the pattern in place. Dust with parting powder, place the pin end of the flask in place, and fill with sand. Invert the flask, separate the halves, and remove the pattern. Put the flask together again, and it is ready for pouring.

FINISHING CAST RINGS

Rings that are cast in sand may be set with stones of various kinds, or initials or emblems may be soldered or engraved upon the various types.

Several different styles of cast rings are shown in Fig. 107. Three of them are designed for initials, emblems, or stones; one is designed for faceted stones. The bezel for the stone set on top of the rings was

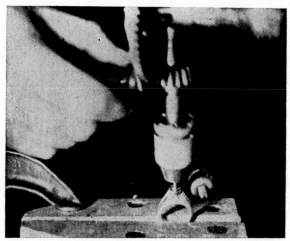

Fig. 114.—Cutting a bearing for a round faceted stone.

made of fine silver and soldered to the ring. After soldering a bezel to a cast ring, avoid sudden cooling of the ring, as it may warp. The carved agate is set flush with the top of the ring. This is accomplished by cutting out the metal and leaving a narrow rim, which is burnished over the stone and holds it in place.

Round faceted stones are somewhat harder to set as the bearing must be cut on an angle. This may be done by filing, but a quicker, as well as an easier, way is to use a bearing burr. The method of cutting the bearing with a burr is shown in Fig. 114. The ring is held in a wood clamp. A hole is bored through the ring with a drill that is a little smaller than the stone. The burr is then inserted in the hand drill, and a seat, or bearing, is cut for the stone.

After the bearing is cut, the prongs are filed thin at the top, the stone is set in place, and by using a burnisher the prongs are forced over the edge of the stone to hold it firmly. Bearing burrs may be purchased singly or in sets. A set of 30 different-sized burrs is shown in Fig. 115.

Fig. 115.—Bearing burrs.

GOLD AND SILVER

Troy weight is used in weighing precious metals—gold, silver and platinum. Silver is sold by the ounce, gold by the pennyweight.

Troy Weight

24 grains = 1 pennyweight (dwt.).
20 pennyweight = 1 ounce (oz.).
12 ounces = 1 pound (lb.).

Comparative Weights

5760 grains = 1 pound troy = 373.2 grams.
7000 grains = 1 pound avoirdupois = 453.6 grams.

1 gram = 15.43 grains = 0.032 ounce troy.

1 ounce troy = 1.097 ounces avoirdupois = 31.1 grams.

1 ounce avoirdupois = 0.912 ounce troy = 28.35 grams.

16 ounces avoirdupois = 14.6 ounces troy = 1 pound avoirdupois.

1 pound troy = 13.2 ounces avoirdupois.

1 carat = 3.086 grains = 0.20 gram.

Fine Gold. Fine (pure gold) is known as 24-karat gold. Gold is the most ductile and malleable of all the metals. Fine gold is very soft and rarely used for jewelry purposes. The melting point of 24-karat gold is 1945°F. The specific gravity of fine gold is 19.3.

Karat Gold. Karat gold is a measure of fineness. Fine (pure) gold is 24-karat gold. If an article is made of 18-karat gold, the fine gold in the article is $\frac{18}{24}$ of the total weight. Likewise, if it is 10-karat gold, it is $\frac{10}{24}$ fine gold by weight. Metals used in alloying fine gold are silver, copper, zinc, and nickel.

Colored Golds. The component metals used in various colored golds are as follows:

Yellow golds for general purposes: gold, silver, copper, small amount of zinc.

Yellow golds for enameling purposes: gold, silver, copper.

Green golds for general use: gold, silver, small amount of copper, small amount of zinc.

Green gold for enameling purposes: gold, silver, small amount of copper.

White gold for general use: gold, nickel, small amount of zinc.

Red gold for general use: gold, copper, small amount of silver.

Melting Points of Golds. Different 10-, 14-, and 18-karat golds vary as to melting points because of the various alloys that are used to obtain certain colors.

The approximate melting points of various karat golds are as follows:

Karat	Yellow	White	Pink	Green
10	1510	1760	1690	1470
14	1555	1690	1650	1590
18	1640	1650	——	1750
20	1810			
22	1850			
24	1945			

Gold-filled and Rolled-gold Plate. Gold-filled plate or wire is made by joining a layer of gold alloy to a base metal and then rolling or drawing to the required thickness.

Rolled-gold plate is made in the same way as gold-filled, but it has a lower gold content.

No article having a gold coating of less than 10-karat fineness shall have applied to it any quality mark. No article having an alloyed gold content of less than $\frac{1}{20}$ shall be marked "gold-filled." For example, "$\frac{1}{20}$ 10K gold-filled" on an article means that the article consists of a base metal covered on one or both surfaces with a gold alloy of 10-karat fineness and that the gold alloy comprises $\frac{1}{20}$ part, by weight, of the metal in the article, exclusive of joints, pin stems, catches, or other findings.

Fine Silver. Fine (pure) silver, like fine gold, is very soft and finds little use in handmade jewelry other than in the making of bezels. Fine silver melts at 1761°F.

Sterling Silver. "Sterling" is one of the best known and the most respected quality markings in use. Sterling silver is made of 925 parts pure silver and 75 parts base metal, which is usually copper.

The copper adds stiffness and wearing qualities. The proportion of pure silver, 92½ per cent, never varies in sterling silver, as it is fixed by law.

The word sterling came from the "Easterlings," which was the name of a band of traders in eastern Germany in the twelfth century. These traders came from five free towns where the people made not only their own laws but their own currency. In trading with English merchants they gave silver coins in payment. The English learned that the coins, which were referred to as the coins of the Easterlings, could be depended upon as containing $925/1000$ fine silver. The original designation, Easterlings, was later abbreviated to sterling.

Silver is hardened by hammering, rolling, or drawing. It is annealed (softened) by heating to 1100 to 1200°F. and either cooled in air or quenched in water.

The melting point of sterling silver is 1640°F.

Coin Silver. Coin silver, the alloy used in making United States silver coins, consists of 90 per cent ($900/1000$) fine silver and 10 per cent copper. The melting point of coin silver is 1615°F.

How to Order Silver. In ordering silver be sure to state whether sterling or fine silver is wanted. Specify whether it is to be sheet or wire and what quantity is needed. Next specify the gauge or thickness. If sheet silver is being ordered, specify the width, if any predetermined width is wanted. If ordering wire, state whether it is to be round, half-round, or square. The tables in Figs. 117 and 118 show the weights of silver in the various gauges. Silver is sold by the troy ounce.

The Brown and Sharpe gauge is used in measuring the thickness of silver. It is advisable, unless a rolling mill is available with which to reduce the thickness, to keep several gauges of sheet silver on hand. The author has found from experience in dealing with students that, in sterling, sheet silver kept in 16-, 18-, 20-, and 24-gauge thicknesses will meet the requirements for most jewelry making, with occasional uses for 12 and 14 gauge.

Many different sizes of sterling wire are used in making jewelry, although the 12-, 14-, 16-, and 20-gauge round wires are those most frequently needed. The heavier round wires, 8 and 10 gauge, are especially useful in making bracelets. Square wires in 8, 10, and 12 gauge find many uses. The larger sized half-round sterling wire, such as ³⁄₁₆, ¼, and ⁵⁄₁₆ inch diameter, is excellent for bracelet making, while the smaller half-round wire such as 10, 12, and 14 gauge, is used in other types of jewelry.

Various sizes of circles, stamped from sterling sheet, are available and have many uses. Order these by specifying diameter and thickness, as well as the quantity desired.

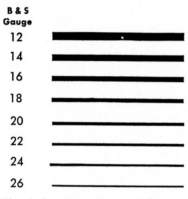

B & S Gauge

12
14
16
18
20
22
24
26

Fig. 116.—Approximate thicknesses of the most popular Brown and Sharpe gauges. (*Courtesy Handy & Harman, New York, N. Y.*)

Sterling silver, although usually supplied in annealed form, may be obtained in various tempers with a spring quality for use where no soldering is required. These tempers are called *half hard*, which means there has been a reduction of 2 gauges without annealing; *hard*, 4 gauges; and *spring hard*, 6 to 10 gauges. The higher the gauge of hardness, the closer the metal is taken to its elastic limit.

Use of Drawplate. By the use a drawplate, it is a simple matter to make any desired gauge by drawing or reducing wire of larger size. Drawplates may be purchased for drawing round, half-round, triangular, square, and rectangular wire.

Sheet Metal

(Weight in pennyweights or ounces per square inch by Brown & Sharpe gauge)

Brown & Sharpe gauge	Thickness, inches	Sterling silver, ounces	Fine gold, pennyweight	18-karat Yellow gold, pennyweight	14-karat Yellow gold, pennyweight	10-karat Yellow gold, pennyweight	Platinum, ounces	Palladium, ounces
1	0.28930	1.58	59.0	47.5	39.8	35.3	3.27	1.83
2	0.25763	1.41	52.6	42.3	35.5	31.4	2.91	1.63
3	0.22942	1.26	46.8	37.7	31.6	28.0	2.59	1.45
4	0.20431	1.12	41.7	33.6	28.1	24.9	2.31	1.29
5	0.18194	0.996	37.1	29.9	25.1	22.2	2.06	1.15
6	0.16202	0.887	33.1	26.6	22.3	19.8	1.83	1.02
7	0.14428	0.790	29.4	23.7	19.9	17.6	1.63	0.912
8	0.12849	0.704	26.2	21.1	17.7	15.7	1.45	0.812
9	0.11443	0.627	23.3	18.8	15.8	14.0	1.29	0.723
10	0.10189	0.558	20.8	16.7	14.0	12.4	1.15	0.644
11	0.09074	0.497	18.5	14.9	12.5	11.1	1.03	0.574
12	0.08080	0.443	16.5	13.3	11.1	9.85	0.913	0.511
13	0.07196	0.394	14.7	11.8	9.91	8.77	0.813	0.455
14	0.06408	0.351	13.1	10.5	8.82	7.81	0.724	0.405
15	0.05706	0.313	11.6	9.37	7.86	6.96	0.645	0.361
16	0.05082	0.278	10.4	8.35	7.00	6.21	0.574	0.321
17	0.04525	0.248	9.23	7.43	6.23	5.52	0.511	0.286
18	0.04030	0.221	8.22	6.62	5.55	4.91	0.455	0.255
19	0.03589	0.197	7.32	5.89	4.94	4.38	0.406	0.227
20	0.03196	0.175	6.52	5.25	4.40	3.90	0.361	0.202
21	0.02846	0.156	5.81	4.67	3.92	3.47	0.322	0.180
22	0.02534	0.139	5.17	4.16	3.49	3.09	0.286	0.160
23	0.02257	0.124	4.60	3.71	3.11	2.75	0.255	0.143
24	0.02010	0.110	4.10	3.30	2.77	2.45	0.227	0.127
25	0.01790	0.0980	3.65	2.94	2.46	2.18	0.202	0.113

(Continued on next page)

Sheet Metal

(Weight in pennyweights or ounces per square inch by Brown & Sharpe gauge)

Brown & Sharpe gauge	Thickness, inches	Sterling silver, ounces	Fine gold, pennyweight	18-karat Yellow gold, pennyweight	14-karat Yellow gold, pennyweight	10-karat Yellow gold, pennyweight	Platinum, ounces	Palladium, ounces
26	0.01594	0.0873	3.25	2.62	2.19	1.94	0.180	0.101
27	0.01419	0.0777	2.89	2.33	1.95	1.73	0.160	0.0897
28	0.01264	0.0692	2.58	2.08	1.74	1.54	0.143	0.0799
29	0.01125	0.0616	2.29	1.85	1.55	1.37	0.127	0.0711
30	0.01002	0.0549	2.04	1.65	1.38	1.22	0.113	0.0633
31	0.00892	0.0489	1.82	1.46	1.23	1.09	0.101	0.0564
32	0.00795	0.0435	1.62	1.31	1.09	0.969	0.0898	0.0503
33	0.00708	0.0388	1.44	1.16	0.975	0.863	0.0800	0.0448
34	0.00630	0.0345	1.29	1.03	0.868	0.768	0.0712	0.0398
35	0.00561	0.0307	1.14	0.921	0.772	0.684	0.0634	0.0355
36	0.00500	0.0274	1.02	0.821	0.689	0.610	0.0565	0.0316
37	0.00445	0.0244	0.908	0.731	0.613	0.543	0.0503	0.0281
38	0.00396	0.0217	0.808	0.650	0.545	0.483	0.0448	0.0250
39	0.00353	0.0193	0.720	0.580	0.486	0.430	0.0399	0.0223
40	0.00314	0.0172	0.641	0.516	0.432	0.383	0.0355	0.0199

Fig. 117. (*Courtesy Wildberg Bros. Smelting and Refining Co., Los Angeles, Calif.*)

Point one end of the wire to be reduced in size by filing or by hammering. Put the drawplate in a vise, the smaller side of the hole nearer you, with copper or other soft metal protecting it from the vise jaws. Insert the pointed end in the hole nearest its size.

Grip the wire with the drawing tongs, and pull through the plate. Annealing is necessary after a few draws to keep the wire from breaking. No silver is lost in the reducing process, because the wire simply becomes longer as its thickness is reduced.

Round Wire

(Weight in pennyweights or ounces per foot in Brown & Sharpe gauge)

Brown & Sharpe gauge	Thickness, inches	Sterling silver, ounces	Fine gold, pennyweight	18-karat Yellow gold, pennyweight	14-karat Yellow gold, pennyweight	10-karat Yellow gold, pennyweight	Platinum, ounces	Palladium, ounces
1	0.28930	4.32	161.0	130.0	109.0	96.2	8.91	4.99
2	0.25763	3.43	128.0	104.0	86.1	76.3	7.07	3.95
3	0.22942	2.72	101.0	81.5	68.3	60.5	5.61	3.14
4	0.20431	2.15	80.3	64.6	54.2	48.0	4.45	2.49
5	0.18194	1.71	63.6	51.2	43.0	38.0	3.53	1.97
6	0.16202	1.36	50.5	40.6	34.1	30.2	2.80	1.56
7	0.14428	1.07	40.0	32.2	27.0	23.9	2.22	1.24
8	0.12849	0.852	31.7	25.6	21.4	19.0	1.76	0.984
9	0.11443	0.676	25.2	20.3	17.0	15.1	1.39	0.780
10	0.10189	0.536	20.0	16.1	13.5	11.9	1.11	0.619
11	0.09074	0.425	15.8	12.7	10.7	9.46	0.877	0.491
12	0.08080	0.337	12.6	10.1	8.47	7.50	0.695	0.389
13	0.07196	0.267	9.96	8.01	6.72	5.95	0.552	0.309
14	0.06408	0.212	7.89	6.36	5.33	4.72	0.437	0.245
15	0.05706	0.168	6.26	5.04	4.23	3.74	0.347	0.194
16	0.05082	0.133	4.97	4.00	3.35	2.97	0.275	0.154
17	0.04525	0.106	3.94	3.17	2.66	2.35	0.218	0.122
18	0.04030	0.0838	3.12	2.51	2.11	1.87	0.173	0.0968
19	0.03589	0.0665	2.48	1.99	1.67	1.48	0.137	0.0767
20	0.03196	0.0527	1.96	1.58	1.33	1.17	0.109	0.0609
21	0.02846	0.0418	1.56	1.25	1.05	0.931	0.0863	0.0483
22	0.02534	0.0331	1.23	0.994	0.833	0.738	0.0684	0.0383
23	0.02257	0.0263	0.979	0.789	0.661	0.585	0.0543	0.0304
24	0.02010	0.0209	0.777	0.625	0.524	0.464	0.0430	0.0241
25	0.01790	0.0165	0.616	0.496	0.416	0.368	0.0341	0.0191

(Continued on next page)

Round Wire

(Weight in pennyweights or ounces per foot in Brown & Sharpe gauge)

Brown & Sharpe gauge	Thick-ness, inches	Ster-ling silver, ounces	Fine gold, penny-weight	18-karat Yellow gold, penny-weight	14-karat Yellow gold, penny-weight	10-karat Yellow gold, penny-weight	Plati-num, ounces	Palladi-um, ounces
26	0.01594	0.0131	0.489	0.393	0.330	0.292	0.0271	0.0151
27	0.01419	0.0104	0.387	0.312	0.261	0.231	0.0214	0.0120
28	0.01264	0.00825	0.307	0.247	0.207	0.184	0.0170	0.00952
29	0.01125	0.00653	0.243	0.196	0.164	0.145	0.0135	0.00754
30	0.01002	0.00518	0.193	0.155	0.130	0.115	0.0107	0.00598
31	0.00892	0.00411	0.153	0.123	0.103	0.0914	0.00847	0.00474
32	0.00795	0.00326	0.122	0.0978	0.0820	0.0726	0.00673	0.00377
33	0.00708	0.00259	0.0964	0.0776	0.0651	0.0576	0.00534	0.00299
34	0.00630	0.00205	0.0763	0.0614	0.0515	0.0456	0.00423	0.00236
35	0.00561	0.00162	0.0605	0.0487	0.0408	0.0362	0.00335	0.00188
36	0.00500	0.00129	0.0481	0.0387	0.0324	0.0287	0.00266	0.00149
37	0.00445	0.00102	0.0381	0.0306	0.0257	0.0228	0.00211	0.00118
38	0.00396	0.000809	0.0302	0.0243	0.0204	0.0180	0.00167	0.00093
39	0.00353	0.000643	0.0240	0.0193	0.0162	0.0143	0.00133	0.00074
40	0.00314	0.000509	0.0190	0.0153	0.0128	0.0113	0.00105	0.00059

Fig. 118. (*Courtesy Wildberg Bros. Smelting and Refining Co., Los Angeles, Calif.*)

Fine Silver for Bezels. Fine silver, used for making bezels, may be purchased by the ounce in various widths and gauges. Either 26 or 28 gauge is a good thickness for bezel making. The widths of ⅛ inch and ³⁄₁₆ inch are the two most used in bezel making, although the ¼-inch width is sometimes used in making rings from sheet silver, where a higher bezel is needed. If desired, fine silver may be purchased in sheet form and cut into various widths as needed.

Fig. 119.—Hand rolling mill.

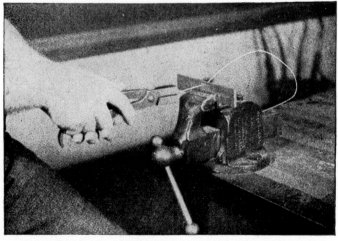

Fig. 120.—Reducing wire with a drawplate.

Cost per Square Inch. It is advisable, when dealing with students, to find out how much your sheet silver costs per square inch and how much the wire costs per inch or foot. Although you will buy it by the ounce, the student will not call for it in that manner. He will instead request a certain size of sheet or so many inches or feet of a certain gauge wire. By knowing the cost per square inch or linear foot, you can eliminate much weighing and save time.

SEMIPRECIOUS STONES

Semiprecious stones, both cabochon and faceted, suitable for use in handmade jewelry may be obtained from various dealers by those who do not care to cut and polish their own. Prices on stones vary, depending upon the quality, color, quantity bought, and other factors.

Fig. 121.—The metric scale, used in measuring many gem stones.

One of the best ways to buy stones is to arrange to have the dealer send an assortment of various stones "on consignment." Then you are permitted to look them over, select what you want, and return the remainder, paying for only those chosen.

Many of the dealers in gem-cutting material cut and polish a large number of stones, especially cabochons.

The carat, which is equal to 3.08 grains troy weight, is the unit of weight for weighing precious and some semiprecious stones. For convenience the carat is divided into 100 parts, each part of which is called a point. Thus a stone weighing 65 points would weigh 0.65 carat.

AGATE-HANDLED TABLEWARE

Many unusual and attractive pieces of tableware may be made by using sterling silver for the metal parts and agate for the handles.

The making of these pieces is well within the ability of the average craftsmen, after he has learned to shape and polish a piece of agate, to use the jewelers' saw and to silver solder. Many of the pieces shown in the following illustrations were made by J. W.

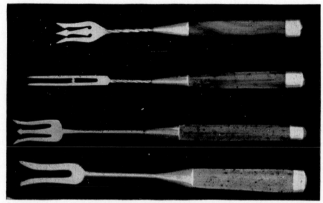

Fig. 122.—Colorful gem stones may be used to decorate the tips of agate handled, hand-made, forks.

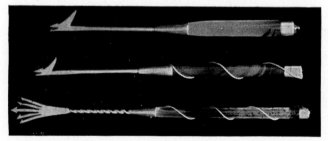

Fig. 123.—Pickle forks may be made in various designs.

Anderson, seventy-three years old, of Baltimore, Md. These pieces were Mr. Anderson's first attempts at silver work, based on the instructions on silver soldering contained in an earlier edition of this book.

Make a full-sized drawing of the piece to be created. If making a fork, fold a piece of paper, and sketch one half of the tines. Cut out the design, and unfold. Using this paper pattern as part of the drawing, sketch the remainder of the fork.

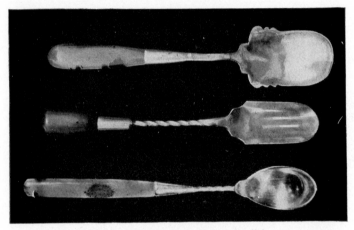

Fig. 124.—Sugar shells, cheese scoops, and relish spoons are a few of the many types of spoons that may be made.

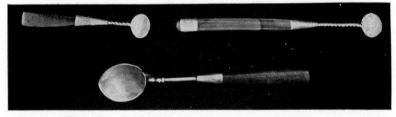

Fig. 125.—Individual salt spoons and mustard spoon.

These pieces may be made any size. The handles for the forks shown in Fig. 122 are 3 to 4 inches in length and were made from slabs $\frac{3}{8}$ to $\frac{1}{2}$ inch wide and $\frac{5}{16}$ to $\frac{3}{8}$ inch thick. The $\frac{3}{8}$- by $\frac{3}{8}$-inch blanks were cut into round handles.

Grind the handle to shape, sand and polish. Make a taper on one end to fit into the ferrule. Sand and polish the taper. All the work can be done upon a smooth grinding wheel, the sander and the felt buff.

Paste the paper pattern upon a piece of sterling sheet 12- or 14-gauge Brown and Sharpe, and saw to shape with the jewelers'

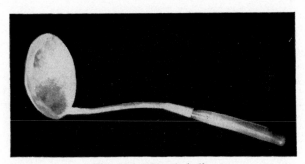

Fig. 126.—Punch ladle.

Fig. 127.—A butter knife made of sheet silver with a colorful agate handle makes an attractive piece of silverware.

saw. File to approximate shape, leaving some of the filing to be done after all soldering is completed.

Make the shank from 8- or 10-gauge Brown and Sharpe round or square wire or from two or more strands of smaller wire twisted together. If using twisted wires, solder the wires together, and flatten slightly at the end where it is to be soldered to the tines or knife blade.

The ferrule, or transition piece, may be made from 24-gauge Brown and Sharpe sheet silver. For most pieces the ferrule may be ¾ to 1 inch in length. Make a paper pattern by carefully fitting the paper around the tapered end of the handle. Cut the ferrule out of sheet silver and carefully file the joint. Bend to shape and silver solder. A piece of wood or metal shaped like the tapering end of the handle helps in shaping the ferrule to fit the handle, before soldering the ferrule to the shank.

The ferrule and shank may be modeled in wax, invested, and cast by using the "lost wax" method of casting.

Fig. 128.—Letter openers make unique pieces for gifts, or for own use.

Solder the ferrule to the shank, allowing the shank to extend into the small end of the ferrule. Remove all oxides by pickling, and, with a smooth-faced metal hammer, hammer the tines or knife blade and the shank, resting the metal upon a smooth metal surface. Unless the silver is hammered, it will remain soft from the heat at the time of silver soldering.

Grind numerous nicks into that portion of the tapered handle fitting down into the ferrule. Cement the handle into the ferrule, using Rapid Stone, Cementstone, or one of the various "stones" that are available at any dental supply house or dental laboratory. Rapid Stone is inexpensive and is used in the dental field for the making of models. It is not a cement, but it holds the agate in the ferrule. Mix the powder with water until it has the consistency of heavy cream. Pack the ferrule with the mix being sure no bubbles are entrapped. Push the handle into the ferrule, and tap the end of the handle gently with a wood mallet or fiber-faced hammer. Allow to harden, and clean off excess stone. There is no contraction when the mix hardens.

The tip of the handle may be left plain, or a colorful stone such as chrysocolla may be used. Make a bezel from 24- or 26-gauge silver that fits the tip of the handle, and grind the stone to fit the

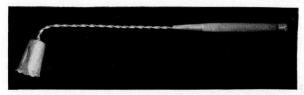

Fig. 129.—Candle snuffer with gem stone set in bezel on end of agate handle.

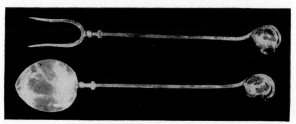

Fig. 130.—Cabochons and hand-made silver leaves burnished over the gem stones were used to decorate these pieces. No. 10 gauge square wire was used for the fork, also the spoon handle.

bezel. Grind nicks on the end of the handle, cement the bezel in place, and press stone into the bezel. Burnish the bezel over the stone after the cement has hardened.

The rope effect on two of the forks shown in Fig. 123 was obtained by twisting two strands of small silver wire. Solder one end of the wire to the ferrule and the other end to the cap before the handle is cemented in place. Cement the handle in the ferrule; after the cement hardens, twist the wire around the handle, and cement the end cap in position. Use a wood clamp on the end cap to keep it in place while the cement hardens.

In making a spoon or ladle, raise the bowl from 16- or 18-gauge sheet, by using a smooth ball peen hammer and a piece of hard wood with a depression cut into it. The shaping may also be done upon a sandbag or in a pitch bowl.

Butter knives and butter spreaders, as well as letter openers, may be made from 14- or 16-gauge sheet silver. Hammer the blade after all soldering is finished, saw to shape, and file to the desired taper.

PRECISION INVESTMENT CASTING

Precision investment casting making use of expendable wax patterns by embedding them in a refractory material known as investment, burning out the pattern, and then forcing molten metal into the mold by centrifugal force or other means is being widely used in manufacturing fields today.

Introduced to the jewelry field from the dental field about 1935, precision investment casting became popular during the Second World War for making small, intricate metal parts that were difficult to machine because of their shape and the hardness of the metal from which they were cast. Investment casting is now standard practice in many fields of industrv and tolerances range from ±0.005 to ±0.003 inch.

Since the mold used in making the cast is broken up and discarded in removing the casting, undercuts present no problem; hence one is able to carve intricate patterns in wax and faithfully reproduce minute detail in silver, gold, or platinum. Because the wax pattern is burned out of the mold—thus completely lost—this method is also called the "lost-wax" method of casting.

Investment casting is well within the realm of the craftsman working in his homeshop or 'the student in the schoolshop. A spring-powered centrifugal casting machine, together with necessary waxes

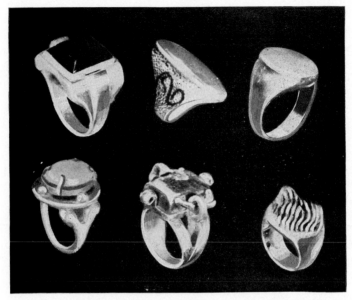

Fig. 131.—Cast finger rings, four of which are in gold. Undercuts present no problem in centrifugal castings.

Fig. 132.—Many unusual pieces of jewelry can be made by making a pattern or model in wax and reproducing in gold or silver by centrifugal casting. This brooch, resembling a crab, was modeled in wax by a high school senior girl student in the author's class and cast in silver. This was her first attempt at wax modeling. The stone used was the first stone the student cut.

and investment, is all that is absolutely necessary to make a good cast, as the wax can be burned out over a Bunsen burner. A gas or electric furnace, with temperature controls and indicator, is however, desirable for the burnout, for thus temperatures can be controlled.

Fig. 133.—Kerr Centrifico casting machine with various size casting rings, sprue bases, and counterweights. (*Courtesy Kerr Manufacturing Co., Detroit, Mich.*)

A spring-powered centrifugal casting machine such as the Vaughan No. 34 or the Kerr Centrifico is excellent for making the cast. Various size casting rings or flasks may be used on either of these machines.

The wax pattern, made entirely by hand or in a rubber or soft metal mold, is fastened to one end of a short wax rod or wire, called a sprue; the other end of the sprue is fastened onto a conical-shaped metal or rubber base, called a sprue base or sprue former. The pattern is then washed with soap and water or with one of the patented solutions to reduce surface tension.

The investment, a powder composed of refractory particles and a binder which sets when wet, is mixed with water, the pattern placed inside a casting ring, or flask, and the investment mix poured into the flask.

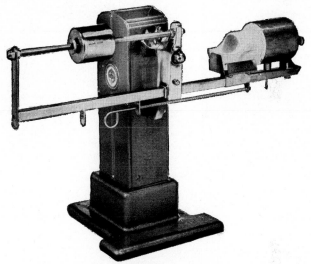

Fig. 134.—Vaughan No. 34 centrifugal casting machine. Various size casting rings or flasks may be used. (*Courtesy Torit Manufacturing Co., Saint Paul, Minn.*)

After the investment sets, the sprue base is removed, and the wax pattern is burned out by heating the flask. The hot flask is placed in the casting machine, which has been wound, the metal to be cast being placed in the crucible and melted with a suitable blowpipe or torch. When the metal is molten, the crossarm is released, and the molten metal is instantaneously thrown through an opening in the end of the crucible and thence through the opening in the mold made by the sprue to the cavity in the mold formed by the burning out of the wax pattern.

In industrial casting many patterns are cast at one time, the patterns being fastened onto wax rods, forming a treelike assembly before being invested. Fifty to one hundred rings may be cast at one time. The craftsman can invest several patterns in one flask and cast them all at the same time (Fig. 141).

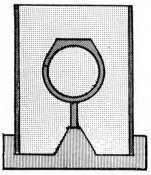

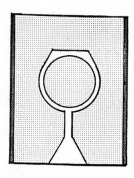

Fig. 135.—Cross section showing wax pattern mounted on rubber sprue base with casting ring or flask in place and filled with investment.

Fig. 136.—Cross section showing invested pattern, after removing the sprue base and burning out the wax pattern and wax sprue.

Wax for Patterns. Wax used for making patterns (models) should be of a type that will burn out of the investment without leaving any carbon residue. This wax should be hard enough to withstand handling and carving, yet capable of being bent and formed to shape when slightly warmed.

Waxes suitable for patterns are available from dealers in precision-casting equipment and supplies or from your local dental supply house. They are available in sheet, wire, and stick form as well as in bulk. Two or more waxes may be blended to produce a wax best suited for a particular purpose. Bulk wax may be melted and poured upon a glass slab to form thick sheets.

Blue inlay casting wax, a dental wax available in sheet and stick form, has many uses. Another dental wax very handy for making ring and other patterns is base-plate wax. Base-plate wax is usually 16 gauge in thickness and is packaged in half-pound and larger boxes. It is available in three grades, soft, medium, and hard. The medium or hard is best for making ring patterns.

Paraffin may be used for small patterns. The original pattern of the sea horse (Fig. 154) was made by a high school student who warmed a piece of paraffin, flattened it against a piece of sheet metal, and cut to outline with a penknife. He used an engraving tool to get the detail.

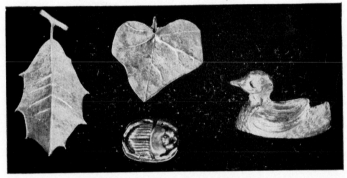

Fig. 137.—Holly and ivy leaves cast in silver, using real leaves for patterns. The beetle was cast from a hand-carved wax model. The duck was cast from a pattern made in a flexible mold.

Making Patterns. The making of a handmade wax pattern is not a difficult task, although it takes time and patience. Sheet wax, for instance, can be cut to shape, slightly warmed, and bent around a ring mandrel to form the base upon which to build a ring pattern. Add thickness where needed by applying more wax with a wax spatula or with a piece of hack-saw blade ground and polished to the shape of the spatula.

Warm the spatula, and touch it to a piece of wax, allowing the melted wax to run down onto the blade; transfer the melted wax to the pattern. A set of cork borers is excellent upon which to shape a finger-ring pattern, as there is no taper and a wide variety of sizes is available.

The ring pattern should be made about one size smaller than the ring size desired, to allow for cleaning and polishing of the metal after the cast is made.

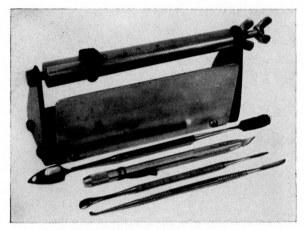

Fig. 138.—A stand for holding ring mandrel, or specially made mandrel, is handy when shaping the wax model. Wax spatulas like those shown find many uses.

Wax wires, round and half-round, are useful in the making of patterns for rings as well as for many other pieces of jewelry, since they are pliable and may be bent to any desired shape. Dental supply houses stock these wires.

To keep wax from sticking to a ring mandrel when making the pattern, coat the mandrel with a thin film of vaseline or Microfilm, a commercial product available from dental supply houses.

Bezels for stones may be formed in the wax; or the bezel may be made of thin silver or gold, set in the wax, and the wax flushed against the metal with the spatula. Bezels made of gold should be of a high karat. Fine silver is better than sterling. The molten metal when cast into the burned-out investment will replace the metal used in the bezel, thus making the bezel an integral part of the cast.

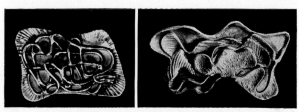

Fig. 139.—Brooches cast in silver from patterns made of wax sheet and wax wire.

Fig. 140.—Rubber sprue base at left, and metal sprue base at right. These sprued models are ready to be invested.

Smoothing Wax Patterns. The finished wax pattern should be as smooth as possible before being invested. Smooth out any irregularities with a slightly warmed wax spatula or ground and polished hack-saw blade. Many irregularities may be removed by scraping or by using abrasive cloth or sandpaper.

The wax pattern may be rubbed with a piece of cotton or cloth while the pattern is held in cold water to keep the wax hard, or the pattern may be flamed.

To flame a pattern, quickly pass it through a small flame. A large hypodermic needle fastened to one end of a rubber tube, the other end of which is connected to a gas outlet, will, when lit, produce a small flame quite handy in smoothing patterns. Do not flame thin patterns or thin sections of heavy patterns.

Another method of smoothing a handmade wax pattern is to rub the pattern with a small piece of cotton moistened with oil of eucalyptus or oil of cajuput (available at drugstores), which softens the wax. Then immediately rub the model with another piece of cotton moistened with acetone to stop the action of the oil.

Spruing and Mounting. The wax pattern, before being invested, must be fastened to a wax rod called a sprue, the other end of which is attached to a sprue base, usually of rubber or metal.

Round wax wires, 10 gauge or heavier, make excellent sprues. Warm the wax spatula, and seal one end of the sprue to the wax pattern; then fasten the other end of the sprue to the sprue base in the same manner. A short sprue is generally better than a long one.

After the pattern is mounted on the sprue and the sprue base, it must be at least $\frac{1}{4}$ inch below the top of the flask or casting ring when the flask is placed in position over the pattern.

In some cases it is best to run several sprues to different places on the pattern. In casting against a silver or gold bezel, three sprues may be used as shown in Fig. 147. Several sprues should be used in casting thin patterns, such as leaves. Attach the sprues to a heavy wax wire or rod fastened to the sprue base. Thin leaves may be backed with 28-gauge sheet wax. Warm the sheet wax, and press against the back of the leaf. Attach the sprues to the back of the leaf. When possible, attach the sprue to the thickest portion of the wax pattern.

In multiple casting the patterns must be separated and, in most instances, sprued to a central sprue or sprues of heavy wax rod (Fig. 141).

Cleaning Patterns. Before being invested, that is, placed in the refractory material, wax patterns must be treated with some solution to reduce surface tension. Otherwise the investment, which is mixed with water, will not adhere to the wax surface, and the surface of the casting will be rough. This is caused by surface bubbles or air pockets formed during the investment, which in turn produce nodules on the casting.

Fig. 141.—Several wax patterns may be attached to a central wax rod and all cast at the same time.

Fig. 142.—Three sprues are attached to this heavy wax model, hand carved by a student.

Paint the entire surface of the wax pattern with a mixture of equal parts of tincture of green soap and hydrogen peroxide. Brush the solution on the pattern with a small artist's brush, or dip the model into the solution; rinse with water, and blow dry.

Another method is to use a small brush and any convenient soap. Wet the brush with water, rub onto a cake of soap, and brush the pattern thoroughly. Keep wetting the brush and scrubbing the pattern until water flows evenly over the entire surface. Dry by blowing. Some dentists clean their wax models prior to casting by brushing them with, or dipping them in, a solution of equal parts of alcohol and household ammonia, rinsing with water, and blowing dry.

Commercial liquids for reducing surface tension, such as Kerr's Debubblizer, are available. Spread the liquid over the entire surface with a small artist's brush; blow off any excess and let dry.

Mixing Investment. Mix the investment with water in a rubber mixing bowl. For general use, a mixing bowl 3 or 4 inches in diameter is best. Investment, which is procurable in 5- and 10-pound tins

Fig. 143.—Mechanical spatulator attached to a rubber mixing bowl for thoroughly mixing the investment. (*Courtesy Kerr Manufacturing Co., Detroit, Mich.*)

and in drums, comes in powder form. Inlay or commercial investment is generally used. Investment is sold under several trade names. Kerr's Cristobalite is widely used for silver and gold. Special investments are used for platinum.

By weight, use 38 to 42 parts Cristobalite to 100 parts water. If no weighing device is handy, add enough investment to the water to produce a creamy mix that will pour readily from the bowl. A thin mix is ideal for casting pieces with fine detail. Pour the water, room temperature, into the bowl first, and then add the investment.

Use a stiff hand spatula, and thoroughly blend the powder with the water, with a rapid stirring motion. When spatulation is complete, the mix will be uniform and free of lumps. This should be completed in 30 seconds to 1 minute. If the mix is too thick, add a few drops of water. Do not add dry powder to the mix.

Vibrate the bowl on an electric vibrator (Fig. 144) for about 30 seconds by holding the bowl on the platform of the vibrator, using very little pressure. This removes air bubbles in the mix. If a vibra-

Fig. 144.—Electric vibrator. (*Courtesy Kerr Manufacturing Co., Detroit, Mich.*)

tor is not available, hold the bowl against, or on top of, any convenient motor-driven machine that has a slight vibration. Attach the mechanical mixer, if available, to the bowl, and spatulate for about 30 seconds. The mechanical mixer removes air bubbles and increases the strength of the investment by thoroughly mixing. If a mechanical mixer is not available, spatulate thoroughly by hand before vibrating.

In commercial casting, the investment, after being thoroughly mixed mechanically, is exposed to a high vacuum under a bell jar for a few seconds to remove air trapped in the mix.

Painting the Pattern. After the sprued pattern has been mounted on the sprue base, paint the pattern carefully with some of the investment mix, using a small artist's brush. Use the ends of the brush bristles to puncture any visible air bubbles. If desired, this coating may be blown off and the pattern repainted to further minimize bubbles. When the pattern is completely covered with investment, it is ready to be invested.

Investing the Pattern. Either of two methods of investing may be used where the small sprue base is employed. Place the sprue base holding the investment-coated pattern on a piece of glass or sheet metal, and set the flask or casting ring around the sprue base, centering the flask with the sprue base.

Pour the investment from the rubber bowl into the flask. Pour the investment to one side of the pattern, and allow it to flow around the pattern to avoid trapping air, which forms bubbles.

The second method is to set the flask upon a piece of glass or sheet metal and to fill the flask with the investment mix. Insert the investment-painted model into the filled flask by holding the edge of the sprue base and gently wiggling the pattern down into the mixture, allowing the excess mix to flow over the edge of the flask. Center the sprue base with the flask, and allow the investment to set.

When using rubber sprue bases that cap one end of the flask, pour the investment around the pattern.

Let the investment harden (which takes about 30 minutes) before removing the sprue base and starting the burnout.

In industrial casting the patterns are usually painted with a surface-tension reducer (such as Kerr's Vacufilm) and invested, and the flask is then placed under a bell jar with a high vacuum for about 15 seconds to eliminate completely any trapped air.

In making castings where precision is critical, line the insides of the flasks with asbestos paper before investing the pattern. Cut the asbestos so that a piece will cover the inside of the flask, with the exception of about ¼ inch at each end. Dip the asbestos-lined flask in water, and press the wet asbestos to the flask. Asbestos lining is not generally used for casting jewelry of silver or gold. It is, however, used for platinum casting.

Preparing for Cast. Remove the sprue base from the invested pattern, and scrape off any excess investment. Place the flask in the casting machine and the metal to be cast in the crucible, and balance the arm. On the Vaughan or the Kerr Centrifico the balancing is done by moving the counterbalance and locking it in position.

Remove the flask from the machine, and then burn out the wax model.

Wind the machine. Two or three revolutions of the arm are usually enough for the Kerr machine. Locking on this machine is done by raising the pin on the base of the machine and engaging it with the arm. There are three speeds on the Vaughan machine. Gold and silver are usually cast on either of the first two speeds, platinum on the third, or high, speed. Engage the pin in the proper ratchet, and turn the arm slightly less than half a revolution and lock it in position.

Asbestos paper may be used to line the inside of the crucible, a new piece being used for each flask; or the crucible may be glazed before using by melting borax in it. If using asbestos paper, cut to shape, dip in water, and press into position. If, after much use, particles of metal are found sticking to the inside of the crucible, remove them by melting with the blowpipe.

Metal to Be Cast. It is essential that the proper amount of metal be placed in the crucible to make the cast. If too little metal is used, the casting will be incomplete. If too much metal is used, it will stick in the mouth of the crucible.

The easiest method, in using small patterns, is to place the wax pattern in a small-diameter glass cylindrical graduate partly filled with water. If necessary, hold the pattern under the water with a wire. Remove the pattern, and place pieces of the metal that are to be cast in the graduate until the water reaches the same height as when the wax pattern was in the water. This is the exact amount of metal needed for the pattern. It is necessary to add more metal for the sprue and the button on the end of the sprue.

If a glass graduate is not available, place the pattern in a can of small diameter, fill to overflowing with water, remove pattern, and put in metal until the water overflows again.

Another method is to weigh the wax model and sprues. If using silver for casting, multiply this weight by 10 to get the proper amount of metal needed, less the amount for the button. For 10-karat yellow gold multiply the weight of the model and sprues by 12.5; for 14-karat yellow gold multiply by 14; for 18-karat yellow gold multiply by 16. Add extra metal for sprues and the button.

Silver scrap may be used, as long as the metal is clean. Buttons and sprues from former casts, when cleaned in pickling solution, may be used for part of the needed metal.

Wax Burnout. After the invested pattern has set for at least 30 minutes (during which time the investment has become hard), remove the sprue base, and burn out the wax from the investment. This leaves a cavity in the investment exactly like the wax pattern into which molten metal will later be cast.

Controlled gas or electric furnaces are generally used for eliminating the wax. The temperature to which the flask is heated is governed by the size and thickness of the wax model and the kind of metal being cast.

For casting gold and silver the usual procedure for 2- and 3-inch flasks is to put the invested flask, after removing the sprue base, in a cold furnace, sprue hole down, and to bring the temperature up to around 1350°F., over a period of 3½ hours. Larger flasks may take longer. After the furnace has been heating for about an hour, during which time most of the wax will have melted and run out, invert the flask with the sprue hole up. Wax that has been absorbed by the investment will go off in vapor.

After the flask has been burned out for at least half an hour at 1300 to 1350°F., the temperature of the flask should be lowered before making the cast.

Fig. 145.—An electric furnace, with three heat ranges, and heat indicator, is excellent for the wax burnout. (*Courtesy Kerr Manufacturing Co., Detroit, Michigan.*)

It is difficult to lay down specific rules for temperatures since patterns and flasks vary. In general a flask temperature of 700 to 800°F. should be used for heavy patterns; 1000°F. for wax patterns of medium thickness; and 1200 to 1300°F. where the patterns are extremely thin. In each case the lowest possible flask temperature that will produce a filled casting should be used.

Manufacturers in casting rings generally use a flask temperature of 700 to 800°F. for men's rings and 900 to 1000°F. for thinner ladies' rings.

Instead of using a controlled gas or electric oven for the burnout, single flasks can be burned out over a Bunsen burner. Place the flask on a ring stand, resting the flask on a wire screen. Cover with a small flowerpot or a tin can with several ventholes punched in the top, and heat for several hours until all traces of wax are gone. Figure 146 shows a gas burner designed for burning out single flasks.

Fig. 146.—Gas-burning wax eliminator. (*Courtesy Torit Manufacturing Company, Saint Paul, Minn.*)

An entirely different procedure was used during World War II by the Kerr Manufacturing Company. It placed the flasks in a preheated furnace whose temperature was 900°F., and they burned out at that temperature for 3 hours. By not raising the temperature, no cooling of the flask was necessary. The wax patterns used were small. If larger patterns are used, it would be necessary to leave the flask in the furnace for a longer time.

The burn-out cycle should completely remove the carbon residue of the wax, thus opening the pores of the mold, so that, at the time of casting, air trapped in the mold can readily pass through the mold. When a mold is completely burned out, there will be no trace of discoloration caused by the wax around the sprue hole.

If a pattern has been invested for any length of time (a day or longer) before it is burned out, place the flask in water and allow the investment to soak up all the water possible before placing the flask in the furnace.

Making the Cast. After completing the proper burn-out cycle of the flask and just before removing the flask from the furnace, heat the proper amount of metal to be cast to a red heat in the crucible of the casting machine. Do this with a blowpipe burning gas and compressed air, gas and oxygen, or oxygen and acetylene or with a Prest-O-Lite torch with a large tip.

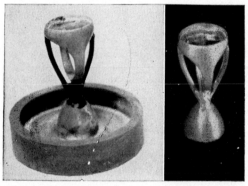

Fig. 147.—Hand-carved wax ring pattern, using a fine silver bezel for stone, mounted on sprue base with three sprues attached to pattern. At right is the cast ring, after removal from investment, before sprues and button were removed.

Remove the flask from the furnace, and place it in the casting machine, using the correct saddle for the size of flask being used. Quickly melt the metal in the crucible. Use borax to prevent undue oxidation.

Remove dross, if any, from the molten metal with a slate pencil.

When the metal is molten, release the crossarm, and the molten metal will instantaneously be thrown through the hole in the end of the crucible and thence through the hole in the investment formed by the sprue, or sprues, and into the mold. Be sure, however, that the metal is molten, not just melted on top, before releasing the revolving arm; otherwise the metal will stick in the crucible or fail to produce a good cast.

At the time of releasing the crossarm, be sure the blowpipe or torch is not in line of rotation, or the crucible may hit the torch and damage either torch or crucible, possibly spilling molten metal.

Remove the flask from the machine when the arm stops revolving, and allow the metal to cool a few minutes. Place the flask in a pail of water. The water on the hot mold will cause the investment to disintegrate, thus freeing the cast. Scrub off any investment sticking to the casting, and clean by boiling in a pickling solution.

WAX-PATTERN DUPLICATION

Duplication of wax patterns is accomplished by the use of molds. These molds are usually made of rubber, low-melting bismuth alloys, hydrocolloids, and other flexible mold-making compounds.

Rubber molds are widely used because they are easy to make and very satisfactory. Metal molds, made of low-melting bismuth alloys, are excellent but require special equipment.

Rubber Molds. Many of the molds used in commercial casting establishments are made from uncured, pure gum sheet rubber, which is usually cured in an electric vulcanizing press. The craftsman can, however, cure or vulcanize the mold in the kitchen-stove oven.

Rubber molds may be made in three general types: (1) split molds made in two sections, with locating pins or locks of some type to align the sections; (2) the solid molds made in one piece and then carefully cut in two with a surgical knife, cutting locks (irregular cuts in the outer portion of the mold), so that the two sections will align; (3) open molds, which may be used for objects having a flat base or back such as the sea horse or the small duck, shown in Figs. 137 and 154.

Split Mold. The split mold, also known as the double vulcanization mold, is usually made in a two-piece vulcanizing frame. These frames are made in openings of several sizes, the range being from 1½ by 2 by ⅝ inches to 3½ by 4¾ by 1½ inches.

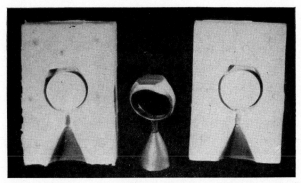

Fig. 148.—Rubber mold for making duplicate wax patterns. Master ring model, with metal sprue attached, shown in center.

Fig. 149.—Aluminum frame for making rubber molds used in casting wax patterns.

Solder a metal sprue and reservoir to the master metal model, the reservoir being a tapered brass rod fitting onto one of the metal sprues. Fill one half of the vulcanizing frame with modeling clay, and embed part of the master model in the clay. Embed that portion of the model which is to be included in the first half of the rubber mold. Place the second half of the frame in position, and fill with Rapid Stone, mixed with water to obtain a heavy cream consistency. After the stone sets, remove the modeling clay, and with a countersink make a number of small conical-shaped holes about $\frac{1}{4}$ inch deep in the stone, which will serve as locators or locks. Remove all dust, and rub talc into the stone.

Replace the second half of the frame—the part that held the clay—and carefully pack with uncured gum rubber, packing deep recesses with small pieces of rubber. Allow the rubber to protrude slightly above the top of the frame and, using a metal plate on each side of the frame and metal C clamps, tightly clamp the assembly.

Fig. 150.—Bard-Parker surgical knife with curved and straight blade used in slitting rubber molds.

Place in the kitchen-stove oven, heated to 300°F. for 30 minutes or longer to cure the rubber. Remove the stone, being careful not to harm the model. Rub talc into the rubber, and pack the second half of the frame with gum rubber, and cure as with the first half. After curing, remove the mold from the frame, and, starting at one corner, gradually separate the two halves by pulling them apart. Remove the master model, and the mold is ready for use. Metal locator pins are available, as are corrugated rubber strips, for use in making the locators or locks, instead of fashioning them as described in the preceding paragraph.

It may be necessary to make certain cuts in the mold with a surgical knife or razor blade to facilitate removal of the wax pattern. It may also be necessary to make, with a sharp knife, one or more ventholes in the form of narrow V cuts, so that the mold may completely fill with wax.

The molds, in industry, are generally filled with a special pattern wax from an electrically heated wax pot equipped with an injector. The craftsman can melt the wax in a suitable container and, using a glass syringe with rubber bulb, pick up the wax and inject it into the mold. A hard casting wax is generally used. Lubricate the mold with Kerr's Vacufilm, using an artist's brush.

Fig. 151.—Perfection casting machine equipped with aluminum crucible and holder for rubber mold for casting of wax patterns centrifugally. (*Courtesy Alexander Saunders & Co., New York, N. Y.*)

The Perfection wax caster is standard equipment in the production of ring and other small patterns in many industrial plants. It makes use of the Perfection horizontal-throw casting machine, equipped with aluminum crucible and a clamp for holding the mold. Wind the machine, warm the metal crucible, transfer the melted wax to the crucible, and release the arm. The wax is thrown centrifugally into the mold. A platform may be made for holding the mold on almost any type of casting machine; the wax may then be melted, placed in a crucible, used only for that purpose, and then cast into the mold.

Solid Mold. The solid mold is made in one vulcanization. Solder the metal sprue and reservoir plug to the master metal model, pack both sides of the model with rubber, and vulcanize. After vulcaniz-

Fig. 152.—Wax pattern made in flexible mold. Several coats of liquid latex were brushed over original model to make the mold.

Fig. 153.—Silver casting made from wax pattern shown in Fig. 152.

ing use a surgical knife to slit the mold, cutting locks into the mold as it is split. The slitting of the mold is a tedious operation, and one is likely to ruin several before becoming adept at this operation. In slitting the mold start near the tapering reservoir plug, slit alongside it, and follow along the sprue pin to the model.

Another method in making a solid mold in one vulcanization is to use a very thin metal shim, cut out in the center to accommodate the model, sprue, and reservoir plug, to provide a partial separation of the two halves. Dimple the shim to provide locks. After vulcanizing finish the separation of the mold by slitting with a knife.

Open Mold. An open mold may be made for objects having a flat base or back by placing the metal master model on an iron plate, putting a suitable metal ring or frame around it, packing with rubber, and clamping and vulcanizing. It may be necessary to slit the mold to remove the model, as well as the wax pattern.

Another method of making an open mold is to use latex liquid rubber and to apply carefully a number of coats to the master model, allowing each coat to dry before applying another. Nylon

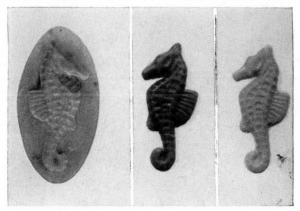

Fig. 154.—Flexible mold at left, wax pattern made in the mold, and at right a silver cast made from one of the wax patterns.

threads are sometimes used to strengthen the mold. The rubber mold can usually be pulled back over the model, as well as over the wax pattern after pouring melted wax into the mold. The pattern shown in Fig. 152 made by a student was produced in a mold of latex, using a carved-ivory figure as the master model.

Hydrocolloids. Hydrocolloids, available in tubes at dental supply houses, may be used in making open molds, if only a few wax patterns are desired. Place the tube in a double boiler filled with water, and boil for 12 minutes. Place the model upon modeling clay or upon a glass or metal plate, and put a casting ring or other suitable ring around the model. Open the end of the tube of colloid, and using an artist's brush carefully coat the model with the colloid, and then fill the ring with the colloid. When cool, the master model can be removed by flexing the mold. When the mold is not in use, keep it in water to prevent shrinkage. The colloid can be re-used by cutting into small pieces, adding a small amount of water, and boiling in a double boiler.

Fig. 154A.—Deer cast from a plastic model.

Allow molten wax to cool below the smoking stage before pouring it into a colloid mold.

Flexible Compounds. Numerous flexible compounds are available from firms specializing in plaster-casting materials. Some are in liquid form; some set when a catalyst is used; others require heating. Many of these make excellent open molds, as they are very pliable, often requiring no slitting of the mold to remove the wax pattern. No lubricant is required with many of these compounds. The disagreeable feature of some is the obnoxious fumes when the material is heated. The mold for the sea horse (Fig. 154) was made from one of these compounds.

Part 3

THE ART OF GEM STONE-CUTTING

FROM TIME immemorial man has been fascinated by the gem minerals found in practically every part of the world. When prehistoric man first went afield, he was undoubtedly attracted by colorful gem minerals, polished by nature with the gravels of a river bed or the sands of the beach. Certainly he could not have resisted a gleaming red ruby or blue turquoise among the unattractive pebbles of a gravel bar. Thus mineral and gem collecting is probably the oldest hobby known to man.

Archaeological investigations indicate that Neanderthal man, living in Europe, worked crystal quartz into weapons and probably into objects of personal adornment. Fashioned fragments of his work have been found in his cave dwellings in France and elsewhere.

Our first record of the utilization of gem minerals as ornaments dates from about 5000 B.C., when turquoise and lapis were cut and polished and widely used by the early Pharaohs of Egypt. From that time on, as man became more skilled in the art of gem stone-cutting, the harder gem materials were brought into use. The cutting and polishing of the very hard gems, such as diamonds, sapphires, and rubies, however, have been relatively recent.

The early lapidary was handicapped by the lack of modern machinery and abrasives. The abrasive grits and polishing agents used by the early artisans were materials found in nature—emery, tripoli, pumice, rottenstone, and a number of others. Late in the nineteenth century the very hard artificial abrasives, such as silicon carbide and alumina, products of the electric furnace, were introduced into the lapidary industry, and since then these materials have been manufactured into grits, grinding wheels, sanding cloths, and similar tools for the gem cutter.

In general, the lapidary industry was rather slow to adopt modern grinding wheels and abrasives. This was partially due to the fact that textbooks published in the last century still described the technique of the art as it was practiced prior to the introduction of

Fig. 155.—Compact gem grinding outfit with 8-inch saw, 8-inch grinding wheels, sanding disk, and felt polishing wheel, equipped with a 4-inch 3-step pulley, enables one to saw, grind, sand, and polish a cabochon gem stone on one machine weighing only 50 pounds. (*Courtesy M. D. R. Manufacturing Co., Los Angeles, Calif.*)

more effective modern methods. Moreover, for centuries the technique of gem stone-cutting was carried on within families, all the members of which worked at the art in their homes. As a result, the secrets of the art were confined to members of the guild and closely guarded. Until recently few data on modern lapidary technique had appeared in print. A search of the libraries will readily reveal the lack of information of this kind.

Fig. 156.—Students at work in jewelry and gem-cutting class of
Woodrow Wilson High School, Washington, D.C.

Fig. 157.—Bench grinder converted into a cabochon-grinding
outfit for school use.

Only within the last 15 years has there been any research on the technique. The data given here are to some extent based on the work of others in addition to methods devised by the author.

While it is altogether possible to cut and polish gem stones by the use of antiquated abrasives and equipment, modern grinding wheels and manufactured abrasives greatly speed and facilitate the

Fig. 158.—Grinding heads are available for either 8 or 10 inch diameter wheels. The Poly arbor shown above is for 8 inch wheels. (*Photo Courtesy Grieger's, Pasadena, Calif.*)

procedure. Although the technique given here is primarily for the amateur working in his own shop with limited equipment, the basic methods are suitable for commercial use, if the additional equipment described is added to increase speed and output.

The home lapidary shop is often equipped with only one or two arbors, on which all work is carried on. This necessitates changing wheels and pulleys to obtain the various speeds required for the different operations; this consequently slows up the work. The homeworker, uninterested in commercial production, will doubtless not find the time loss a serious handicap.

CLASSES OF WORK

In general, the lapidary art is divided into two phases. The first is cabochon cutting, which includes curved- and flat-surfaced styles applied to the less precious stones. These are usually referred to as semiprecious and include agate, turquoise, jasper, opal, lapis, and numerous others. The second division, facet cutting, is confined mainly to the transparent gems having a hardness of 7 and greater. Diamond and zircon, for example, are always cut in facet styles to bring out the brilliance and play of colors and other features that enhance their beauty and value.

PRECIOUS GEM STONES

Five gem stones are generally recognized as belonging to the group of precious stones, namely, diamond, ruby, emerald, sapphire, and opal, although only the best quality of opal can actually be compared in value with the other members of this group. Pearls, although of organic origin, are usually considered among the precious group, because of their beauty and rarity in good quality.

BIRTHSTONES

Different months of the year have long been represented by certain gem stones. These stones are known as birthstones and are said to bring good luck to the wearer. The following stones have been officially adopted by the Precious Stone Dealers Association:

```
January  ..................... Garnet
February  .................... Amethyst
March ........................ Aquamarine or bloodstone
```

April .... Diamond
May .... Emerald
June .... Pearl or moonstone
July .... Ruby
August .... Peridot or sardonyx
September .... Sapphire
October .... Opal or tourmaline
November .... Topaz
December .... Turquoise or lapis

WHERE TO FIND MATERIAL

The home lapidary will doubtless confine his first efforts to cabochon cutting, and fortunately a great deal of rough material of this type is available at a reasonable cost. Further, semiprecious gem minerals are found in virtually every part of the country and can often be collected at no more cost than that of visiting the various localities. The beaches, especially those of the Pacific Coast states, yield a great variety of material, mainly from waterworn pebbles cast up on the beach.

In the glacial drifts of the Middle West quantities of suitable material are available. Often a rock quarry or excavation within a large city will yield superb gem-cutting material. Similar rough material may also be found lying loose on the great deserts of the West. River gravels are often good areas where the treasure hunter may search.

Most of the material the craftsman will use belongs to the quartz group. Detailed descriptions of these materials as well as the localities where they are to be found are contained in the book *Quartz Family Minerals* by Dake, Fleener, and Wilson (McGraw-Hill Book Company, Inc.). A complete description of gems is found in *Gems and Gem Materials* by Kraus and Slawson (McGraw-Hill Book Company, Inc.).

Gem materials may be purchased in the rough by the pound from dealers. Many dealers also have pieces available in sizes suitable for cabochons for those who want to grind and polish their own gem stones but who do not care to saw the rough material.

Information with regard to available gem material can be obtained from the *Lapidary Journal* or one of the other magazines that carries advertisements of dealers handling rough gem material, slabs of gem material, and lapidary equipment and supplies. Some of these dealers are listed on pages 322–325.

CUTTING MATERIAL

Of the materials that can be cut and polished into beautiful cabochons, the agates, jaspers and petrified woods found in many localities are popular with amateur lapidarists. Some of the most frequently used will now be described.

Montana Agates. Agates from Montana offer the lapidarist great variety. They are available in white with black moss spots or with black or red markings, which are sometimes in ribbons. Often scenic stones can be cut. This material is excellent for cabochons, (Fig. 161).

Beach Agates. Many of the beach agates, especially those of our northwest coast, when cut have an attractive pattern and make good gem stones.

Brazilian Banded Agates. This is one of the most popular agates as it comes in a wide variety of patterns and natural colors. It is excellent for rings and for the larger cabochons, such as hearts, pendants, and crosses.

Orbicular Jasper. Known also as California-poppy jasper, this material, which comes from near Gilroy, Calif., is available in a variety of markings, usually red and yellow.

Jasperized Arizona Wood. Selected scenic wood that is free from cracks works well into cabochons. By careful study of the sawed slabs, one can cut many unusual scenic stones. This type of stone is being used in much of the "Indian" jewelry of the Southwest.

Vesuvianite. This mineral is found in various shades of green, yellow, and brown. The green variety suitable for gem cutting is known as californite and is sometimes referred to as "California jade."

Tigereye. This chatoyant yellow material from South Africa saws easily and works into beautiful cabochons. It will turn a cherry red when heated, which may be done in the kitchen stove.

Jade. The nephrite variety of jade from Wyoming, which is available in many shades of green, works into nice cabochons. The light green, without dark inclusions, and the jet-black varieties are very popular.

Rutilated Quartz. Most of the rutilated quartz, or sagenite, used for gem cutting comes from Brazil. It is a rock crystal that contains long fine needles of rutile. It is also known as Venus or Thetis hairstone.

Turquoise. Good-quality turquoise for gem cutting is hard to obtain, although it is sometimes available in small nodules. Much of the turquoise used in commercial jewelry is dyed.

Lapis Lazuli (*Lazurite*). Although too soft for use in men's rings, as its hardness is 5 to 5½, this blue-colored mineral is very popular for ladies' jewelry. Most of the material available for cutting comes from Chile.

Malachite. Although too soft for use in rings, this green mineral makes beautiful cabochons for brooches and pendants. Most of the material suitable for cutting comes from Siberia and Africa.

HARDNESS OF MINERALS

The hardness of a mineral is usually given on Mohs' scale, where talc, No. 1 on the scale, is the softest and the diamond, No. 10, is the hardest.

Mohs' scale of hardness indicates the relative hardness only and not the degree of hardness of any one mineral over another. The relative hardness of any substance can be ascertained by finding which mineral on this scale will just scratch the material being tested.

After many tests with the Knoop Indenter, a sensitive diamond-indenting tool developed at the National Bureau of Standards, Dr. Chauncey G. Peters and the late Dr. Frederick Knoop of the National Bureau of Standards assigned hardness numbers to the various minerals listed on Mohs' scale. From these numbers the comparative degree of hardness of two minerals can be determined.

By using the diamond microhardness indenter cut in the form of an elongated pyramid, the hardness of all materials from pitch (2) to diamond (6500) can be placed in their relative positions on this single scale. The minerals on Mohs' scale of hardness are shown in Fig. 159, which also shows the hardness on the National Bureau of Standards scale.

The hardness number on the National Bureau of Standards scale is defined in terms of the ratio of the applied load to the area of the indentation and is not dependent on calibration with material test blocks.

Minerals that can be scratched with a copper coin have a hardness of 3 or less on Mohs' scale. A knife blade has a hardness of approximately $5\frac{1}{2}$, which is about the same as window glass; thus any mineral that a good knife blade will not scratch must be over 5½ in hardness. A steel file has a hardness of 6 to 7 on Mohs' scale.

Mohs' scale		National Bureau of Standards scale
1.	Talc	
2.	Gypsum	32
3.	Calcite	135
4.	Fluorite	163
5.	Apatite	360–430
6.	Orthoclase	560
7.	Crystalline quartz	710–790
8.	Topaz	1250
8.	Spinel	1240–1300
9.	Sapphire, natural	1400–1450
9.	Sapphire, synthetic	1650–2000
	Alundum	1620–1670
	Black silicon carbide	2050–2150
	Green silicon carbide	2130–2140
	Molded boron carbide	2250
10.	Diamond	6200–6500

Fig. 159.—Hardness of Mohs' minerals and abrasive materials. For crystalline materials like apatite, quartz, and sapphire there is a great deal of difference in the hardness number on the National Bureau of Standards scale depending upon whether the long diagonal of the indentation is parallel or perpendicular to the optic axis. This is caused by the fact that such materials fracture more readily in one direction than in another.

ABRASIVES

Any hard, sharp material that will wear away a softer material when the two are rubbed together is known as an abrasive. There are two broad classifications of abrasives, natural and artificial.

Natural Abrasives. Flint, garnet, and emery are the best known natural abrasives and are today used primarily in the manufacture of coated abrasives.

Flint-coated paper, more frequently referred to as sandpaper, is the oldest type of coated abrasive. Garnet-coated abrasive paper and cloth are superior to flint in that the garnet is harder and tougher. Emery, a mixture of iron oxide and corundum, is used in coating both cloth and paper and finds its use primarily in metal-working. Before the discovery of artificial abrasives emery was used in making grinding wheels.

Natural abrasives are not used today in the grinding and polishing of gem stones to any appreciable extent, having been supplanted by the harder artificial abrasives.

Artificial Abrasives. There are three artificial abrasives, all of which are products of the electric furnace. They are silicon carbide, aluminum oxide, and boron carbide. Silicon carbide and aluminum oxide are both made into grinding wheels, as well as being available in grit sizes.

Silicon Carbide. Silicon carbide was first made by Dr. Edward Goodrich Acheson, in a little shop at Monongahela City, Pa., in 1891. Dr. Acheson had just completed a number of experiments for Thomas A. Edison and conceived the idea of making an abrasive to replace emery, corundum, and other natural abrasives. Most abrasive wheels at that time were made of emery.

Putting a mixture of clay and coke into a small iron bowl, Dr. Acheson ran two wires from a generator to the bowl. He grounded one of the wires to the iron bowl, attached the other to a carbon rod, which he placed in the clay and coke mixture, and started the generator. After heating the mass for several hours, he allowed it to cool. Upon breaking open the mass, he found that he had something different. Tests proved that the material was extremely hard. Dr. Acheson took samples to New York City and prevailed upon gem cutters to give them a trial. He received a small order at 40 cents a carat—$880 a pound.

Today silicon carbide is made in brick furnaces approximately 50 feet long, 10 feet wide, and 10 feet high. They have permanent ends and demountable sides. A charge of coke, pure glass sand, sawdust, and salt is placed in the furnace. When the furnace is half filled, a trench is made and filled with granulated coke to serve as a resistor. The furnace is then filled.

Electric current is passed through the core, and the mixture is heated to 4700°F. for 36 hours. The fused center of the mass, after cooling, is crushed, cleaned, and sized for use as an abrasive grit or made into grinding wheels.

Silicon carbide, both grit and wheels, is sold by manufacturers under several trade names. The Norton Company products are termed Crystolon, while those of the Carborundum Company of America are known as Carborundum.

Aluminum Oxide. Aluminum oxide was first made in 1899 by Charles B. Jacobs. It is made from bauxite, a clay that contains aluminum. The bauxite is mixed with coke and iron filings, which are purifying agents, and put into circular-arc-type furnaces. Two electrodes are placed in the mixture, and a current of 5,000 amperes heats the mixture to 3000°F.

Aluminum oxide, although harder than natural abrasives, is not so hard as silicon carbide. Its grains are not so sharp, but it is tougher. It is used widely in the metal industry, and many optical powders are made from it.

The Carborundum Company of America sells aluminum oxide products under the trade name of Aloxite. The Norton Company sells them under the trade name of Alundum, with the exception of the alumina polishing powders.

Boron Carbide. Boron carbide, sold under the trade name of Norbide, is the hardest material made by man for commercial use, ranking next to the diamond in hardness. Developed by the Norton

Company in 1934, it is made from coke and boric acid at a tremendously high temperature. It is available only in grit.

Hardness of Abrasives. On Mohs' scale of hardness quartz is rated as 7, topaz 8, corundum 9, and diamond 10. The hardness of the various artificial abrasives is shown in Fig. 159 on the National Bureau of Standards hardness scale.

Grain, or Grit Size. After being crushed and cleaned, the various-sized grits must be separated, or graded. This is accomplished by sieving them through screens having a different number of meshes to the linear inch.

Grit that is classed as No. 100 grit has passed through a screen having 100 meshes to the linear inch. Grit finer than No. 240 is separated either by air flotation or by sedimentation.

The size of the abrasive grain that is to be used depends largely upon the nature of the work and the finish desired. This is true whether the grains are to be made into wheels or used on laps or coated abrasives. Grits finer than No. 100 are used in the cutting of gem stones.

Standard sizes of silicon carbide grain, listed from coarse to fine, are as follows:
  Screened sizes: 8, 10, 12, 14, 16, 20, 24, 30, 36, 46, 60, 70, 80, 90, 100, 120, 150, 180, 220, and 240.
  Unclassified flours: *F, 2F, 3F, 4F, and XF.*
  Classified flours: 280, 320, 400, 500, and 600.
  Aluminum oxide is made in the same grit sizes as silicon carbide.
  Boron carbide is made in the following grit sizes: 8, 10, 12, 14, 16, 20, 24, 30, 36, 46, 54, 60, 70, 80, 90, 100, 120, 220, 240, 280, 320, 320*F*, 400, 500, 600, and 800.
  Silicon carbide and aluminum oxide grain are packaged in 1-, 5-, 10-, 25-, and 50-pound cans and in kegs of 100 pounds or more.

Abrasive Grain Sizes

Manufacturer	Manufacturer's designation	Approximate average particle size, microns	Type of abrasive
	Screened abrasives		
	50 mesh	297	
	60 mesh	250	
	70 mesh	210	
Available from almost any abrasive manufacturer	80 mesh	177	Synthetic aluminum oxide or silicon carbide
	100 mesh	149	
	120 mesh	125	
	150 mesh	100	
	180 mesh	88	
	220 mesh	62	
	Fine abrasives		
Carborundum Co.	F	50	Synthetic aluminum oxide
Norton Co.	F	50	Synthetic aluminum oxide
Norton Co.	FF	45	Synthetic aluminum oxide

Bausch & Lomb	No. 500	31	Corundum
Carborundum Co.	No. 320	30	Synthetic aluminum oxide or silicon carbide
Norton Co.	No. 320	30	Synthetic aluminum oxide or silicon carbide
Carborundum Co.	*FF*	30	Synthetic aluminum oxide or silicon carbide
Carborundum Co.	No. 400	26	Synthetic aluminum oxide or silicon carbide
Norton Co.	No. 400	26	Synthetic aluminum oxide or silicon carbide
Bausch & Lomb	No. 600	26	Corundum
Norton Co.	*FFFF*	23	Synthetic aluminum oxide
Carborundum Co.	No. 225 optical powder	22½	Synthetic aluminum oxide
American Optical Co.	No. 203	22	Corundum
Carborundum Co.	No. 500	20	Synthetic aluminum oxide or silicon carbide
Carborundum Co.	No. 200 optical powder	20	Synthetic aluminum oxide
Norton Co.	No. 500	20	Synthetic aluminum oxide or silicon carbide
Carborundum Co.	*FFF*	20	Synthetic aluminum oxide
Bausch & Lomb	No. 750	20	Corundum

Abrasive Grain Sizes—*continued*

Manufacturer	Manufacturer's designation	Approximate average particle size, microns	Type of abrasive
		Fine grinding powders	
General Abrasive Co.	No. 24	19	Synthetic aluminum oxide
American Optical Co.	No. 302½	18	Corundum
Bausch & Lomb	No. 850	18	Corundum
General Abrasive Co.	No. 21	17	Synthetic aluminum oxide
Carborundum Co.	No. 175 optical powder	17½	Synthetic aluminum oxide
Bausch & Lomb	No. 950	16	Corundum
Bausch & Lomb	No. 1000	15½	Corundum
American Optical Co.	No. 303	15	Corundum
General Abrasive Co.	No. 18	15	Synthetic aluminum oxide
J. H. Rhodes Co.	No. 1015	15	Synthetic aluminum oxide
Carborundum Co.	No. 145 optical powder	14½	Synthetic aluminum oxide
Titmus Optical Co.	3X fine emery	13½	Synthetic aluminum oxide
Bausch & Lomb	No. 1150	13½	Corundum
Bausch & Lomb	No. 1200	12¾	Corundum
Titmus Optical Co.	4X fine emery	12½	Synthetic aluminum oxide
Carborundum Co.	No. 125 optical powder	12½	Synthetic aluminum oxide

J. H. Rhodes Co.	No. 1012	12	Synthetic aluminum oxide
American Optical Co.	No. 303½	11	Corundum
Carborundum Co.	No. 95 optical powder	9½	Synthetic aluminum oxide
J. H. Rhodes Co.	No. 1009	9	Synthetic aluminum oxide
Bausch & Lomb	No. 1600	9½	Corundum
American Optical Co.	No. 304	8	Corundum
Bausch & Lomb	No. 2100	7½	Corundum
Bausch & Lomb	No. 2600	6	Corundum
American Optical Co.	No. 305	5	Corundum
Rhodes Rouge	No. 487	1–1.5	Rouge

Fig. 160. Approximate grain size in microns of many of the grits and optical powders used in grinding, lapping, and polishing. Information available shows that No. 600 grain size measures approximately 17½ microns; No. 700 approximately 14½ microns; No. 800 approximately 12½ microns; and No. 900 grain size approximately 9½ microns.

181

Grinding Wheels. A grinding wheel has three physical characteristics: (1) the abrasive grains that do the cutting; (2) the bond that holds the grains together so that they may cut; (3) the spacing of the abrasive grains in the wheel to provide clearance for the chips cut by the abrasive grains.

There are two abrasive grains used primarily in the manufacture of grinding wheels, aluminum oxide and silicon carbide. Wheels made from silicon carbide are used for cutting cabochons as silicon carbide grains are both hard and sharp.

There are five general types of bonds used in making grinding wheels: (1) vitrified, (2) silicate, (3) rubber, (4) shellac, and (5) resinoid.

More than 75 per cent of the grinding wheels manufactured are made with a vitrified bond. Such wheels have great strength and porosity and are not affected by water, acid, or oils. Vitrified grinding wheels are used in gem cutting.

Ceramic materials—clay, feldspar, and flint—are used in making vitrified bonded wheels. The abrasive grains are mixed with the ceramic materials and molded to shape under high pressure. As very little water is used, the wheels are fired at once in a kiln. They are heated to 2400°F. for 4 or 5 days and then bushed with lead, trued, and submitted to speed tests, after which they are ready for use.

The hardness, or grade, of a grinding wheel is determined by the amount of bond used in the making of the wheel. A hard wheel is made by increasing the amount of bond.

Manufacturers of grinding wheels now use a standard system of marking their wheels as to hardness. The wheels increase in hardness as the letters progress from the beginning to the end of the alphabet. This system was adopted in 1944. Prior to that time no standard system of grading as to hardness was in effect; in fact two systems were used, and they were exactly opposite. Following is the system in use today:

Very soft	Soft	Medium	Hard	Very Hard
E, F, G	*H, I, J, K*	*L, M, N, O*	*P, Q, R, S*	*T, U, W, Z*

Medium-grade bonded wheels are used for grinding cabochons. The Norton Company recommends *L* or *M* grade. In general use soft wheels for cutting hard material and hard wheels for cutting soft material. A wheel that is too hard will glaze; one that is too soft will show excessive wear.

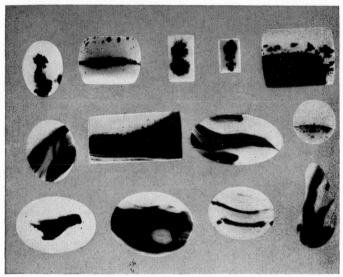

Fig. 161.—Cabochons of many designs are cut from agate.

The structure of a grinding wheel is determined by the spacing of the grain. The Norton Company recommends No. 8, which is a wide spacing. Its system of spacing is as follows: Close spacing: 0, 1, 2, 3; medium spacing: 4, 5, 6; wide spacing: 7, 8, 9, 10, 11, 12.

CABOCHON CUTTING

The cutting of cabochons—the stones most frequently used by the student and craftsman—is a relatively simple process. It does not require long experience to produce beautifully polished stones suitable for many types of jewelry. A little practice will enable the novice readily to fashion attractive gem stones from the softer classes of gem minerals ordinarily used for cabochon styles.

So popular is the hobby of gem stone-cutting that persons in all parts of the country are turning to this delightful and fascinating recreational activity. Many colleges and high schools have installed lapidary equipment for use in connection with jewelry work. Doubtless there are home lapidarists in your locality, or you may learn of them through the periodicals devoted to the hobby.

Fig. 162.—Cabochon ground from orbicular jasper.

The cabochon mounted in the ring in Fig. 162 was the author's first attempt at cabochon cutting. He was assisted by a high-school student, who later mounted the stone. The handmade leaves decorating the ring were the student's first attempt at leaf making. This semiprecious stone was ground and polished from a fragment of orbicular jasper, found in California, neither author nor student having previously seen lapidary equipment in operation.

EQUIPMENT FOR GEM CUTTING

Cabochons can be cut on either vertical- or horizontal-running silicon carbide wheels. The craftsman may build a unit using arbors (Fig. 158) upon which he can perform the various operations, or the outfit may be purchased complete.

Horizontal-running lap units are available either in kits, where the purchaser builds his own bench, or in complete machines, such as the Covington Multi-Feature Lap Unit, where grinding on silicon carbide wheels, sanding, and polishing are all done with various attachments. The lap unit can also be used for flat lapping and polishing of specimens and for sphere cutting. The lap units are popular in schools, as more than one student can lap at one time.

Bench grinders (Fig. 157), such as are found in most school shops, are ideal for converting into grinders for cutting cabochons, as they are fully protected by heavy cast-iron guards. The bench grinder using wheels 10 by 1 inch is ideal. The water used on the wheels does not enter the bearings as it is thrown out toward the periphery of the wheel. Drill a hole in the bottom of the cast-iron guard so that the water will drain out.

In a school shop separate arbors should be used for the grinding, sanding, and polishing, but the home lapidary may, if desired, use one arbor for all operations.

If funds are available, it is well to construct a sturdy bench and equip it with several ¼-horsepower electric motors with grinding heads (arbors) for the different lapidary operations. Or, a line shaft may be installed and all units driven from the line shaft, which is usually powered with a single ⅓- or ½-horsepower motor.

For those with limited means and space the following equipment will enable the lapidary to turn out satisfactory work:

One ¼-hp. motor and grinding head (arbor), or a lap unit.

One silicon carbide wheel, 1 inch thick, 6 to 12 inches in diameter, No. 100 or No. 120 grit.

One silicon carbide wheel, 1 inch thick, 6 to 12 inches in diameter, No. 220 grit.

Several sheets of silicon carbide sanding cloth, No. 220 grit.

One hard felt buff, preferably 6 or 8 inches in diameter, with a width of at least 1 inch.

A supply of polishing powders.

A few sticks of dop cement.

A few pounds of No. 120 grit silicon carbide, for "mud" sawing, or a diamond-charged metal disk.

The sawing of gem-cutting material into blanks suitable for cutting cabochons causes beginners more trouble than any of the other operations. The beginner is in a hurry. He is eager to see a finished stone and does not master the technique of sawing. The author recommends that beginners use small pieces or buy a few blanks from a dealer and grind and polish them before attempting the sawing. Get acquainted with the technique of grinding, sanding, and polishing. If you are not acquainted with the materials used in cabochon cutting, buy an assortment of blanks. After you have mastered the grinding, sanding, and polishing, then turn to sawing, if you care to saw your own material.

Cabochon blanks that have been rough ground are known as "preforms" and are available from many dealers.

FOUR MAIN OPERATIONS

There are four distinct operations in the production of a cabochon gem. They are (1) sawing, (2) grinding, (3) sanding, and (4) polishing. Each of these operations is carried out at different speeds in commercial production, but for the student and home craftsman, the grinding and sanding can be carried out on a single arbor at the same speed. The same is true of sawing and polishing.

The use of a single arbor in this way simplifies the installation of equipment for the home or school shop.

SAWING

Rough gem material is usually sawed into slabs, and the slabs are then resawed into suitable-sized blanks from which gem stones are cut. A saw is also used where a large flat surface upon a specimen is to be polished.

There are two general methods of sawing: one uses the "mud" saw; the other, the diamond-charged disk. The diamond saw is by far the better and is used almost exclusively today, whereas the mud saw, employing a revolving disk and silicon carbide grit, was widely used around 1935.

The diamond method of sawing is much faster and cleaner. A diamond saw is always ready for use, whereas with the mud saw the abrasive mix must be of proper consistency before the saw can be

Mot. pulley size, inches	Pulley on machine: Size, inches												
	2	2¼	2½	2¾	3	3½	4	5	6	7	8	10	12
2	1725	1498	1325	1187	1075	905	781	614	505	425	371	295	245
2¼	1828	1725	1525	1360	1235	1040	897	684	577	490	426	327	282
2½	2120	1875	1725	1542	1402	1180	1019	794	655	556	483	372	319
2¾	2330	2120	1880	1725	1562	1317	1148	887	732	624	542	416	356
3	2550	2260	2040	1860	1725	1452	1252	980	807	685	596	458	392
3½	2990	2650	2380	2165	1985	1725	1489	1162	958	815	708	543	466
4	3800	3300	2920	2605	2360	2000	1725	1345	1100	940	820	650	540
5	4875	4230	3750	3350	3040	2560	2205	1725	1425	1210	1050	835	695
6	5900	5140	4550	4060	3700	3105	2680	2095	1725	1480	1250	1010	840
7	6950	6050	5340	4775	4350	3650	3160	2460	2025	1725	1500	1190	990
8	8000	6950	6150	5490	5000	4200	3600	2825	2320	1985	1725	1350	1135

Fig. 163.—Speed Table.

This table will enable one to select the proper pulleys for the approximate speeds listed. Motor pulley speeds are based on motor speed of 1725 r.p.m. (*Courtesy of Delta Manufacturing Co., Milwaukee, Wis.*)

used. Most lapidary supply houses stock diamond-charged disks, as well as sawing outfits, but none, to the author's knowledge, handles sawing outfits for mud sawing.

Sawing Outfits. Sawing is best done upon a machine designed and made for that purpose, although one can section an occasional small stone by improvising a saw with any available arbor.

There are two general types of outfits for the use of the diamond-charged disk: the sliding-carriage type, and the swinging-arm type. A vise. which can be moved laterally, mounted on the carriage, makes it easy to cut slabs of any thickness. On the swinging-arm-type saw, the vise, or clamp, is mounted to the arm, which is movable laterally. Both types of sawing outfits are widely used.

Diamond-saw outfits being made today use either mechanical feed, springs, weights, or hydraulically controlled pressure to pull

Fig. 164.—Power-feed sawing outfit. (*Courtesy of Covington Lapidary Engineering Company, Redlands, Calif.*)

the specimen into the revolving blade. The mechanical feed makes use of gears or of gears, belts, and pulleys. The spring feed uses a tension spring tied to carriage or arm with a cord tied to the other end of the spring. Tension is applied by stretching the spring and fastening it in position.

The weight feed usually consists of a sash cord tied to carriage or arm, running over a pulley and fastened to a pail filled with rocks or other suitable weights. The weight can be varied with the material being sectioned.

The hydraulically controlled feed makes use of a double-action hydraulic cylinder and weights. The cylinder is mounted back of the carriage or swinging arm, and the piston rod is connected to the swinging arm or carriage. Feed lines of small tubing or flexible hydraulic hose connect the two ends of the cylinder, with a needle valve placed in the hydraulic line.

Hydraulic fluid in one end of the cylinder is forced to the other end by means of a weight feed, previously described, the speed being governed by the opening of the needle valve in the oil line. When a cut is made, the needle valve is opened and the fluid is returned to the opposite end of the cylinder by pulling the arm or carriage back, preparatory to making another cut. A quick-operating cock valve, placed in a by-pass oil line, permits return of the arm or carriage without changing adjustment of the needle valve.

As a rule, power or hydraulically controlled feed greatly increases the cutting life of the blade, as the smooth, steady pressure allows the blade to cut cleanly and to clear itself as it progresses. There is no shearing or breaking of the specimen as the blade nears the end of the cut.

Saws designed to use the diamond blade cannot be employed for grit or mud sawing, because the arbor bearings are too near the blade and the carriages are not covered to protect them from grit. An arbor used in mud sawing should have the blade some distance from the nearest arbor bearing. A swinging arm of some sort is generally used to hold material being sectioned by the grit method in order to remove the mechanism from the field of grit.

Material being sectioned on the swinging-arm type of saw can be held in place on the arm by being clamped between boards, or a steel-spindle adjustable wood clamp can be bolted to the arm and used to hold the work. To start the operation, reverse one of the spindles on the wood clamp. This is readily done by removing the handles, which are held in place with metal pins, removing the spindles, exchanging positions with the two metal screw plugs of one spindle, and replacing the spindles.

Fig. 165.—Swinging-arm sawing outfit built by the author for 10 inch diameter diamond saw blades. This machine, plans of which are shown in Fig. 166, has no end play and permits easy lateral movement for sawing gem material into slices of desired thickness.

Saw carriages and arbors for the blade are available from lapidary dealers for those who wish to build their own diamond-sawing outfit. A ball-bearing saw mandrel may be used as the arbor in making a diamond-saw outfit.

The swinging-arm sawing outfit, shown in Fig. 165, may be made by anyone having the use of a metal screw-cutting lathe. Thread one end of a 24-inch length of ¾-inch ground steel shafting for a distance of 7 inches with N.F. (16) threads. The shaft support, or bearing, at the left end of the shaft may be made of a pipe flange reamed to fit the shaft; or the flange may be bored, fitted with brass, and then reamed to fit the shaft.

The stationary nut may be made from a pipe flange by boring and threading with ¾-inch N.F. (16) threads. The crank may be made of iron, ¾-inch wide by ¼ inch thick and 6 inches long.

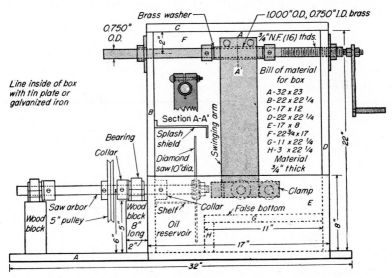

Fig. 166.—Drawing of the swinging-arm-type of diamond sawing outfit shown in Fig. 165.

The swinging arm is a piece of 2 by 4 maple, 16 inches long. Bore a 1-inch hole through one end for the brass bearing, which is 5½ inches long, with a 1-inch outside diameter, and an inside diameter which makes a bearing fit with the ¾-inch shafting. The brass should be reamed with an expansion reamer to fit the shaft. True both ends of the tubing, face the collars, and make two brass washers, $\frac{3}{16}$ inch wide.

Saw a slot in the end of the maple arm, insert the tubing in the hole in the arm, and clamp in place by using two carriage bolts to draw the sides of the slot together. Very little tension is required. Too much distorts the tubing.

Build the box, insert the swinging-arm mechanism, and install the arbor. Test for alignment by placing a metal ruler or pointer in the specimen clamp, adjusting the swinging arm laterally until the ruler touches the saw blade. If the arm is in alignment with the

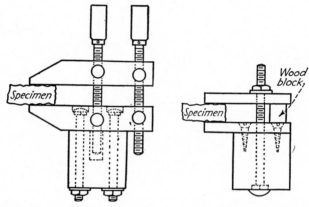

Fig. 167.—Two methods of holding a specimen while it is being sawed.

saw blade, the ruler will touch the saw blade all along as the arm is moved back and forth. If it is not in alignment, move either the arbor or the ¾-inch shaft until the saw blade is aligned with the swinging arm.

The ¾-inch holes for the shafting are 5 inches from the inside of the back of the box.

A sawing outfit built as described, with the brass bearing accurately fitted to the shaft, makes an ideal sawing outfit for 8- and 10-inch diameter diamond-saw blades. It permits easy adjustment for any thickness slab, as each revolution of the crank moves the swinging arm ¹⁄₁₆ inch laterally. By increasing the length of the swinging arm and raising the height of the box, a 12-inch-diameter blade may be used.

In general, a pressure of about 10 pounds is used in sawing a specimen of average size. Large ones require a greater pressure, smaller ones less. This can be adjusted with experiment.

In starting the cut, do not apply too much pressure. Permit the blade first to cut a slight slot, and then increase the pressure.

Fig. 168.—Saw carriage and vise with cross-feed adjustment may be used in building a sawing outfit. (*Courtesy Vreeland Manufacturing Company, Portland, Ore.*)

Mud Saws. The disk used in the mud saw is usually made of sheet metal. The disks vary in diameter from about 8 up to 50 inches or more. The smaller disks are 20, or 22-gauge metal and are operated at speeds of 300 to 450 r.p.m. Higher speeds tend to throw the mud mixture from the blade and thus slow down the cutting.

The blade revolves in an aqueous mixture of silicon carbide and water, No. 100 or No. 120 grit ordinarily being used. A small amount of clay flour or similar substance is added to the mixture to give greater viscosity, making it adhere more readily to the blade. The effectiveness of the saw depends upon the ability of the blade to carry the mixture to the point of cutting. The mud mixture is held in a metal reservoir below the saw, thus permitting the periphery of the blade to pass through the mixture. A water-soluble oil, added to the abrasive mix, stops rust and corrosion and does not impair the cutting.

Diamond-charged Saws. Metal disks, charged on the edge with diamond powder, or grit, and termed diamond saws are used today by most amateur as well as professional lapidaries in sectioning gem material.

The diamond saw is far superior to the mud, or grit, saw. A 10- or 12-inch-diameter diamond-charged blade, which will section most of the gem material used by the amateur lapidary, costs $15 to $20 and will, if properly used in a correctly aligned sawing outfit, generally section several thousand square inches of material.

There are numerous diamond-saw outfits on the market, or the craftsman may obtain the parts and build his own if he is adept with tools. The diamond saw must be used on an arbor that is free from end play, and the blade must be in alignment with the sliding carriage or the swinging arm, or its cutting life will be short, as the set will soon be worn off and the blade will bind in the cut.

When in operation, the diamond saw must be lubricated to keep the blade cool and to wash the rock dust off the cutting edge and from the cut. On most sawing outfits this is done by running the lower edge of the blade through a mixture of equal parts of kerosene and lubricating oil or a water-soluble oil and water, held in a sump, or well, underneath the saw blade. The saw should be shielded to prevent splashing of the coolant. There are many advocates of each coolant or lubricant. If using a water-soluble oil and water, choose one that has been tested and tried out for this purpose, or experiment to find out whether or not it is satisfactory.

One question frequently asked in regard to diamond sawing of agate and similar material is, "How fast will it cut?" The speed of sawing depends upon two factors, the speed of rotation of the diamond-charged disk and the amount of pressure used. Manufacturers of diamond-charged saws recommend a speed of 2000 to 2500 s.f.m., which is around 1000 r.p.m. for a 10-inch blade and 800 r.p.m. for a 12-inch blade, to get maximum life of the blade. For the amateur, a slower rather than a higher speed is recommended.

A saw blade operated at, or below, the recommended speed will usually last much longer. The author has, as this is being written, a standard 10-inch-diameter saw blade that has been used daily for more than a year in sectioning agate and similar material, the use varying from half an hour to 3 hours daily, and the blade is still cutting. It is being used in a swinging-arm-type saw, with kerosene and motor oil for a lubricant, operating at 800 r.p.m. The author tried out one blade, a 10-inch-diameter, operating at faster than motor speed, and found that, although it would cut through an agate in record time, the life of the blade was short.

Most diamond-saw blades purchased today will cut properly on first use. If not, dress the blade by sawing into a wheel-dressing brick, a piece of old grinding wheel, or a hard brick. This will wear off enough metal to expose the diamond. Some materials, such as malachite, tend to clog up a blade, and the blade must be dressed after every two or three cuts.

A saw in use will eventually lose its set and bind or stick in the cut. Remove the blade from the arbor, and hammer the periphery carefully to give it another set. Do not start a newly hammered blade in an old saw cut.

If your diamond saw fails to function properly or does not give long service, do not condemn the tool, but look into your technique of sawing and check your equipment for alignment and end play.

Pointers on Sawing. Do not use a diamond-charged disk on an arbor that has end play. Side play wears off the set of the blade.

Do not saw large specimens on a small saw and expect to get the maximum "mileage" out of your saw.

Be sure that the blade fits the arbor snugly and that there is no grit on the inside of the flanges.

Do not force the saw, or you will shorten the life of the blade.

Start a cut on as smooth and even a surface as possible. Often it is necessary to grind a smooth place on the specimen.

Allow the blade to cut a groove before applying tension or weight. Stop the machine, and check the alignment of the blade and the groove it has cut. If necessary, move the specimen laterally, without removing it from the clamp, to align the cut with the saw blade. A blade that is cutting to the side will soon wear off the set.

Do not operate the saw too fast. A 10- or 12-inch blade should operate satisfactorily at a speed of 800 to 1000 r.p.m.

Watch the level of the lubricant—half kerosense and half motor oil—and do not let the saw run dry. The blade should dip down into the lubricant approximately ½ inch.

If the blade heats while there is plenty of lubricant, the blade needs hammering or rolling to give it a set.

Never start a new blade or a hammered or rolled blade in an old cut. To do so will shear off the set of the blade.

Never start a cut until you are positive that the specimen is securely clamped. If the specimen slips, the blade is likely to be bent and thus damaged. Small kinks caused by the specimen's slipping can often be hammered out by holding a hammer on one side of the blade and hammering the blade on the opposite side with a small hammer. The hammered portion must then be reset. A blade that has been bent and straightened is often good for small specimens but may bind in deep cuts.

Sometimes particles of diamond work out of the notches and become embedded in the side of the blade, causing it to bind in the cut. When this happens, back the saw out of the cut, and remove the diamond particles by scraping with a knife blade.

As the blade nears the end of the cut, release most of the tension, and allow the blade to cut until it is nearly through the specimen. Lift the specimen from the blade, and press the slab in toward the cut to snap it off. By carefully watching the beginning of the cut, the finishing of the cut, the clamping of the specimen, and the tension, most operators can greatly increase the life of their diamond-saw blades.

Trim Saw. A trim saw is very useful in sawing slabs into desired cabochon blanks and in sawing corners off cabochon blanks prior to starting work on the grinding wheel. It may be also used to saw small pieces of rough gem material.

Trim saws are small in size and use diamond-charged blades of 4 to 6 inches in diameter. All sawing is done freehand, without use of mechanical clamps, by sliding the slab into the blade.

Silicon Carbide Cutoff Saws. Thin disks of silicon carbide, either resinoid- or shellac-bonded, have in past years been recommended by some manufacturers for the sectioning of gem material.

In the author's opinion these disks are dangerous to use for sectioning any gem material, especially material of the hardness of quartz. They are used in some commercial establishments for cutting glass and materials softer than quartz. They must be used at high speed, kept cool by a spray of water, and well guarded. The diamond-charged saw blade is much better for the sectioning of gem material.

Metal-bonded Diamond Cutoff Saw. The metal-bonded diamond cutoff wheels, or saws, are undoubtedly the best diamond saws made. The diamond in these saws is actually embedded in solid metal and fused to the rim of the blade. The saws are available in sizes from 3 to 18 inches in diameter. Saws with bronze centers are available in 100 diamond concentration in depths of either $\frac{1}{16}$ or $\frac{1}{8}$ inch. Saws with steel centers are available in both 25 and 50 diamond concentration, to a depth of $\frac{1}{8}$ inch. These saws cost much more than the diamond-charged metal blades. A 10-inch steel center blade, with diamond concentration of 50, to a depth of $\frac{1}{8}$ inch, sells for more than $100.

Charging a Diamond Saw. A steel disk can be charged with diamond by the average craftsman, and it will give fair service, but as a rule it will not compare with the modern charged disk commercially made for such a purpose.

The method used by the author in charging a saw blade is similar to that used by other lapidaries. The same method, modified slightly, can be used in charging a circular cutter (Fig. 196), used for cutting paperweights or buttons.

With a knife blade or old hack-saw blade sharpened like a wood chisel and a small hammer, notch the periphery of the disk at regular intervals. Cut 8 to 12 notches to the inch, making each notch about $\frac{1}{16}$ or $\frac{3}{32}$ inch deep. Make the notches at a slight angle rather than straight in toward the arbor hole. For an 8-inch disk use a full carat of diamond. Number 60 mesh diamond bort is a satisfactory size of grit or powder to use. Less than a carat of the powder can be used, but skimping of diamond impairs the cutting quality of the blade. The diamond powder may be purchased ready crushed and graded as to grit size.

Mix the diamond powder with a small amount of olive oil or vaseline. With a sharpened toothpick apply the diamond to the notches, and work it into the bottom of the notches. A magnifying glass (mounted above the work) aids in placing the diamond, or a magnifying headpiece may be worn. Use a lightweight hammer to close the notches by tapping lightly on the periphery of the blade, taking care to use approximately the same pressure around the circumference. The hammering will embed the diamond in the notches and give the saw a set so that it will cut its own clearance in the work. Place the hammered blade on a flat metal surface, and lightly hammer each side of the periphery. This closes the notches on the sides and gives the blade an even set.

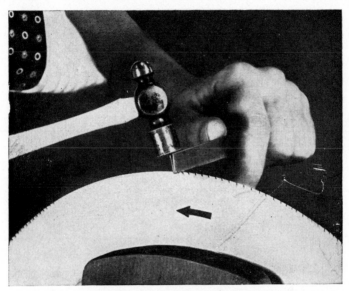

Fig. 169.—Diamond-charged sawing disks may be made by cutting nicks in the disk with a hack-saw blade, sharpened like a wood chisel and a hammer, working diamond grit into the nicks and hammering the nicks closed.

Start the saw cutting a smooth piece of quartz or agate, and it will soon wear smooth, exposing the embedded diamond, which then starts cutting the quartz. A wheel-truing abrasive stick or piece of old abrasive wheel may be used instead of the quartz.

If a saw blade tends to wobble sideways, this can be corrected to some extent by "massaging" the side of the saw with a flat 2-inch width of hardwood, applied to the side when the saw is in motion.

Start the operation near the arbor, and work toward the periphery, using pressure in the proper direction.

GRINDING

After the specimen has been cut to the desired shape, it is ready for the grinding wheels to shape the stone properly. Gems of different hardness require different grades of bond in the wheels. This,

Fig. 170.—Grinding a gem stone on a silicon carbide wheel.
Water is sprayed on the wheel.

however, is not an important matter for the amateur, since wheel wear is not the large factor in the home shop that it is in commercial shops.

Two grits of silicon carbide wheels will suffice for the home shop, namely, No. 100 and No. 220. All grinding wheels should be operated at surface speeds (s.f.m.) of approximately 5000 feet per minute for maximum efficiency. This means that a 6-inch wheel should revolve at about 3000 r.p.m. and a 10-inch wheel at about 1900 r.p.m.

Dealers in lapidary equipment handle properly bonded wheels for cutting cabochons. Silicon carbide grinding wheels are sold under various trade names, including Crystolon and Carborundum.

Wheels 1 or 1½ inches thick are generally used. They are available in any size of diameter, from 6 to 12 inches. The 8- and 10-inch-diameter wheels are the most popular sizes for cutting cabochons, unless the work is being done on a commercial scale when wheels of larger diameter are generally used.

If using a ½-inch-diameter arbor, do not use a wheel larger than 6 inches in diameter. Wheels 7 and 8 inches in diameter can be safely used on a ⅝-inch-diameter arbor; 10-inch wheels require arbors at least ¾ inch in diameter; and 12-inch wheels should not be operated on arbors less than 1 inch in diameter.

The grinding wheels should be kept wet with running water and well shielded to prevent splashing. Water may be sprayed on the sides of the wheels by the use of regular city water pressure, with valves controlling the amount of water. An air-pressure hose is useful in connecting the water pipe line to the small tubing used to direct the water on the wheels. Another method is to elevate a large pail to be used as a water reservoir, from which the water may be turned on the wheels. A 5- or 10-gallon milk can is an excellent container.

Provision must be made to take care of waste water. If this is run into a sink or drainpipe, make provisions to catch the sediment before the water is released. Run the water into a container that holds several gallons, and make a connection near the top of this container to carry the waste water to the drain. Much of the sediment will remain in this improvised trap, instead of being carried into the drain. The container, or trap, must be cleaned out occasionally.

Small, compact grinding units can be constructed with watertight compartments made of galvanized iron or sheet copper. Two such compartments are needed, a right- and a left-hand unit. They should be provided with a drain and shielded to keep the water from splashing onto the bearings. Pour water into each compartment until it touches the bottom of the wheel. When the wheel is rotating, the suction will lift the water onto the wheel.

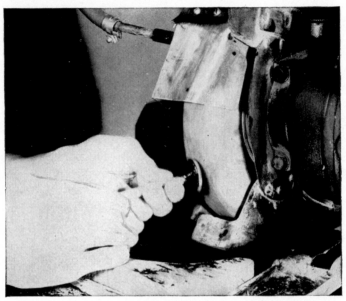

Fig. 171.—Grinding a cabochon that has been rough-ground and cemented to a dop stick. The dop stick facilitates movement of the stone.

Wheels should never be allowed to stand in water before being started, for the part that is in the water is heavier and throws the wheel off balance. If it is started under such conditions, the wheel may explode, causing serious injury.

Always use a compressible washer between the flanges and the wheel. Before installing new wheels, inspect them carefully to see that they were not damaged in transit. When starting the wheels, stand to one side for a minute.

After much use, grinding wheels often get out of round and become full of grooves; this makes the grinding of a cabochon difficult and increases the danger of the stone being chipped. Such wheels must be trued, which is usually done with a diamond wheel dresser or a coarse, hard abrasive stick.

The diamond wheel dresser is the quickest means of truing a grinding wheel. These tools are available in various sizes, depending upon the size of the diamond crystal used in making the tool, and in a type in which clusters of diamond are cemented in tungsten carbide. The cluster-type tool is easier to use and will generally last longer. In using a diamond-wheel truing tool, take light cuts, and avoid shocks. Use plenty of water to keep the diamond cool.

The Huntington or the Norton type wheel dressers have replaceable revolving metal cutters, which, when used correctly, give a grinding wheel a good cutting surface. Many cutters use this type of dresser after truing a wheel with a diamond tool, since it will generally make the wheel cut faster. Hard abrasive sticks are also available for truing wheels, but this method takes much longer.

When using the grinding wheel, try to keep the surface smooth. Make a practice of using the entire surface, and avoid cutting grooves in it.

The ratio of the weight of the grinding wheel to the material being ground is very important. The ratio should be very large. Cabochons can be ground on a 6-inch grinding wheel without knocking the wheel out of round, but if you grind specimens weighing ½ pound or more on the small wheels, you are likely to have trouble.

This can be offset to some extent by placing a good heavy block in front of the wheel and using the same technique as though you were truing the wheel. The majority of wheel troubles are no doubt caused by grinding specimens too large for the wheels. When grinding large specimens, use larger (heavier) grinding wheels.

Plenty of water passing over the wheel will tend to keep the wheel surface flushed and clean for fast work. The water will also keep down frictional heat in the gem being ground, preventing it from cracking, and it will help to avoid dust.

Cabochons are generally ground from small pieces of gem-cutting material or from blanks or slabs cut from larger pieces. Study the piece of material very carefully for unusual markings, and cut the stone to show them to the best advantage.

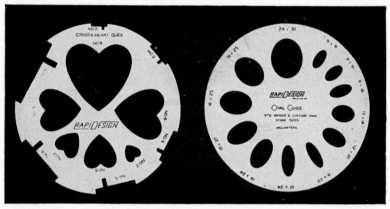

Fig. 172.—Accurately made templates facilitate the laying out of cabochons, enabling one to cut stones to a standard size. (*Courtesy George T. Davey, Van Nuys, Calif.*)

Mark out the outline of the stone on the bottom side of the blank, using a pointed piece of aluminum wire or a strip of aluminum cut from a sheet. Marks made by aluminum will not wash or rub off easily. Outlines of stones may be drawn on cardboard, and the cardboard may be cut out and used as a template; or finished cabochons may be used as outlines.

Gauges or guides, made of plastic, for use in outlining stones can be obtained from supply houses. They are available in standard jewelry ring-stone sizes for commercial mounts; in standard costume-jewelry sizes; in standard cushion, octagon, and antique shapes or in shapes for hearts and crosses.

If the blank is thin, much of the waste material can be pinched off with a pair of blunt-nosed pinchers. It is necessary when using the pinchers to remove a very small portion at a time. One soon becomes adept at this, and one can thus save much wheel wear.

To shape a cabochon properly is a matter of experience and practice, although it is possible to cut some of the more difficult ones, such as a double-cabochon heart, on the first attempt. The author, in his experimenting, has found this true with exceptional students, though as a general rule it is best for beginners to stick to the conventional oval style.

Most grinding is done by holding the work by hand against the wheel, using a steady rest for the arms. The preliminary rough grinding is done on the No. 100 grit wheel and the final grinding on the No. 200 grit wheel.

Keep the stone in motion as it is held against the wheel. All grinding should be done from the base of the stone toward the crown to avoid possible chipping at the edge. While most of the work is done on the periphery of the wheel, the sides are brought into use for obtaining flat surfaces.

Grasp the stone with the thumb and index finger of each hand, holding it tightly, yet not too rigidly. Allow the stone to rotate on the index finger of the left hand.

In grinding to the outline marked upon the blank, it is good practice to grind off the bottom edge first—in this case the top of the stone, as it is being held bottom upwards—and then grind off the waste around the outline. This will eliminate to a large extent any possible chipping on the crown side, as it reduces the area of the stone in contact with the wheel.

After grinding the stone to the general outline desired, shape the crown side, always grinding from the edge toward the crown, or center, of the stone. When the blank has been shaped on the coarse-grit wheel, take it to the fine-grit wheel, and shape further, removing many of the irregularities left by the rough grinding.

Cement the stone to a dop stick 3 or 4 inches in length, and further grind on the No. 220 grit wheel. With the aid of the dop it is possible to move the stone more quickly, giving it a brushing stroke and thus smoothing the stone.

Valuable and fragile gems should be cut entirely upon the fine-grit wheel. Soft gems, such as opal, turquoise, malachite, and lapis, are generally cut on the finer grit wheel.

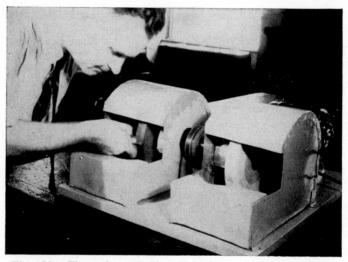

Fig. 173.—The author grinding a cabochon on a small, compact gem-cutting outfit. Grinding wheel is at left and felt polishing buff is at right.

The sides of any cabochon-style gem stone should be slightly tapered to permit clamping in the bezel mounting. An improperly sloped stone will present difficulties in some styles of mounting. Never slope the edge to the very bottom of the stone, thus making a knife-edge, for such edges are easily broken when being mounted. Stones that are cut with a very high crown generally work loose in the bezels. Through experience in mounting gems one will soon gain an appreciation of the proper shape for the stone and the correct slope at the girdle (edge).

After the stone has been properly shaped to size and form and all dull-looking matrices and blemishes have been ground away, it is ready for the sanding operation. Hearts and crosses are ground and polished in the same manner as any other cabochon. If a horizontal lap is available, the stone can be roughed out on the grinding wheels and smoothed up on the lap plate. The lap plate is especially useful in making crosses.

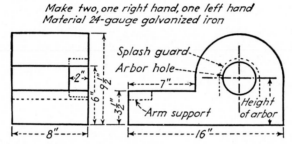

Fig. 174.—Detail drawing of the splash pans shown in Fig. 173
Dimensions may be changed to make pan fit your arbor.

After grinding the cabochon on the No. 220 grit silicon carbide grinding wheel it may be further smoothed by lapping on a flat lap with No. 220 silicon carbide grit. The flat lap is especially useful in the school shop for smoothing cabochons just prior to sanding inasmuch as it is difficult to keep grinding wheels true.

Diamond Grinding Wheels. Metal-bonded cup-shaped diamond grinding wheels are used by many lapidaries for the grinding and shaping of their cabochons, all the grinding being done upon one grit wheel. Number 150 diamond grit is commonly used.

These wheels are made by mixing diamond powder with powdered metal, which is then sintered in a hydrogen furnace.

The wheels are available in several sizes, the 5- and 6-inch diameters being preferred, because of the extremely high cost of the larger sizes. The cost of the wheel is in proportion to the amount of diamond used. The larger the wheel diameter, the greater the depth of the diamond and the higher the diamond concentration, the greater the cost of the wheel. Three factors make the wheel cost high: diameter, depth of the diamond on the face of the wheel and the diamond concentration (25, 50, or 100 concentration).

Wheels used in the home lapidary usually have a diamond concentration of 25 or 50 per cent, a depth of $\frac{1}{32}$ or $\frac{1}{16}$ inch, and a working face of about an inch in width. They may be used with good results at almost any speed, employing water as a coolant. One of these wheels will cut thousands of cabochons, and, on a cost per stone basis, they are undoubtedly as cheap as or cheaper than silicon carbide wheels.

SANDING

Regardless of the fineness of the grit of the grinding wheel used in grinding a cabochon or rounded specimen, there will always be small ridges and wheel marks on the stone when all grinding is completed. These must be removed before the stone can be given a high gloss on the polishing buff.

Sanding is usually done upon either a disk-type or a drum-type sanding wheel, using fine-grit silicon carbide coated cloth stretched over a backing of firm sponge rubber, cork, or felt, which is cemented to the wheel. The backing gives resiliency to the working surface. All work on the disk-type sander is done on the side of the disk; all work with the drum-type sander is done on the periphery of the wheel.

Practically all commercial sanding wheels available today are made of aluminum, which has replaced the wood wheels formerly used. The aluminum wheels are machined, and balanced, and they run true. Both disk and drum sanders are available in 7- and 8-inch diameters. Drum sanders are usually 2 or 3 inches wide.

Disk sanders are available in convex, concave, and hollow-head shapes. The hollow-head sander has no backing. When the cabo-

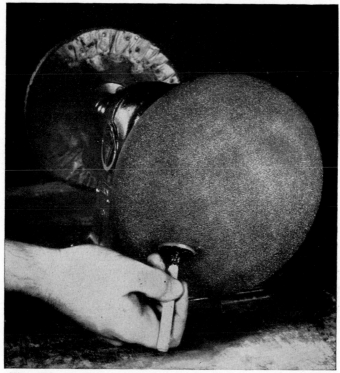

Fig. 175.—Sanding a cabochon on a vertical running convex wood disk covered with sponge rubber, canvas, and silicon carbide grit No. 220. The abrasive is held to the canvas with hot cabinet-maker's glue.

chon, or rounded specimen, is pressed against the abrasive cloth, the cloth conforms to the curvature of the stone and quickly sands the surface to an even curvature.

Sanders of 7- and 8-inch diameters should run at a speed of

about 1000 r.p.m. or less. High speed will heat a stone too quickly and cause it to crack.

The type of sander purchased depends to a large extent upon the type of work being done. If you plan to do cabochon gem cutting, the convex disk sander is undoubtedly the best buy. If the cabo-

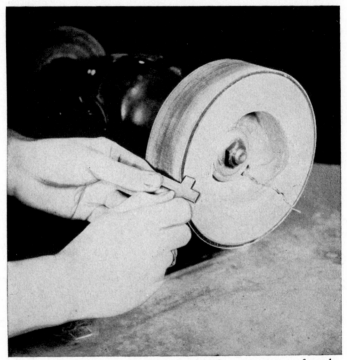

Fig. 176.—Drum-type sanders are ideal for many types of work, such as sanding crosses cut from agate.

chons are to be round or oval and are to be produced in quantity, the concave or the hollow-head disk sander will prove timesaving. Straightedged, square, and rectangular cabochons cannot be sanded properly on the concave or hollow-head sander. Drum sanders are excellent for large specimen sanding, as well as cabochon sanding.

A perfectly flat top stone cannot be sanded properly on any type sander. The top will not stay flat, as the abrasive cloth will cut first on the outer portions of the stone; by the time the stone is sanded in the center, it will be slightly rounded. Flat top stones should be worked on a flat lap. Faceted stones are not sanded, all the work being done upon flat laps.

Fig. 177.—Hollow head sander (left) and leather buff (right) are used by many lapidaries. Uncovered metal head is shown in center. (*Courtesy Allen Lapidary Equipment Co., Los Angeles, Calif.*)

Sanding may be done with the wheels running in either a vertical or a horizontal position. If a large number of cabochons are being made, it is best to secure an arbor and equip it with two or more sanding wheels.

When gem cutting started as a hobby in the United States, practically all sanding with abrasive cloth was done dry, and undoubtedly more dry sanding is done today than wet sanding. Both methods—wet and dry—are effective. Wet sanding, however, is becoming more and more popular as it eliminates the flying dust and keeps the sanding cloth free of dust, thus making the sanding operation quicker and minimizing breakage of stones caused by heating. In wet sanding the cloth may be kept damp by using a brush dipped in water, or a spray with suitable shields may be used.

Abrasive coated cloth, suitable for sanding, is available in several grit sizes. Abrasive coated cloth for dry sanding cannot be used for wet sanding, as the grit is cemented to the cloth with a water-soluble glue. Cloth for wet sanding may be used for dry sanding. The most popular grades of sanding cloth are Nos. 120, 220, 320, 400, and 600.

Fig. 178.—Cast aluminum sanders are machined and are true running. Drum sander is shown at left. The convex disk sander, right, may be converted to a leather buff by using a leather disk instead of the silicon carbide cloth. (*Courtesy Grieger's, Pasadena, Calif.*)

The selection of the proper grit size depends upon the type of material being sanded and upon the smoothness of the surface prior to sanding. If desired, the cabochon can be smoothed on a flat lap, using No. 220 grit, after all grinding is completed. It may then be sanded, using No. 220 grit abrasive cloth. This may be followed by sanding on the finer grit abrasive cloth, if desired.

If the dry-type sanding cloth is being used, wet the back of the cloth with a rag or sponge, and when it becomes pliable (which is usually in 1 or 2 minutes), place it on the sanding disk, smooth out all wrinkles, and allow it to dry before using. Trim off the edges after the cloth dries.

A new sanding cloth cuts much faster than an old one. A new cloth must be broken in before a good finish can be given the cabochon. A sanding cloth, worn smooth, is excellent for the final sanding before the stone is put on the polishing buff. A worn No. 220 grit sanding cloth will give a better final sanding than a new No. 400 or No. 600 grit cloth.

A well-worn, dry-type sanding cloth can be brushed lightly with a stiff brush dipped in water. This removes the dust and loosens the grit, exposing new cutting edges. Allow it to dry before using.

In sanding cabochon-style gems it is best to mount the stones on dops to facilitate handling. The correct technique in using the sander is to brush the stone against the cloth, using a rotary and wiping action, to keep from sanding too long at any one spot. Apply very little pressure, for if a heavy pressure is used for any appreciable length of time the stone may crack or burn, small white spots, or "moons," appearing. Use a light touch, and keep the stone moving at all times. If the stone becomes too warm, it will soften the cement or wax holding the stone to the dop. Grind a half-dozen or more stones at one time; sand each stone for a few seconds, put it aside, and sand another. This allows the stones to cool and minimizes burning or cracking.

Time spent in sanding is well spent, for if all the deep scratches are removed by sanding, considerable time will be saved at the polishing buffs. The sander removes the scratches much faster than the polishing buffs. Proper sanding will give a near polish, or shine, to the stone, and only a short time will be needed to attain the final high glossy finish on the polishing buff.

If you have many persons, especially students, using the same sander, it may be advisable to make your own, as follows: Obtain an 8-inch wood disk that is at least an inch thick, mount a faceplate to the disk, and place it on the sanding arbor.

True the disk with a chisel, making the work face slightly convex. Cut a circle, slightly larger than the disk, from a piece of firm sponge rubber, about ¼ inch thick, and glue this to the disk. After the glue dries, trim the circle to the size of the disk. Cover the rubber with canvas, tacking the canvas to the back of the wood disk, at the same time keeping the canvas free of wrinkles.

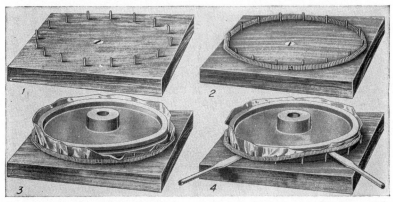

Fig. 179.—One method of replacing sanding cloth on a cast aluminum disk sander, using a spring to hold the cloth in place, is to use a jig made from a board and headless nails, as shown above. (*Courtesy Grieger's, Pasadena, Calif.*)

Coat the canvas with No. 220 grit silicon carbide. Hide glue, also known as hot cabinetmaker's glue, is a good adhesive for holding the grit to the canvas. Cold, liquid prepared glue does not work so satisfactorily as the hot glue. Casein or the synthetic resin glues are unsatisfactory as they cannot be washed off the canvas in recharging the sander.

Soak the glue overnight in water, and then heat it, using a double boiler to keep it from overheating. Make the glue rather thin. Apply the glue to the canvas with a brush, and immediately dust the canvas with the grit. A small screw-top jar, with small holes punched in the top, partly filled with the correct grit silicon carbide, is an excellent means of applying the grit to the glue-covered canvas. Allow the canvas to dry overnight before using it. If this type of sander is used, it is advisable to have several so that all may be recharged at the same time. Before recharging, wash off all glue and remaining grit with hot water, scrubbing with a stiff brush; allow the canvas to dry.

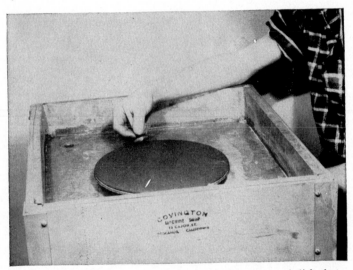

Fig. 180.—Sanding a cabochon on an abrasive-covered disk that screws to vertical spindle of a lap unit.

Convex sanders made of wood may be made for using the silicon carbide coated cloth. After truing the wood disk cut a groove in the periphery and glue a piece of firm sponge rubber or felt to the face. The cloth may then be held in place with a string, a heavy rubber band cut from an old automobile inner tube, or a coil spring of suitable size and length made into a circle. Another method of holding the cloth is to taper the periphery of the wood disk and to use a hoop made from a metal band cut to proper length with ends brazed or silver soldered together.

If a faceplate is not available to fit your sanding arbor, one can be made by welding or riveting a nut to a circular disk cut from heavy brass or sheet iron.

Felt buffs (used with fine silicon carbide grit or one of the finer optical finishing powders mixed with water into a paste) are excellent for removing fine scratches prior to polishing. Muslin buffs are also sometimes used. Wood disks, with grooves cut in the face or on the periphery, are sometimes used to remove fine scratches from crystal-clear cabochon gem stones cut from rock crystal or rutilated quartz, prior to the final polishing. Use a wet abrasive paste of the desired grit, and apply it to the disk or felt as needed. The use of felt buffs, muslin buffs, or wood wheels, with abrasives mixed with water requires proper shields.

Rubber-bonded abrasive wheels, such as Cratex, are used by many lapidaries for the entire sanding operation. The Cratex wheels are available in coarse, medium, and fine grits. Wheels 6 or 8 inches in diameter and 1 inch thick are generally used. They may be used on either vertical- or horizontal-type mountings at speeds of from 2000 to 5000 s.f.m. In general, the slower speed is better as it eliminates the danger of overheating. The wheels should be used wet. Stones of all hardness, including ruby and sapphire, may be sanded upon the Cratex wheels.

Examine the sanded stone with a magnifying glass. If there are no pits or deep scratches, the stone is ready to be polished; otherwise it will require more sanding.

Wash the stone and dop stick thoroughly when you are through sanding so that no abrasive grit will be carried to the polishing buff.

POLISHING

A high, glossy finish on the surface of a gem stone makes it more attractive and is the ultimate aim of the cabochon cutter.

If the gem stone has been properly sanded with fine-grit abrasive and all pits and scratches have been removed, the polishing operation is rather easy. On the other hand, if scratches or pits are still in the gem stone, the polishing can be long and tiresome, and the surface will never appear as you would like it. Be sure the stone is ready to be polished before starting the polishing operation.

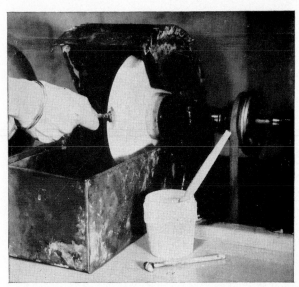

Fig. 181.—Polishing gem stone on felt buff wheel.

Polishing may be done upon felt, muslin, leather, or canvas buffs. The speed of the buff depends upon the type and size of the buff being used.

For general all-round usage the hard wool-felt wheel is recommended. Felt wheels are made by manufacturers in varying degrees of hardness from soft to rock hard, the degree of hardness being governed by the amount of shrinkage. The soft felt wheels are not so satisfactory as the hard wheels.

Wheels 6 or 8 inches in diameter and 1 inch thick are good for general use, the polishing being done on the periphery of the wheel. Larger wheels are available and will, of course, enable one to work with large specimens. A felt wheel 8 inches in diameter, operated at approximately 450 r.p.m. will give excellent results.

A muslin buff, of the type used for polishing jewelry and metal, is excellent for polishing practically all kinds of cabochon gem stones. This type of polishing buff is used in many commercial shops. An 8-inch buff may be mounted on an arbor directly on the

Fig. 182.—A bench arbor when properly shielded makes a good polishing arbor.

end of the motor shaft. With a motor of 1725 r.p.m. the buff will be reasonably stiff as it revolves and will work excellently. Obtain several sewed buffs, remove the outer two rows of stitches, and place them on the arbor. If your motor runs at 3450 r.p.m., use 6-inch buffs.

The muslin buff is excellent for polishing many of the softer stones such as turquoise, malachite, variscite, onyx, and serpentine, which do not acquire a high polish on the felt buff. Another advantage of the muslin buff is that it does not easily heat and burn the specimen.

Leather buffs, made of elk hide, of the disk type are used for polishing both hard and soft stones. The leather is usually stretched, while wet, over one of the aluminum disk-type or hollow-head sanders. If desired, you can make the leather buff by covering a wood disk, mounted upon a faceplate that fits the arbor, with firm sponge rubber and then leather. Leather buffs, of 8-inch diameter, should turn around 1725 r.p.m.

Heavy steer-hide leather is generally used for polishing jade. One Wyoming jade dealer uses a leather buff made by cementing together leather disks to form a cylinder about 4 inches in diameter and 6 inches high. A hole was bored through the center, and the buff is operated on a vertical spindle.

Ten-ounce canvas, stretched over a rubber-backed convex disk sander, is used for polishing many types of material, because canvas has a lower polishing temperature than leather or felt buffs.

Many polishing agents are in use. These include tin oxide, cerium oxide, tripoli, chromium oxide, zirconium oxide, Linde "A" powder, rouge, and many special polishing powders made by abrasive- and optical-goods manufacturers.

Tin oxide is one of the oldest polishing agents, and it is still used extensively.

Cerium oxide which is used extensively in the optical trade, is an excellent all-around, all-purpose, polishing agent. Zirconium oxide is a very good substitute for tin oxide and its cost is only about half that of cerium oxide.

Levigated alumina, an unfused aluminum oxide, is perhaps the cheapest polishing agent in general use. It will give good results on most gem material.

Chrome oxide, chemically pure, is used extensively in the polishing of jade, rhodonite, vesuvianite, and lapis on leather buffs. It is good for most gem materials, but its use is limited because it is difficult to remove it from the hands; it leaves a green stain.

Linde A-5175 alumina powder, known as Linde A powder, is widely used as a polishing and buffing compound. It is made by Linde Air Products Company, makers of synthetic sapphire, ruby, and spinel; it appeared during World War II. Each particle is about 0.3 micron in size, or 0.0000117 inch. It is packed according to rigid requirements and costs more than other polishing agents. It is however, very light, and a small amount will go a long way. Linde A powder is now being used to polish spinel, zircons, and other gem stones that formerly were polished with imported Damascus ruby powder.

Fine rouge powder is an excellent polishing agent. Many lapidaries use it to put the final gloss on their cabochons after using one of the other agents. Rouge powder is used as the abrasive in the final polishing of a perfectly flat glass surface, the polishing being done upon a pitch lap. The polished surface is tested under a controlled wave length of light to see if it is perfectly flat.

The polishing agent is mixed with water, and it is usually applied to the polishing buff with a brush. Place some of the polishing agent in a jar, cover with water, stir thoroughly, and allow to settle for a few minutes. Use from the top of the jar. First wet the polishing buff, and then apply a small amount of the polishing agent. The best polishing is usually done when the buff begins to run dry. Be careful, however, that the buff is not too dry, for the stone may heat and crack.

Tigereye is best polished with a felt buff, the polishing being done at right angles to the fibers.

Oxalic acid crystals, added to the polishing mixture, aid in the polishing of onyx and serpentine. Dissolved in water, the oxalic acid will remove iron stains from many specimens.

Thoroughly wash the stone, the dop stick, and your hands after the sanding operation to remove any grit, thus keeping grit off the polishing buff. It is much easier to keep abrasive grains off the buff than it is to remove them from the buff; the latter may be done by scraping.

Felt buffs, after continuous use, may be scraped with a blunt wood chisel to present a new surface.

A polishing buff should not be placed near a sander if equipment is set up permanently; under no circumstances should it be left exposed where grit will fall upon it.

Arbors for buffing may be purchased from dealers. A good low-cost polishing outfit can be made by using two pillow-block bearings (either ball-, babbit-, or bronze-bearings), a piece of ¾-inch-diameter shafting (30 inches long), four collars, and two nuts. The motor can be placed behind the unit or under the table.

Fig. 183.—Polishing outfit made from pillow bearings, shafting and collars. The hinged covers protect the buffs when not in use.

Thread both ends of the shaft with right-hand threads, if a left-hand die or screw-cutting lathe is not available; place two nuts on the left-hand side, using one nut as a lock nut, or drill a hole through the nut and shaft, and use a cotter pin.

The polishing outfit shown in Fig. 183 was made in this way. By using a long shaft two people can easily polish at the same time. An arbor with a wheel or buff on each end is handy for individual use because two polishing agents can be used without changing buffs.

Sometimes a stone has a pit or pinhole that cannot be ground out. During the polishing operation the agent becomes firmly embedded in the flaw and cannot be easily washed out with a brush. Soaking the stone in acetone will generally loosen the agent. Some cutters leave the polishing agent in the pit, but use black waterproof drawing ink to color the agent.

DOPPING

After a cabochon gem stone has been ground on the grinding wheels, it is advisable to dop, that is, mount on a small stick called a dop. This will facilitate handling in the further smoothing of the stone on the fine-grit grinding wheel or flat flap, during the sanding and the final polishing.

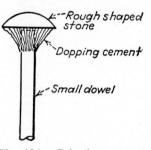

Fig. 184.—Cabochon cemented on dop stick.

Small dowel rods make excellent dops when cut into 3- or 4-inch lengths. These may be purchased at most hardware stores or lumberyards. For cabochon cutting wooden dops are generally used, but in facet cutting metal dops are best.

Dopping cement may be purchased from supply houses, or sealing wax may be used. If the wax or cement softens too quickly during the sanding, melt the wax and stir into it flake shellac or powdered stick shellac. The shellac increases the holding power of the wax. If, on the other hand, the wax is too brittle, melt it, and add a small amount of paraffin, being careful by testing it not to add too much.

Stick one end of the dop stick into hot cement, and coat about ¾ inch of the stick. Warm the stone by placing it upon a piece of metal, flat side up, and heat the metal from the underside, if possible, until the stone will melt the cement. A small piece of shellac, cement, or sealing wax, placed on the stone, will melt when the stone becomes warm enough to dop. Warm the cement on the end of the dop stick by holding it in a flame; when it begins to melt, press it against the base of the stone. If you do not place cement on the base of the stone and melt the cement, touch the base of the warm stone with a dop stick covered with cement, and coat the stone with the cement. With *damp* fingers mold the cement around the dop onto the stone. Keep the cement back from the edge of the stone; otherwise during the sanding operation the cement will get on the sander and ruin the cloth. If the cement is not back far enough from the edge of the stone, trim it off with a knife. The stone will not stick to the cement on the dop stick unless it is warm enough to melt the cement.

When molding the cement around the stone, be sure to center the stone on the dop stick, and hold the stick perpendicular to the base of the stone; otherwise it is difficult to grind and sand the stone properly.

Make up an assortment of dop sticks, and keep them on hand, ready for use. Place some dopping cement in a tin can, and heat until the cement melts. Dip one end of the dop stick in the melted cement, allowing it to remain in the cement for a few seconds. Remove, and immediately roll the waxed end of the stick on a flat piece of iron. Flatten the end by pressing against the iron, and cool by dipping in water.

After the stone is given its final polish, it is ready to be removed from the dop. Warm the stone, being careful not to overheat, by moving back and forth into a flame, and lift off the stone. A sharp knife may be used to scrape off any cement that remains on the base of the stone. Fine steel wool is good for removing particles of cement from the harder gem stones. Another method of removing stones from dops is to place a few pieces of ice in a pan and to put the dopped stones on top of the ice. When the ice melts, the stones in most instances will be separated from the dop sticks. A cloth dampened with alcohol, turpentine, or acetone will remove particles of cement left on the stones.

CABOCHONS FROM SYNTHETIC BOULES

Synthetic ruby, sapphire, and spinel are now being manufactured in the United States and the material is being made into both faceted and cabochon gem stones by commercial and amateur lapidaries.

The synthetic material is made in the form of boules in a specially constructed refractory furnace using an inverted burner with oxygen and hydrogen for fuel. The corundum boules are split lengthwise to relieve strain, the half boules weighing between 50 and 150 carats. Spinel boules weigh 50 to 250 carats each.

Corundum boules are split by grinding the base of the boule— the small end—on a grinding wheel. When a small amount of the boule has been ground off, the boule will suddenly split lengthwise, usually making a clean break. Spinel boules are split by sawing.

Corundum boules are available in the following colors: ruby, white sapphire, green sapphire, golden sapphire, rose sapphire, topaz sapphire, blue sapphire (Ceylon, Burma, and Cashmere), alexandrite, garnet, kunzite, and padparadschah, or danburite, which is orange colored.

Spinel boules are available in the following colors: blue spinel, erinite or green spinel, aquamarine, green zircon, peridot (emerada), and tourmaline.

For all practical purposes these synthetic materials are identical in physical and chemical composition with the natural minerals. The ruby and sapphire are in the corundum group and have a hardness of 9 on Mohs' scale of hardness. Spinel is 8 in hardness on that scale. For comparison with diamond and other minerals as to hardness, see Fig. 159.

Synthetic corundum and spinel boules may be sawed with diamond-charged metal blades; they are usually ground by the conventional techniques with diamond powder as the abrasive.

Spinel (which is not so hard as sapphire, yet harder than agate and most of the other materials that the lapidary will cut into cabochons) may, after being sawed into blanks, be ground on a No. 100 grit silicon carbide wheel, smoothed on a No. 220 grit wheel, and then sanded on a new No. 220 grit silicon carbide cloth sanding wheel. Follow this with sanding on a well-worn sanding cloth. The "orange peel" surface left by sanding may be removed by using heavy pressure on a slow running (350 to 500 r.p.m.) 8-inch hard felt buff, using No. *FF* or No. 320 silicon carbide grit mixed with water to a crumbly consistency. Continue this operation until all small pits are removed.

The final polishing may be done on a 4- or 6-inch hard felt buff, running at motor speed (1725 r.p.m.), using Linde A powder or Norton's levigated alumina as the polishing agent. Avoid overheating during this operation.

George T. Davey, a commercial lapidary of Van Nuys, Calif., uses the following methods for polishing ruby, sapphire (corundum), and spinel cabochons. Mr. Davey uses Cratex rubber-bonded abrasive wheels for sanding. Water is used as a coolant in each procedure. Amateurs may, without loss of anything but time, omit those steps for which their equipment is inadequate.

Corundums

1. Rough-shape the blank on No. 150 grit diamond powder in a metal-bonded wheel or on a lap at 2000 s.f.m.

2. Grind on No. 400 grit diamond in a metal-bonded wheel or on a lap at 2000 s.f.m.

3. Smooth on a coarse-grit rubber-bonded wheel, using heavy pressure.

4. Smooth on a medium-grit rubber-bonded wheel, using heavy pressure.

5. Smooth on a fine-grit rubber-bonded wheel, using heavy pressure.

6. Polish with 4-micron diamond powder on a zinc lap at 2000 s.f.m.

7. Superpolish, using 4-micron diamond powder on the hardest leather obtainable at 2000 s.f.m. Be careful during this step not to overheat the stone.

Spinels

1. Rough-grind on No. 100 grit silicon carbide wheel.

2. Smooth on No. 220 grit silicon carbide wheel.

3. Smooth on a coarse-grit rubber-bonded wheel, using heavy pressure.

4. Smooth on a medium-grit rubber-bonded wheel, using heavy pressure.

5. Smooth on a fine-grit rubber-bonded wheel, using heavy pressure.

6. Semipolish on a hard felt buff, using plenty of pressure with No. 500 emery as the abrasive. If using a 6-inch buff, run at motor speed.

7. Polish on a hard felt buff, at 700 to 800 s.f.m., using No. 1000 emery.

8. Superpolish on a hard felt buff, at 700 to 800 s.f.m., using Linde A polishing powder.

DRILLING

To mount a cabochon as a pendant (without using a bezel) or an initial or other ornament on top of the ring set, is is necessary to drill a hole into or through the stone. A small metal tube and an abrasive provide a very satisfactory method of drilling.

Tubing for drilling stones is easily made from a narrow strip of tin plate or from metal cut from a tin can, by drawing the strip through a drawplate. Taper one end of the strip, bend the strip lengthwise to form a V, and pull it through the large hole of the drawplate. Continue pulling the strip through smaller holes, thus reducing the size, until the desired size is obtained. Drill tubes made from tin plate are excellent because they usually last longer than those made from brass.

Any drill press can be used for drilling, or drilling outfits may be made by using one's ingenuity. Drills are now available that are automatic after the starting of the operation. The author has seen

Fig. 185.—Drilling a hole in a gem stone with a small, hollow metal tube and silicon carbide grit. (*Courtesy Gordon's Mineral and Lapidary Supply Co., Long Beach, Calif.*)

various homemade automatic drilling outfits in home workshops. Some were elaborate, others quite simple, but each was capable of drilling a hole in a gem stone with a minimum of attention.

If using your regular drill press, be very careful not to get grit into the chuck. This can be accomplished to a large extent by closing the top of the drill tube with soft solder or using one of the drill collets available from Grieger's and other dealers. These collets hold the tube firmly without crushing.

Diamond powder is the fastest abrasive to use in drilling, but the cost per drilled hole is greater than in using silicon carbide grit or

Norbide, which is boron carbide. If using diamond powder, mix it with olive oil, and apply it sparingly with a toothpick to the gem stone at the point where the hole is to be drilled; gently lower the drill tube onto the stone.

Silicon carbide, No. 100 or No. 220 grit, may be used for most tube drilling. Norbide is faster, but it is also messier. The author has drilled hundreds of gem stones with a homemade automatic drilling machine that raises and lowers the drill tube against the stone, using silicon carbide as the abrasive. This machine was made before commercial drilling outfits were available and is somewhat similar to them. It raises and lowers the drill tube about 50 times per minute. Using a light pressure to avoid chipping, the usual time to drill a $\frac{3}{16}$-inch-depth hole is around 40 minutes. By using more pressure this time could be shortened, but the likelihood of chipping the stone is much greater.

Mount the stone on a board, using hard dopping cement or sealing wax. Be sure to get the cement under that portion of the stone where the hole is to be drilled if the hole is to go through the stone; this will support the stone in the final drilling and minimize chipping.

Place a spot of white or black ink, depending upon the color of the stone, at the point where the hole is to be drilled, and cement a ring, about $\frac{3}{8}$ inch diameter (made from a narrow strip of thin sheet metal), on the stone, centering the ring over the ink spot. Modeling clay may be used to form a ring to hold the abrasive.

Place the board on the drill-press table, align the stone with the drilling tube, and clamp the board to the table.

Mix the abrasive, silicon carbide or boron carbide, with light lubricating oil, and place the mixture inside the metal ring. Start the drill press, and with a very light pressure bring the tube down upon the stone. Lift the tube every few seconds to allow new grit to get into the hole.

Diamond-charged drills in small sizes are available. They are very delicate and must be used with extreme care. They should be operated at a high speed and kept cool with water.

Ornaments or initials may be mounted on drilled stones by soldering a short length of silver or gold tubing to the ornament, letting the tube extend just through the stone and burnishing on the underside. If the tubing is too large for the hole, it may be reduced in size by pulling through a drawplate, or the hole may be enlarged by using a nail or a piece of drill rod in the same way the tube was used. A nail or drill rod can, in an emergency, be used to drill a hole, but they do not work so satisfactorily.

Eye pins can be attached to stones, such as hearts, crosses, or teardrops, by drilling the hole into the stone and cementing the pin in place with pearl cement.

HOW TO CUT A SPHERE

The grinding of a sphere is not a difficult task, and it can be accomplished on the grinding wheels, followed by grinding or lapping in a metal tube, or pipe, with various-sized grits. Many craftsmen cut spheres to add to their collections because they are odd, and when accurately cut and given a high polish they have a high value, representing a quantity of work well done.

Select good material that is free from cracks and flaws. Some of the softer materials, such as onyx, are excellent for the first sphere. The first step is to saw out a cube. If a small sphere is being made, take the cube directly to the grinding wheel. If the cube is of any size, cut off the 12 cube edges, which leaves a regular rhombic dodecahedron.

Round off all sharp corners on the grinding wheel until the material resembles a sphere. It is possible, if one is adept at shaping cabochons, to grind a fairly accurate sphere on the silicon carbide wheels. The author has had students grind spheres, doing the final grinding on a No. 220 grit wheel, that were so nearly perfect as to be almost unbelievable. For the final grinding be sure that the wheel is perfectly true.

Hold the spherical-shaped material with the thumb and index-, or forefinger, of each hand. In the final stages of grinding hold the material in such a manner that when placed against the fine-grit wheel it will tend to rotate. Guide the spinning sphere with the hands.

Fig. 186.—Lapping a sphere in a metal cutter mounted on a vertical spindle.

The sphere is ready for the lapping in the tube or pipe with the various-sized grits when it is ground as nearly accurately as possible on the grinding wheels. Tubes of various sizes, made to fit your arbor, are available from lapidary supply dealers.

If a machinists' lathe is available, you can make your own lapping tubes from pipe caps and short lengths of pipe threaded on one end. The piece of pipe should be about 3 inches in length. Center the pipe in the lathe chuck, screw the pipe cap onto the pipe, drill the correct-sized hole in the end of the cap, and thread it to fit your arbor. Bevel the inside of the top of the pipe. One can, by using one or more bushings, make a large-sized cap that will accommodate several different-sized pipes.

To keep the grit from going through onto the threads, cement a cork into the bottom of the pipe. Dopping cement or sealing wax will do, or pitch may be used. Some craftsmen use half of a rubber ball of the proper size in the larger sized pipes, cementing it in place.

In making a small sphere, a piece of pipe or tubing can be mounted on a wood arbor and used in the drill press, although this method is not so good as mounting the tube on a horizontal or vertical arbor. The ideal mounting is on a vertical shaft, such as a horizontal lap-unit shaft.

Use a tube smaller in diameter than the sphere being lapped. Only one tube is necessary, for, by holding the sphere in the hand (wearing a rubber glove for protection), you can keep the work under better control. If two pipes are used, the sphere is at all times stationary in one of the pipes.

Hold the sphere in your hand, apply grit mixed with water to the sphere with a small paintbrush, and slowly turn it into the revolving tube. The grit tends to stick to the material as though held by electrostatic force.

Work the sphere through several grits, using Nos. 100, 220, 320, and 500. Wash both tube and sphere when going from one grit size to another.

Inspect the sphere frequently while lapping. If it shows frosty spots or pits, continue the lapping until they disappear. Do not try to remove the pits on the next-sized grit; it will take much longer, and this technique often results in poorly finished work.

One of the final-lapping compounds will remove many of the fine scratches, leaving a semigloss surface; this results in a quicker and better polish on the buff. Polish with the felt or muslin buff, using a good polishing agent.

Students in the author's classes have cut and polished spheres that were accurate to within less than one-half of a thousandth of an inch.

MAKING A DOUBLET

Much of the remarkably beautiful black (fire) opal used in the jewelry trade is in the form of doublets. Frequently the "fire" in Australian opal occurs in very thin layers and seams; and in many instances the only way to obtain a suitable stone for wear is by strengthening the back to obtain the added thickness necessary for mounting. This is done by cementing a piece of black obsidian or other material to the piece of opal.

The technique of making an opal doublet is quite simple. Grind down the rough piece of opal on a smooth-faced No. 220 grit or finer silicon carbide wheel, and flat-lap it, using No. 320 grit. Semipolish both sides of the piece of opal. Cut a piece of black obsidian or other material into a cabochon with a flat bottom the size of the opal specimen. Polish the flat bottom.

Cement the opal to the black obsidian, placing the best side of the opal against the obsidian. Flake shellac makes a good cement. Lampblack may be stirred into melted shellac to make a black cement, which many cutters prefer. Place a piece of the shellac on the flat surface of the obsidian, gently heat the obsidian until the shellac melts, and spread it over the surface. Allow it to cool until tacky, press the unheated piece of opal onto the obsidian, and gently press the two pieces together, using a circular motion to eliminate air bubbles. If necessary, reheat the obsidian until the shellac is tacky, and press the two pieces together again.

Dop the doublet, being careful not to heat too much. If liquid shellac is brushed on the back of the obsidian and allowed to dry, the doublet may be dopped cold on a slightly warmed dop stick.

The doublet may be shaped on a No. 220 grit or finer wheel to the desired shape and then sanded on a well-worn fine-grit cloth, using very little pressure. The opal may be polished on a felt, muslin, or leather buff. Use extreme caution in polishing as friction from the polishing buff can generate enough heat to fracture the stone.

Purchasing rough fire opal is a matter of some speculation. Valuable gem stones are often cut from an inexpensive rough specimen. A great deal of the cost of fire opal is in the cutting, handling, and waste.

Many pieces of Australian opal are thick enough to cut cabochons in the conventional manner.

HORIZONTAL LAPS

The polishing of flat surfaces can be done to best advantage on a horizontal lap plate made of cast iron or steel. Lap kits consisting of a cast-iron plate, shaft, bearings, and splash pan are available for those who wish to build their own outfit.

With some of the modern lap units, such as the Covington Multi-Feature Lap Unit, or the Hillquist Compact Lapidary Unit, one can use their various attachments to grind and polish cabochons; to cut faceted gem stones; to flat-lap specimens and flat surfaces; to sand, polish and make book ends and spheres.

Cabochon cutting is done with silicon carbide grinding wheels mounted to steel plates that fit the arbor spindle (Fig. 189) or on regular grinding wheels, depending upon the type of machine being used; or with the aid of a special grooved lap that is available from dealers. The cabochons can be cut more quickly upon the grinding wheel, although some cutters prefer the grooved laps. Sanding and polishing are done with special plates that fit the arbor.

The Multi-Feature Lap Unit has two speeds, 250 and 1725 r.p.m. The low speed is for flat lapping, on the 16-inch lap plate, and for faceting, and book-end work. Grinding, sanding, polishing, and tube grinding of spheres are done on the high speed.

Contrary to popular belief and usage, a perfectly flat lap plate is the poorest type to use. A tapered lap is much better. When used with the coarser grits, Nos. 100 to 220, the flap lap offers no diffi-

Fig. 187.—Multi-Feature Lap Unit. (*Courtesy of Covington Lapidary Engineering Company, Redlands, Calif.*)

culty. However, when grit sizes No. 400 and finer are used, the lap tends to grab the specimen, and it is almost impossible to finish it.

The surfaces are in such close contact that the small-sized grit acts like a paste, and the specimen adheres to the lap-plate surface. The specimen is pulled out of the operator's hand and in many instances is broken. To overcome this, many cutters use an increased volume of water or lubricant, and in this way the grit is washed from the lap. On the flat lap the close contact of the specimen and the lap tends to wipe off the grit before it can do its work.

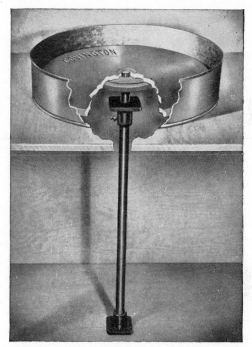

Fig. 188.—A lap kit consisting of plate, shafting, bearings, and splash pan is available for those desiring to build their own outfit. (*Courtesy of Covington Lapidary Engineering Company, Redlands, Calif.*)

If the surface of the lap is machined with a slight taper, practically all specimen grabbing is eliminated and the lapping can be done with a small amount of water. By the use of a tapered lap, specimens can be quickly and economically lapped. A 16-inch tapered lap should have its center approximately $\frac{3}{32}$ inch higher than the periphery. As the center of a lap is practically stationary, it should be relieved to a depth of ⅛ inch, making the cut about 1½ inches in diameter.

A flat lap after it has been in use a short time will be ground away between the center and the rim, and the small grains will

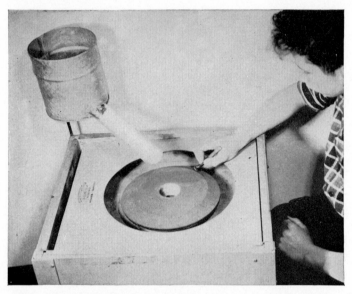

Fig. 189.—Grinding a cabochon on a plate-mounted silicon carbide wheel screwed to the vertical shaft of a lap unit.

slide underneath the specimen. This tendency is not so pronounced on the tapered lap. Occasional large specimens lapped with coarse grit will, however, tend to true a lap plate.

If a large specimen is being lapped, it can be done much more easily on a tapered lap, as part of the specimen can extend over the center of the lap and not be in contact with the lap. By rotation of the specimen a perfect surface is obtained.

In this discussion it is assumed that the lap is revolving counterclockwise and that the operator is seated directly at the 6 o'clock position. Hold the work with the right hand. Apply pressure to the back edge of the specimen, as this lifts up the front and allows the cutting grit to get underneath the specimen. Before placing the specimen on the lap, wet the lap to prevent grabbing.

Fig. 190.—Grinding a cabochon on a silicon carbide wheel mounted on a lap unit spindle. (*Courtesy Lapidary Equipment Co., Seattle, Wash.*)

The grit and water can best be applied to the lap with a paint-brush about 1½ inches wide. A metal can is best to keep the grit and water in, as glass containers are easily broken if a specimen gets away from the operator. Cans made from sheet copper or brass are ideal because they will not rust. If the lap plate becomes dry, apply a few drops of water with the brush. If the cutting action becomes too slow, apply some fresh grit with the brush.

Keep the specimen moving from the center to the periphery of the lap, and rotate. This changes the direction of approach of the grit and speeds the grinding. It also tends to prevent "dishing" of the lap plate. Lap until all saw marks, pits, bad spots, and other irregularities are removed, applying grit and water as necessary.

The length of time for making the first lap depends upon the condition of the specimen. A specimen cut with a diamond saw, which leaves a smooth cut, naturally takes less time. With a 16-inch lap, at 250 to 300 r.p.m., 1 minute per square inch, with a minimum

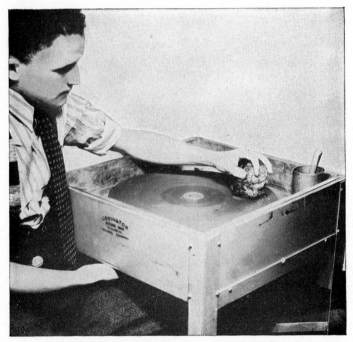

Fig. 191.—Lapping a mineral specimen on a cast-iron lap using silicon carbide grit.

time of 4 or 5 minutes, for any size of specimen should be sufficient lapping time.

The failure of the operator to understand just what is taking place on the lap plate is the cause of many poorly polished specimens. The following discussion may aid the cutters to obtain better results.

It is common belief that the abrasive grains plane away a surface just as a metal planer cuts down a metal block. The grains are said to scratch the material and in this way to reduce the level. This is incorrect.

It is possible to lap a specimen with No. 100 grit silicon carbide and not have a scratch on the surface. The grains of abrasive roll beneath the specimen and dig out small craters or pits. If the specimen is next lapped with No. 220 grit, it must be lapped long enough to remove all the pits left in the previous lapping. Each lapping with a new grit size should be continued until all pits made in the surface by the grit previously used are removed. This must be carried out through the finest grit operation.

Here is where most polishers make their mistake. They are in a hurry and do not lap long enough. The result is that the surface, when polished, has a grainy appearance, or what is known in the optical trades as a "lemon-peel" surface or "ice marks."

Another cause of "lemon peel" or "ice marks" in some types of materials is the generation of heat during the polishing. The heat causes minute chips to break off the surface. These chips are so small that they can hardly be seen without magnification. Leather for polishing buffs has a high friction-heat factor and if used it should be kept wet at all times. Wool or felt buffs are better. Cotton and canvas are good for polishing, as they have a low heat factor, thus eliminating "ice marks" caused by heat.

After using No. 220 grit, use No. 320 grit. Remember that the surface must be lapped long enough to remove all pits left by the No. 220 grit.

If each step is done properly, the specimen cannot help having a fine, smooth gloss when polished. If the lapping in each stage is not properly done, the polished specimen will show craters holding the polishing agent.

The best way to check each stage is to lap the specimen the length of time needed, figuring 1 minute per square inch. Allow the specimen to dry, and hold it in the light. If it has been lapped long enough, it will have an even texture. If it has not been lapped long enough, you will see spots that are frosty in contrast with the other areas.

Never say, "I'll take that out with the next-sized grit." That is the hard way. It is much easier to remove pits left from No. 100

Fig. 192.—An adjustable guide aids in the lapping of book ends. Inset shows finished book ends.

grit with no. 220 grit than to remove them with No. 400 or No. 500 grit.

Do not leave scratches and pits to be taken out on the polishing buff. In some of the softer materials, such as malachite and onyx, it is almost impossible to lap the specimen so that it is free from scratches. These scratches can be "pulled" out on the polishing buff.

Scratches have a mysterious way of appearing. Most cutters

blame the grits, but in most instances the scratches are caused by breaking or crumbling of the specimen edges.

Small pieces breaking off the edges will work under the specimen and cause a bad scratch. When you place the specimen on the lap and accidentally touch the front edge to the rotating lap, small pieces will crumble and scratch the material being lapped. Materials such as thunder eggs are especially bad because of the soft matrix. Crystal quartz has such a strong cleavage that the slightest pressure on an edge will cause small cleavages to break off. Many cutters bevel all edges slightly to prevent chipping.

Another cause of scratches is embedded grit in the lap. Embedded grains cannot roll and will scratch, but if the grains are free to roll they will not scratch. Embedded grains may be removed by scraping the lap. Place an old safety-razor blade in a holder, and hold it edgewise against the lap as it revolves. Another method is to wash off all grit on the lap and to hold a flat agate slab against the lap as it revolves. Use a good deal of pressure.

As the grits become finer, a lighter pressure must be used. A cushion of the abrasive mixture must at all times be between the lap and the specimen. If you have trouble with the grit being thrown from the lap, use a lapping compound (such as Old Miser, made by Covington) to hold the grit to the lap.

Grit can also be made to stick to the lap by using a mixture of clay flour and water, as the clay gives a body to the lapping mixture. Water-soluble oil is sometimes used with the clay flour. In using the fine grits and optical powders, clean water and soluble oil are the only materials added to the abrasive.

When changing from a coarse to a finer grit, wash all the coarse grit from the specimen, lap, and splash pan to avoid contaminating the finer grit. Use a good scrubbing brush. Grit becomes embedded in cast-iron laps much more easily than in steel laps. Many cutters line the splash pan with several layers of old newspapers, replacing them with each change to a finer grit.

Oily and greasy specimens can be washed more easily by adding 2 teaspoonsful of trisodium phosphate to a pail of warm water. The trisodium phosphate emulsifies the oil and dirt, breaking them down into particles than can easily be washed off. A better cleaning solution can be made by adding aerosol to the trisodium phosphate solution. Obtain 1 ounce of aerosol OT 100 per cent and dissolve

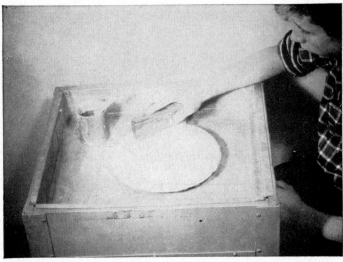

Fig. 193.—Polishing a book end on a horizontal running canvas-covered disk mounted on a lap unit spindle.

part of it in alcohol. Pour a very small amount of the aerosol solution into the pail. Aerosol reduces surface tension, as it is the most powerful "wetting agent" made commercially. It is inexpensive and available at drugstores. One part in 10,000 parts water reduces the surface tension by half.

Many of the synthetic soapless washing powders are excellent for washing specimens. Many of these contain a wetting agent.

Many specimens will show to best advantage if the surface is rounded. A curved or rounded surface is much easier to polish than a flat surface. By rocking the specimen back and forth, it is quite easy to grind a rounded or curved surface upon the flat lap.

The grit sizes used for flat lapping depend to a large extent upon the hardness and size of the specimen being lapped. For average-sized specimens of agate hardness the following silicon carbide grit sizes may be used: Nos. 100, 220, 320, and 600.

Fig. 194.—Cutting gem stones on large water-driven sandstone wheels at Idar, Germany, where the art has flourished for centuries with but few changes. (*Illustration from "Gems and Gem Material," Kraus and Slawson, McGraw-Hill Book Company, Inc.*)

If a specimen is about 3 by 4 inches in size and has been cut on a diamond saw that is running true, start with No. 220 grit. If there are any deep saw marks on the surface, start with No. 100 grit. Malachite, which is very soft, may be lapped with No. 400 grit if there are no deep scratches or saw marks on the surface.

It is extremely difficult using only silicon carbide grits, regardless of how fine the grit, to properly flat-lap a surface so that it can be easily polished. One of the fine optical powders should be used, just prior to the polishing of the specimen.

Silicon carbide grit is used in the lapping of the specimen because it is sharp. The individual grains will break down, through use, into smaller sized grains, but the smaller grains have sharp edges, and they dig into the surface being lapped.

Most of the fine grinding powders, often termed emeries, are either corundum or synthetic aluminum oxide. These grits are very much alike, in that they are both somewhat rounded and do not have sharp edges like silicon carbide grit. In use they do not fracture and break into smaller sized grits. They reduce in size, as they are used, by rolling and wearing away.

After using No. 500 or No. 600 silicon carbide grit for lapping a specimen, a semifinal polish may be obtained by lapping with one of the optical emeries, such as Bausch & Lomb's No. 303, No. 1200, or No. 303½. A comparison of the grit sizes is found in Fig. 158.

Polishing is done upon muslin, canvas, felt, or leather buffs. Use any of the standard polishing agents. If more than one agent is employed, use a separate polishing buff for each agent, and keep the buff free of other grits or polishing agents.

INLAID PAPERWEIGHTS

Attractive paperweights can be made with various materials, such as serpentine, onyx, agate, and jasper. They can be square, round, hexagonal, octagonal, or any desired shape; they may be plain or inlaid by placing a piece of contrasting material in the center of the top. The thickness is usually 1 to 1⅜ inches.

The circular paperweight, 2½ to 3 inches in diameter, with inlaid top is popular. Much of the work can be done with a drill press, using metal pipe or tubing and diamond or silicon carbide for abrasive.

A piece of metal tubing about 3 inches long with a wall thickness of $\frac{1}{16}$ inch or less makes a good cutter. Make the cutter as shown in Fig. 196.

If using diamond, charge the cutter by making nicks in the cutting edge, work No. 60 diamond grit into the nicks, and hammer the nicks closed. Grind an old hack-saw blade until the edge is shaped like a wood chisel. Make nicks in the cutting edge of the tubing

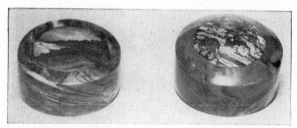

Fig. 195.—Circular paperweights made with contrasting inlays are very attractive.

about $\frac{1}{16}$ inch apart and $\frac{1}{16}$ inch deep. Place the sharpened blade in position, and hit the blade gently with a small hammer. Mix the diamond with olive oil or vaseline, and use a sharpened toothpick to place the grains in place. Hammer the nicks closed.

Place the slab of material being cut upon a piece of firm sponge rubber in a suitable pan; keep a small stream of water directed upon the cutting end of the tube as it revolves in the drill press and goes down through the material.

If using silicon carbide, mix No. 100 grit with water, and apply to the cutter with a small paintbrush.

To center the circle for the inlay, obtain a piece of tubing of the same diameter as the cutting tube (about 2 inches long). Make a template from wood or plastic, as shown in Fig. 196. Make several slits $\frac{3}{4}$ inch long in the base of the 2 inch length of tubing. Place the paperweight base in the tubing, with slits down, and place the template on top of the base. Hold the assembly with a wood clamp while cutting for the inlay, using another diamond-charged tube of the desired size. Silicon carbide may also be used for this cutting. Make the cut about $\frac{5}{16}$ inch deep. Using a smaller diameter cutter, make a second cut the same depth. The smaller circle need not be concentric with the base.

Break out the center of the paperweight, holding the base in slitted tubing to avoid cracking the base. Pour a thin mixture of

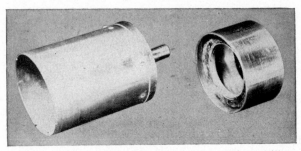

Fig. 196.—Cutter (left) charged with diamond is used in a drill press to cut circular paperweight bases. Tubing (right) with template is used with smaller cutter for cutting top of base for the inlay.

plaster of Paris or patching plaster and water in the base; let it set, keeping the top of the mixture about $\frac{3}{16}$ inch from top of base. This will level the bottom of the cut.

The inlay may be carefully ground to fit into the base, or tubing, and diamond or silicon carbide may again be used. The inlay should be $\frac{1}{4}$ or $\frac{5}{16}$ inch in thickness. If agate is used for the inlay, paint the underside of the inlay with white enamel, and allow it to dry.

Use sealing wax to hold the inlay in the base. Place a piece of the wax in the base, and slowly heat the base until the wax melts and covers the entire surface. Warm the inlay, and gently press it into place. If necessary, let wax flow around the inlay. Green sealing wax is excellent to use with many of the materials selected for the base, especially serpentine.

Grind the top to shape, and sand and polish the entire surface.

CAMEO AND INTAGLIO STONE CARVING

The mechanical equipment for cutting a stone cameo or any other ornamented stone may be very simple in construction.

Fig. 197.—Cameos and an intaglio, top center, cut by Raymond M. Addison, San Jose, Calif. (*Photograph courtesy The Lapidary Journal, Palm Desert, Calif.*)

One of the small polishing motors which has several different speeds controlled by a switch built into the base, or a jewelers' lathe motor with a rheostat will, when equipped with a small, true-running, three-jaw chuck or a small collet chuck, provide an excellent means of holding the laps, diamond tools, abrasive wheels and points, buffs, and other small tools used in carving cameo and intaglio stones. Mount the chuck on the right-hand spindle. The use of a flexible shaft is not recommended.

One can make his own grinding head with shafting, bearings, and cone pulleys, using any small motor. The wheels should be well guarded to protect the face in the event a wheel should break.

There are two methods of cutting the stone. One method makes use of the many diamond tools that are available. The other uses small metal laps, which can easily be made, and silicon carbide wheels and points. The metal laps can be charged with diamond powder, or they may be used with silicon carbide as the abrasive. Small, mounted grinding wheels are handy in removing excess material. Use them wet.

To those who have done some stone carving or to the beginner who is planning to take up carving seriously, an investment in diamond tools will pay rich dividends as they cut faster and are much cleaner to use. There are many diamond wheels and points made for the dental profession that are adaptable to stone carving. They are available from dental supply houses.

All diamond wheels, to do their best work, must be run wet. A diamond wheel will clog up and glaze over like any other wheel if used dry. Keep the dust and grit washed off the wheel by dipping a small artists' brush in water and wiping it over the revolving wheel.

A small copper or steel disk can be silver soldered on the end of a steel rod and turned or filed down to the desired shape and size, the size and shape depending upon the type of cut to be made. The disk can be charged with diamond bort by rolling the disk in the diamond powder, or it may be used with silicon carbide abrasive grits. One can make very useful and efficient equipment in this way.

Very good work can be turned out with the mud-wheel method— using abrasive grits on the revolving disk. In the past all stone carving was done with the mud wheel, but, with the cost of diamond bort brought within reach of the amateur lapidary, better and faster cutting laps can be made or purchased.

In the mud-wheel method the grits are applied with a small brush. Suspend the grits in some liquid. Water is good. Thin machine oil, olive oil, kerosene, turpentine, and glycerine are sometimes used. A little experimenting with the several mixtures will soon reveal the one best for the job you are doing.

Fig. 198.—A small high speed motor, using a rheostat to control speed, converted into a lathe for gem stone carving. An extension on right end gives more freedom of the hands. The motor is mounted on an old casting. (*Courtesy R. M. Addison, San Jose, Calif.*)

All the equipment described may be used in carving other stone objects as well as cameo. You can get a lot of fun out of trying your hand at carving stone. Raymond Addison has whiled away many an hour fashioning grape clusters, acorns with cups attached, buds, beetles, books, and various other objects.

Cameos may be carved from almost any material such as sea shell, lava, jasper, obsidian, or agate. Of all materials, banded agate is the best. Inasmuch as many hours will be spent in carving a cameo, the selection of the material is a very important step. The choice of a good piece of material will contribute a great deal toward the quality of the finished piece.

If you have decided upon the subject to be carved, consider carefully all the appropriate materials before making a selection. Or if

Fig. 199.—Carving a flower from a piece of richly colored petrified wood with a small diamond wheel. The work is held in the hands and brought to the wheel. (*Courtesy R. M. Addison, San Jose, Calif.*)

you have found a nice piece of material, take your time in choosing a suitable subject. In after years you will not be sorry that plenty of time was spent selecting subjects as well as materials. A fine, well-made piece will grow more valuable to you as the years go by.

If banded agate is the material to be used, first cut well into the rock to learn which way the bands run. If the rock is large enough, usually there is a spot where the bands run clear and even. Bands with a slight curve work just as well. If the curve or bulge is just right, quite often it can work out to your advantage.

The best results are obtained from blanks with a darker layer for the background, leaving a light layer for the head. The blank should be shaped to the desired size in the same manner you would grind a cabochon, with the exception that the top is left flat with a soft mat surface. Polish the back, and bevel the edges so that the completed cameo may be set. If the blank is large enough, it may be worked in the hands; but if it is small, it should be mounted on a small wood block, with any good dopping cement, to ensure a good grip in the hands and to facilitate handling.

The beginner should choose a comparatively simple design for his first work. A complex design will bring up problems rather difficult for the beginner. Study another cameo to learn how the cuts were made. It is good practice to copy another cameo for your first

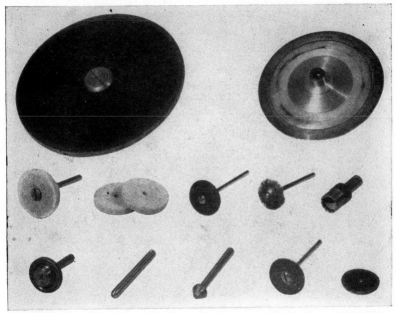

Fig. 200.—Top row: Diamond wheel for heavy carving and removing excess material, and a ¹⁄₃₂ inch, 3-inch diameter metal bonded diamond saw for making fine lines and narrow cuts.

Center row: Felt wheels, rubber bonded silicon carbide wheels and hair brush, all used for polishing. At right is a diamond core drill, useful in making flowers.

Bottom row: Diamond wheel, ⅛ inch by 1-inch, single pointed diamond, oval metal bonded diamond tool and 1-inch diamond disks. (*Courtesy R. M. Addison, San Jose, Calif.*)

attempt at cameo cutting, in order to get the feel of the tools and to develop skill in handling them.

Sketch the design or silhouette on the blank with a sharp, hard pencil. Make the sketch somewhat larger than the finished head. The excess material outside the sketch may be removed on a large grinding wheel. The wheel should be perfectly true, with sharp edges, to enable one to cut clear down to the background or, in the case of a one-colored material, deep enough to leave material on which to carve the head. Now a small island remains on the blank where the silhouette should be redrawn, this time with more detail and more proportion. With a small wheel again remove all the material outside the sketch, clear down to the background.

After this step has been completed, one can readily see where more material may be removed, rounded off here, brought in a little there; and soon shape will begin to take place. As soon as form begins to appear, the carving will progress more slowly. The cuts must be lighter, and one must take more care with detail, always keeping in mind never to overcut. The whole must be carved down together to avoid overcutting and to avoid getting the features out of proportion. Material once removed can never be replaced; it is gone forever. It is very easy to damage features already carved; therefore, as the work progresses and nears completion, patience becomes a great virtue.

At a point where the artist feels that he has about reached the limit of his skill at carving, the polishing process may be started. If one has had experience polishing cabochons, he has the process well in mind, for it is very similar. The grits and polishing powders are about the same, though the grits are usually finer because the laps are much smaller.

At a dental supply house you may purchase small polishing disks of felt and leather and mandrels for holding these disks. It is well to have a number of assorted sizes at hand to use with the various grits and polishing powders.

It is a matter of personal opinion, but Raymond Addison believes that a cameo looks better when the head or face is left with a soft mat finish on a polished background. This gives the piece more character, a little more contrast, and somewhat of a two-toned effect. Other carvings may also be enhanced by giving some portions a mat finish. It should be tried whenever possible, if the design permits a two-toned effect.

Cameo carving will come much more easily to the experienced lapidary than to the beginner, but it will take either of them a little time to become proficient in the use of new tools and to develop a technique.

If your first efforts do not result in the perfection hoped for, remember that fine cameo carving is one of the highest forms of sculpturing and is a challenge to anyone with a creative nature.

Intaglio carving is a carving-out process. The material for an intaglio may be almost any type of stone. Translucent materials such as sard, amethyst, or carnelian are always good. The beginner could start with softer material in order to get the feel of the tools. One of the one-colored jaspers might be good for the first trial.

The blank for an intaglio should be shaped to the desired size, about $\frac{1}{4}$ inch thick, and polished all round. Leave the top with a smooth-lapped surface. Since intaglio carving is a carving-out process, care must be taken not to draw the sketch too large. Also, as the carving is done from the inside out, care must be taken not to overcut. To enable one to examine his work, a piece of plastic wax may be used. From time to time push the wax into the carving, and withdraw. The image formed on the wax will show the progress being made.

The tools and equipment for intaglio work are essentially the same as for cameo work. The laps may vary somewhat (most of them are smaller), but the process is about the same. Intaglio carving is more difficult than cameo work since the carving is done in reverse. It takes a steady hand and great patience to carve a really fine intaglio. It is, however, a challenge to those who like the difficult.

Very interesting pieces may be made along the lines of cut glass. A thin section of clear material is shaped to the desired size, usually a well-shaped oval flat, and polished on both sides. A flower or other design is sketched on the front side with India ink or any other material that will stick to a polished surface. The piece is held over the small lap and pressed down, the lap cutting on the back of the blank. As the lap cuts into the material, one can see the progress being made.

Wash the grit off the work frequently so that the design can readily be followed. Beautiful pendants can be made in this manner It is another way to put into use some of your clear materials.

One of the best materials for this type of carving is clear optical quartz. Smoky quartz and clear agate are also good. For quick results this type of carving is recommended. It is easy and fun. Each piece will be progressively better until you are doing really fine work.

FACET-CUT GEMS

Facet cutting of gem stones is fast becoming one of the most popular phases of the lapidary art. It ranks with intaglio and cameo cutting as work of high accomplishment. With the modern faceting equipment and up-to-date information now available, anyone can do very creditable work in a short time. As relaxation and diversion, as well as a means of livelihood, facet cutting of gem stones is becoming increasingly popular. The following information is presented to help those in either of these categories.

Selection of Material. The selection of faceting material is very important because, fundamentally, the finished gem stone can be no better than the material from which it is cut, regardless of the perfection of the cutting and polishing. If good quality rough material is used in the beginning, much valuable time will be saved later.

In selecting rough material, whether it be amethyst, citrine, topaz, garnet, beryl, spinel, kunzite, sapphire, or one of the many

Fig. 201.—Faceting head and lap mounted on a desk. (*Courtesy M. D. R. Manufacturing Co., Los Angeles, Calif.*)

others, the important properties to consider are (1) clearness, or transparency; (2) solidness, or freedom from fractures or cracks; (3) color; (4) size and shape.

Transparency. The ability of a material to transmit light is called transparency. Since the brilliance of a gem (considering one of perfect cut and polish) depends upon its ability to transmit most of the light which enters the crown, there must be nothing behind the crown to absorb or hinder the progress of the light through the gem. If the material is cloudy or includes foreign substances, it is not first-grade faceting material.

Fig. 202.—Portable faceting unit. (*Courtesy M. D. R. Manufacturing Co., Los Angeles, Calif.*)

Solidness. Solidness is an important factor in selecting rough faceting material. If a piece of material has a fracture in it, from the standpoint of faceting it is considered to be two smaller pieces. A fracture within a stone disrupts the light ray to such an extent that it causes an ugly blemish.

Color. The color of light coming from a gem is one of the qualities that makes it beautiful and pleasing. Some stones are cut for color quality alone. Others are cut for brilliance, with color only a secondary factor. If both good color and brilliance can be obtained, an outstanding gem will be the result. This is best accomplished by selecting material that is not too dark.

Hue is the color of the stone as compared with the colors of the spectrum—violet, indigo, blue, green, yellow, orange, and red. Tone is the darkness or lightness of the hue. Both hue and tone should be given consideration in selecting good faceting gem material.

Size and Shape. Inasmuch as 50 to 70 per cent of the rough material is ground away in the process of cutting, it is important to select rough material of the size and shape that will result in a minimum of waste in the cutting of the gem.

Sawing. The diamond saw is the only practical tool to use in the sawing of faceting material. It is a precision machine and does the work quickly. For faceting work, the smaller sized saws are used.

The trim saw is the most popular. This saw uses a blade 3 or 4 inches in diameter and approximately 0.015 inch thick, running at a speed of about 4200 r.p.m. It has a flat table, with the blade protruding through a slot. Below the table is a tank of coolant in which the lower portion of the blade is immersed. The stone is held in the hands and pushed against the blade.

Be sure that the blade is always running in the coolant, which should be plentiful but not high enough in the tank to run into the bearings. A large tank is better than too small a tank.

Determine where the cut is to be made, and mark the place with a piece of pointed aluminum wire. In order to determine where the cuts should be made, locate the optic axis, and examine the stone carefully for fractures and the best color. The polariscope is used to determine the optic axis if it cannot be established from the crystal faces. To examine for fractures and color, it is often a help to cover the surface of the stone with kerosene or Asteroil (developed during World War II for examining quartz), which permits a clearer vision of the interior of the stone.

Saw the stone so that the optic axis is perpendicular to the table of the gem. If there is any variation in color, the darker tone should,

Fig. 203.—A trim saw with a thin blade is useful in sectioning valuable gem material. Trim saws are widely used in cabochon work in the resawing of sawed slabs. (*Courtesy M. D. R. Manufacturing Co., Los Angeles, Calif.*)

if possible, be in the culet at the bottom of the stone. Fractured parts of the stone should be cut away. A great deal of grinding can be saved by using the saw to partly preform the stone.

There are several kinds of blades available for use in the trim saw. For sawing expensive material, the thin, sintered blade, 0.015 inch thick, is best although it is the most expensive.

Preforming. The first step in the facet cutting of a gem stone is rough shaping, usually called preforming.

Grind the rough stone as near to shape and size as possible, leaving it about 10 per cent oversize. The grinding may be done on a silicon carbide wheel of medium grit and of a bond recommended for lapidary work. The wheel should revolve 1750 to 2000 r.p.m.

Preforming is speeded up and is also much easier to do on a diamond-impregnated wheel of 150 to 200 grit. Grinding is done on the periphery of the wheel, with one side of the wheel charged for flat surfaces. The initial cost of this wheel is high, but if one wants a clean, safe cutting wheel, this is the best.

Fig. 204.—Shaping a preform on a diamond-charged lap with the aid of a mechanical head. (*Courtesy M. D. R. Manufacturing Co., Los Angeles, Calif.*)

All grinding must be accompanied by a good supply of coolant, preferably water, at all times.

Preforming can also be done on a mechanical head; the dopped stone is inserted into the head, the desired angle selected, and the stone fed by mechanical means into a high-speed diamond-charged lap (Fig. 204). With this machine the stone is perfectly preformed in just a few seconds. These machines are expensive, and the hobbyist will no doubt prefer to grind or prepare the stone by hand.

Carefully examine the rough stone for flaws, color, and cleavage and to find a suitable area for the table. Grind the flat surface for the table, and, using one of the methods outlined, grind the stone round, oval, triangular or whatever shape the girdle is to be. If it is to be of a given size, work should be checked frequently to avoid grinding it too small.

After the girdle shape is ground, then the angle on the crown is established. If the material is quartz and the gem is to be a standard round brilliant, the angle should be 42°. The width of the table

Fig. 205.—Inspecting a preform that is being shaped on a diamond-charged lap. (*Courtesy M. D. R. Manufacturing Co., Los Angeles, Calif.*)

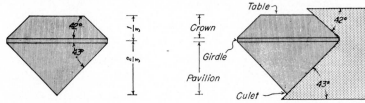

Fig. 206.—Preform for a round brilliant cut faceted stone.

Fig. 207.—A template may be made to check the angles of a preform. Angles shown are for quartz.

should be about half the total width of the stone. Now grind the pavilion (the lower part of the stone from the girdle to the culet) at 43°. These angles are very easily determined by using a bevel protractor, set at the desired angle, using the flat table of the gem stone as a reference, or by making a simple template to use as a guide, as shown in Fig. 207.

In grinding the preform leave a girdle of generous width because the facets will cut into the girdle more than the beginner will realize; thus, there is the possibility that there will not be enough material on the pavilion to place the facets at the proper angles, and a badly proportioned stone will result.

Special care should be used in preforming topaz, amethyst, kunzite, feldspar, or similar material with a weak cleavage. Topaz should be oriented about 5 to 10° off the cleavage, and when the table is ground, an aluminum pencil should be used to mark clearly the direction of cleavage. It is important to remember this when the table is set up for grinding and polishing, because it is nearly impossible to polish topaz against the grain but quite easy with the grain.

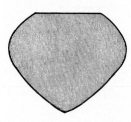

Fig. 208.—Preform for an emerald cut stone.

Amethyst should be oriented with the best color in the pavilion as near the center as possible, to obtain the greatest beauty in the finished gem.

Kunzite should be oriented so that the table is at right angles to the C axis or the long way of the rough, as that is in the direction of the most pleasing color. Some amateurs preform kunzite, but it is a very fragile stone and will not withstand much shock. Less trouble will be encountered if the stone is ground on a faceting lap without preforming.

Some of the feldspars make beautiful gems, but those of the plagioclase group have a parting plane, and if they are not oriented correctly, one will encounter facets that will be impossible to polish. Orienting this group about 15° off the parting plane will prevent this happening.

One thing to keep in mind is that, the less one has to grind off the stone in the final grinding on the facet lap, the less time will be required to complete the gem.

Emerald-cut preforms should have a soft curve from the girdle to the table and from the girdle to the culet. If one studies the arrangement of the facets on the emerald cut, one will find that they form a soft, graceful curve.

Dopping. The dopping wax or cement for facet cutting should have tackiness and strength as well as a high melting point. Special jewelers' wax has been found very satisfactory. Sealing wax mixed with flake or stick shellac may be used. Chaser's cement and pumice, in equal parts and thoroughly mixed, are also used.

Fig. 209.—Use a V block to align the preform on a dop stick, also to change dop sticks from pavilion to crown. (*Courtesy M. D. R. Manufacturing Co., Los Angeles, Calif.*)

In dopping and in transferring the stone from one dop to another, the conventional V block is generally used. A great many stones reaching the amateur have already been preformed (or if the cutter preforms his own, the table is usualy ground flat) and have a flat table. Put the small faceplate furnished with V-block sets in one end of the V block, and press the pavilion of the preform into warm wax on the countersunk end of the metal dop stick. Place the dop stick in the other end of the V block, and press the table of the stone against the faceplate. This helps to center the stone and brings the table at a right angle to the dop stick. Heat both wax and stone to ensure perfect adhesion, and build up the wax around the stone with the fingers, which should be wet. Do not let the wax cover the girdle.

After the crown of the stone is cut and polished, it must be transferred to another dop for the cutting and polishing of the pavilion. Remove the dop from the faceting device, wash the stone thoroughly to get rid of any abrasive or polishing compound, and wipe with a cloth dampened with alcohol to be sure all foreign substances are eliminated. Clamp the dop with the stone in the V block.

Build up enough cement on another dop stick, the same size as the one in use, so that when warm it will spread out over the crown

Fig. 210.—Metal dop sticks are used for faceting gem stones. (*Courtesy M. D. R. Manufacturing Co., Los Angeles, Calif.*)

of the stone but will not extend far enough to reach the girdle. The girdle of the stone must be left exposed.

Heat the wax on the new dop stick, and while warm lay the dop stick in the V on the V block, and press firmly against the stone. Clamp in position. Warm the new dop stick and stone, being careful not to warm the dop stick holding the stone. A little practice will soon enable one to know how much to heat the dop and stone to ensure a bond between the new dop stick and the stone. Remove both clamps after the cement has cooled, and while holding the two dop sticks by hand, warm only the old dop stick itself—not the wax—until the heat softens the wax and permits removal of the old dop stick. Remove any surplus wax with a knife or any sharp instrument by holding the stone between the thumb and fingers, allowing no pressure to be put on the dop stick itself.

It is necessary to leave the crown facets exposed where they meet the girdle, so that the pavilion facets can be properly lined up with the crown facets.

If the wax curves under and inward from the girdle of the stone, the stone is not properly cemented. If the wax edge curves and flows outward toward the girdle, then the stone is properly cemented. In dopping, heat both stone and wax slowly over a flame. Do not overheat the stone or burn the wax.

Jamb Peg and Jam Board. The jamb peg is undoubtedly the oldest faceting device. It is still used by some professional cutters today, but it takes years of experience to master this tool. Today those interested in faceting gems want perfect results with their first gem.

The peg is a piece of wood turned into a frustum of a cone and mounted with the large end up. On one side of this cone there is a series of holes approximately $\frac{3}{16}$ inch apart. These holes are used to give the various angles in relation to the lap, the gem being dopped to a wood stick (called a dop) about 5 inches long and shaped somewhat like a pencil. The small end of the dop is held in one of the holes of the jamb peg.

All angles are determined by eye in using the jamb peg. The indexing, or placing of the facets, is also done by eye. This method has great lap-stick freedom; in fact, so much freedom exists that one does not know where he is most of the time.

The jamb board is a device similar to the jamb peg. It is made out of a piece of hard wood approximately $3\frac{1}{2}$ by 4 inches with a series of holes at an angle of $1°$ in relation to one another. The board is hinged so that it can be tipped forward or backward for slight correction of the angles.

The jamb board is operated in the same way as the jamb peg. Both may be operated either right- or left-handed.

Facet Heads. The facet head is a mechanical device which has nearly replaced the jamb peg and jamb board in modern gem cutting.

There are a number of facet heads on the market today, and each makes use of an index plate or gear to space the facets properly

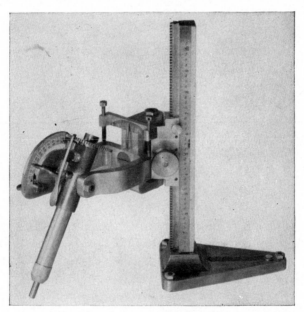

Fig. 211.—Master faceting head. (*Courtesy M. D. R. Manufacturing Co., Los Angeles, Calif.*)

on the gem-stone blank. Many cutters prefer a facet head in which the dop-rod assembly pivots.

The angle to be cut on the gem is readily determined by raising or lowering the head, of which the dop assembly is a part. A 64, 72, 80, or 96 gear is attached to the dop-rod shaft, allowing the cutter to place the facets in any arrangement desired.

In the past, the main fault with facet heads constructed by

amateurs has been that no provision was made to compensate for wear on the tool. In a short time the tool would wear in certain places from the constant contact with abrasives, and this would render the head useless for fast, accurate work. On the better facet heads provision is made for wear.

Weight is also a factor in the make-up of facet heads. A head should be light in weight but rigid. Dural aluminum, developed during the Second World War for aircraft, is exceptionally good for this purpose. A facet head should be so constructed as to have a sensitive touch for cutting small stones—stones of 0.01 to 0.20 carat—such as those used in side mounts for larger stones.

After the beginner becomes adept, he will depend more and more on the feel and sound of the gem on the lap.

Rigidity in a facet head is an important factor. In polishing nearly all gems a heavy pressure is exerted, and if the head is not rigid enough to withstand the pressure, it is almost impossible to achieve flat facets, the mark of good gem cutting. Rounded facets do not give the maximum of brilliance of the flat facets.

In grinding a gem on a diamond-impregnated copper lap, the outer side will be ground more than the inner side because there is more diamond passing under the stone at a higher speed, which cuts off more of the gem. When the grinding operation is finished and the polishing operation started, this off-grind must be compensated for, or the polishing will be a long operation; for the facet will start to be polished on one side and will be actually cut down by the polishing agent before the entire surface is polished. There is danger, therefore, of polishing facets out of alignment.

To eliminate this off grind, the facet head should be equipped with a compensator. This can be accomplished in two ways. One method makes use of an arrangement on the index gear, enabling the operator to move the dop rod in relation to the gear. Another method, which is much faster and better, is to have the dop-rod assembly mounted to a yoke which is pivoted. Simple screw adjustments may then be used to obtain perfect alignment for polishing. This same arrangement will be found invaluable in the cutting of fancy-shaped stones and in the pointing up of facets. Using this type of compensator with a degree scale, any type of cut possible on a flat lap can be made, including hearts, pendeloques, and the novelty cuts.

A facet head should be so constructed that different index gears can be used for the cutting of various shapes, such as a five- or a six-sided stone. To do this, the index gears must be of the same diameter, and the index-gear trigger must be designed to mesh with different-sized gear teeth.

Various means are used to raise and lower facet heads in relation to the lap in order to obtain various angles. One of the best methods makes use of the rack and pinion as found on microscopes.

Nearly all beginners in gem cutting feel that there should be a stop incorporated in the facet head in order to grind the facet to the desired depth; but it has been found that if the cutter will learn to cut freehand, without the aid of a stop, he will, after practice, do better and more accurate work. The facet head should be adjustable through zero (table) to 90° (girdle), and the scale should be clearly visible to the eye.

Using a facet head constructed along these lines, such as the Master facet head, and working with predetermined angles, it is possible for a beginner to do very creditable work from the start.

Cutting or Grinding Laps. Until recent years most cutters, both professional and amateur, have used loose abrasives—silicon carbide, Norbide, and other materials—on copper or cast-iron laps. The loose-abrasive method is messy and the hazard of contamination is great. It is difficult to keep a uniform amount of abrasive on the lap, since it is usually applied with a brush from time to time. These factors are detrimental to accurate cutting.

Today nearly all cutters have discarded the loose-grit method and are using diamond-impregnated laps, which are not only far faster in cutting but have also practically eliminated the hazard of contamination.

The action of the two abrasives seems to be entirely different. The loose grit seems to get under the gem on the lap and roll, thus

Fig. 212.—The cutting of a faceted gem stone is relatively easy with a modern faceting head and a diamond-charged lap. (*Courtesy M. D. R. Manufacturing Co., Los Angeles, Calif.*)

Fig. 213.—Cutting the table of a faceted gem stone with the aid of a 45° angle dop. (*Courtesy M. D. R. Manufacturing Co., Los Angeles, Calif.*)

crushing the surface away. The diamond, being impregnated in the lap with sharp points sticking up, has a planing action which results in a cleaner cut.

Diamond laps are constructed in different ways. First, the sintered method can be used. Diamond grit of the desired size is mixed with a metal in colloidal state and molded into shape usually on an aluminum or plastic disk, forming a rim varying from ½ to 1½ inches, the size depending upon the manufacturer and the purpose for which the wheel is made. This diamond-impregnated surface is usually about $\frac{1}{16}$ inch thick and of varying concentrations of diamond and metal, usually 50-50. One objection to these laps, other than their high cost, is that they lack the toughness of other metal laps; therefore grooving will result unless special care is taken in using them.

Second, another lap of similar construction can be made with plastic. Diamond or other abrasive is mixed with liquid plastic (such as lucite) and molded onto the surface of a lucite disk. This lap is apt to groove or get out of parallel, and from time to time it must be trued by holding a coarse piece of silicon carbide truing brick in the hand and pressing it against the revolving lap. This lap must be run very wet as the lucite generates a great amount of heat.

The last method—and the one recommended here—uses the lap of cold-rolled copper, bell metal, bronze, or brass charged with diamond.

The charging is done by mechanical means, pressing the diamonds into the lap. The lap is malleable, and the diamonds are locked into the lap, leaving just enough exposed to give it a grinding or planing action.

Of all the laps, those made by the last method described are undoubtedly used most. Over a period of years, the original cost will no doubt be the least, and the quality of work will be the best. These laps, charged with various grit sizes, are available from lapidary supply dealers.

As a general rule a large number of stones can be cut before the lap will need to be recharged. As the sharp points of the diamond exposed at the surface will in time be dulled by the cutting action, the lap must be recharged to increase the cutting speed. Wet the lap with water, and apply diamond grit (powder) of the desired size to the lap with the finger tip. Using an agate with a round surface, rub the diamond into the lap. Do not rotate the lap by power when doing this, for some of the diamond may be thrown off the lap. Work the surface of the lap until all the diamond is embedded.

The longer one uses this type of lap, recharging it from time to time, the better it will be, because the cutter can keep it in the condition which gives the best results. Many professional cutters

Fig. 214.—Cutting a faceted gem stone on a diamond-charged copper lap. (*Courtesy M. D. R. Manufacturing Co., Los Angeles, Calif.*)

Fig. 215.—Inspecting a gem stone. (*Courtesy M. D. R. Manufacturing Co., Los Angeles, Calif.*)

have used the same lap for as long as 15 or 20 years, recharging it from time to time as needed.

Cold-rolled copper seems to be the best metal for these laps, as it has the desirable toughness and malleability. Cast copper does not seem to have the density or toughness found in the cold-rolled copper.

If these laps are kept clean, they will work better. Do not grind into dopping wax and leave it on the lap, as it will glaze over the diamonds and keep them from coming in contact with the stone. Always trim the wax away from the edge of the stone, but if some happens to get on the lap, wash it off with alcohol.

Apply water to a copper lap with a square of white, hard felt, such as is used in felt buffing wheels. The material should be about $\frac{1}{2}$ inch thick and 2 inches square. This will keep the lap bright and clean and will supply just the right amount of coolant.

Indexing. Faceted gem stones are usually divided into two general classes—round and square—depending upon the general shape of the girdle of the stone. There are many variations.

The brilliant cut and the emerald cut (also known as the step or trap cut) are the two basic styles of cuts.

The angle that each facet makes with the girdle of the stone is controlled by raising or lowering the end of the dop stick as the facet is being cut. In using a mechanical faceting head, this is accomplished by raising or lowering the head.

The arrangement of facets on each row of facets is controlled by a gear or index plate. The number of teeth on the index gear is always a multiple of the number of facets to be cut on each row. For instance, if there are 4, 8, or 16 facets to be cut, the index plate will usually have either 32 or 64 teeth.

Standard Brilliant. The standard brilliant-cut gem stone should be carefully studied so that one will become acquainted with the different facets and their positions.

There are 57 facets on the standard brilliant-cut gem stone. Including the table, there are 33 facets on the crown—that portion of the stone above the girdle. These are divided into three rows that encircle the crown. There are 8 main crown facets, 8 table facets, and 16 crown girdle facets.

The pavilion, that portion of the stone below the girdle, has 24 facets, comprised of 8 main pavilion facets and 16 pavilion girdle facets.

After cutting the rough gem material into a preform and dopping, cut and polish the table by using a 45° angle dop (Fig. 213). If the material is quartz, set the faceting head to cut at an angle of 42°, and use a 64 index gear (which is standard equipment on a Master facet head) to cut the 8 main crown facets, using indexes 64, 16, 32,

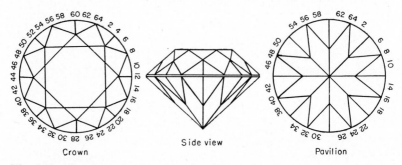

Crown   Side view   Pavilion

Fig. 216.—Standard round brilliant faceted gem stone. The numbers designate index positions for cutting corresponding facets when using a 64 index plate. (*Courtesy M. D. R. Manufacturing Co., Los Angeles, Calif.*)

48, 8, 24, 40, and 56. There is special significance in cutting the facets in this order. If the first 4 facets are cut in uniform size, the last 4 will be much easier to cut, and at the same time a uniform size is maintained on all 8 facets.

Next, cut the 8 table facets at an angle of 27°, using indexes 4, 12, 20, 28, 36, 44, 52, and 60. The 16 crown girdle facets are then cut, using indexes 2, 6, 10, 14, 18, 22, 26, 30, 34, 38, 42, 46, 50, 54, 58, and 62. The crown girdle facets are cut at an angle of 44 to 47° depending upon the diameter of the table and the diameter of the girdle.

Polish the 8 crown table facets first, the 8 main crown facets next, and then the 16 crown girdle facets.

Redop the stone, using the V block, and cut the facets on the pavilion. Cut the 8 main pavilion facets, at an angle of 43°, with the same indexes used in cutting the crown main facets. Next cut the 16 pavilion girdle facets, with the same indexes used in cutting the crown girdle facets. These are cut at an angle of 45°.

Polish the 8 main pavilion facets first, then the 16 pavilion girdle facets.

Cut the girdle, using an 86 to 90° angle. This is facilitated by use of the girdle grinder attachment, which fits the base of a Master facet head (Fig. 222). Polish the girdle. The width of the girdle should be approximately 2 per cent of the depth of the stone, the distance from the table to the point of culet. Cut and polish the girdle first if a stone of a predetermined size is desired.

Emerald Cut. Fewer steps are necessary in cutting an emerald-cut gem stone than a standard brilliant, but more angles are used, especially on the corner facets. The following angles are for quartz.

Cut and polish the table in the 45° angle dop. Place the dopped stone in the facet head, and cut the 42° facets, using indexes 64, 16, 32, and 48, on a 64 index plate. Cut the 27° facets. These may be made very narrow, if desired. Next cut the 55° facets. These may be the same width as, or wider than, the 42° facets.

Cut the corner facets, using indexes 8, 24, 40, and 56. The angles on the corner facets vary considerably from those on the other facets.

Polish the 27° facets first, the 42° facets next, and then the 55° facets.

Transfer the stone to another dop in the V block, and align by making very light trial-and-error cuts on the pavilion at 63°, until the facet cuts parallel the girdle. If difficulty is encountered, use the two compound angle screws on the Master head for alignment. Use the screw on the side corresponding to the wider end of the facet. Cut the 53° facets next and then the 43° facets.

Use the same indexes in cutting the pavilion facets that were used in cutting the crown facets.

Polish the 43° facets first, then the 53° facets, and the 63° facets last.

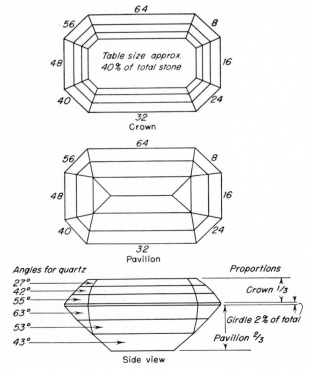

Fig. 217.—Emerald cut gem stone. The numbers designate index positions when using a 64 index plate. (*Courtesy M. D. R. Manufacturing Co., Los Angeles, Calif.*)

Cut and polish the girdle. If a predetermined-sized stone is desired, cut the girdle first.

Modified Brilliant—Horizontal Split Mains. The modified brilliant with horizontal split main facets deepens the color in light material and is especially effective in a light amethyst, citrine, aquamarine, white quartz, topaz, and beryl. The angles given are for quartz, beryl, and natural aquamarine.

Cut and polish the table in a 45° angle dop. Place the dopped stone in the facet head, and cut the girdle.

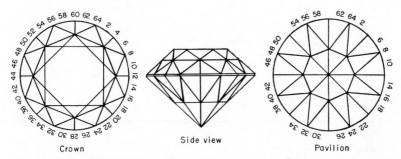

Fig. 218.—Modified brilliant gem stone with horizontal split main facets. (*Courtesy M. D. R. Manufacturing Co., Los Angeles, Calif.*)

Cut the 8 crown main facets, using a 64 index plate, with the facet head set to cut facets at 42°. Use indexes 64, 16, 32, 48, 8, 24, 40, and 56. Grind the break facets at 35°, using indexes 64, 8, 16, 24, 32, 40, 48, and 56. Make the breaks approximately one-third the depth of the main facet.

Cut the 8 table facets at 27°, using indexes 4, 12, 20, 28, 36, 44, 52, and 60. These facets should point up and meet at the break between the 35 and the 42° facets.

Cut the 16 crown girdle facets, using indexes 2, 6, 10, 14, etc. The angle for these facets will be between 45 and 50°, in order to point up at the girdle and table facets. Determine the angle by trial and error. If the facet touches the upper corner before the facets cut at indexes 2 and 62 meet at the bottom, the angle is too great. Lower the facet head to correct this. If the facets overlap at the girdle before they touch the upper corners, increase the angle by raising the facet head.

Polish the table facets, the mains, and then the girdle facets.

Transfer the stone to another dop in the V block, and cut the 8 main pavilion facets at 48°, using the same indexes as those for the crown main facets. Change the angle to 43°, and cut the lower part of each main, bringing it up one-third of the total pavilion depth.

Cut the 16 pavilion girdle facets, changing the angle, which is 50 to 55°, until the facet meets the vertical break line and the girdle.

Polish the pavilion mains first, the breaks next, and then the pavilion girdle facets.

Modified Brilliant—Vertical Split Mains. The modified brilliant with vertical split mains is recommended for citrine, zircon, topaz, beryl and synthetic aquamarine. The angles given here are for quartz and beryl.

Cut and polish the crown of the preform in the 45° angle dop. Place the stone in the facet head, and cut the girdle with a 64 index gear, using indexes 2, 6, 10, 14, etc., at an angle of 86 to 90°.

Cut the 8 crown main facets at a 42° angle, using indexes 64, 8, 16, 24, etc. Still using the 42° angle, regrind the 8 crown main facets to get the vertical splits. Use indexes 63 and 1, 7 and 9, 15 and 17, 23 and 25, 31 and 33, 39 and 41, 47 and 49, and 55 and 57.

At an angle of 27°, cut the 8 table facets, using index numbers 4, 12, 20, 28, 36, 44, 52, and 60.

Cut the 16 crown girdle facets, using indexes 2, 6, 10, 14, 18, etc. Find the angle by trial and error.

Polish the table facets (27°), the main facets (42° at indexes 63, 1, 7, 9, etc.), and then the girdle facets (indexes 2, 6, 10, 14, etc.). Polish the girdle.

Transfer the stone to another dop in the V block, place it in the facet head, and align with the crown. The vertical split in the crown main facet must be in the center of the pavilion main facet.

Using index settings 63 and 1, 7 and 9, 15 and 17, etc., make light trial cuts, at 45°, to the same depth, until the center lines are in alignment with the splits in the crown main facets. Then grind all pavilion main facets.

Cut the 16 pavilion girdle facets. They should be approximately two-thirds the depth of the pavilion. The angle is 45 to 50° and it is found by trial and error.

Polish the main pavilion facets, then the girdle pavilion facets.

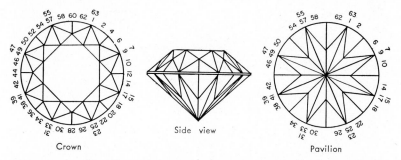

Fig. 219.—Modified brilliant gem stone with vertical split main facets. (*Courtesy M. D. R. Manufacturing Co., Los Angeles, Calif.*)

Brilliant-cut Heart. Grind and polish the table of the preform in the 45° dop. Check in the V block to make certain the table is at right angles to the shank of the dop.

Place the stone in the facet head, using a 72 index gear, and align the stone so that the top is on the 72 index. Set the facet head so that at the finish of the cut the angle will be 42°. The angles given here are for quartz.

Using the same angle, 42°, cut the remaining main crown facets, cutting them in pairs and making sure that each pair is the same width. Use indexes 64-8, 56-16, 52-20, 48-24, 44-28, and 32-40.

Using index 72, cut at 90° a large flat which will be part of the girdle. Disengage the index gear, and cut the girdle freehand. If each pair of facets was ground the same width at the table, the girdle should be symmetrical.

Cut the table facets, using indexes 1-71, 12-60, 18-54, 22-50, 26-46, and 30-42. The angles for these facets will have to be changed so that each facet will be about one-third the height of the crown and point up at the table. The angles are usually between 30 and 37°.

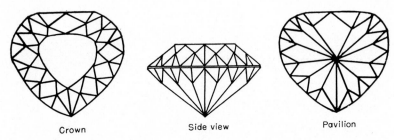

Crown   Side view   Pavilion

Fig. 220.—Brilliant cut heart. (*Courtesy M. D. R. Manufacturing Co., Los Angeles, Calif.*)

The next step is to cut the crown girdle facets, using indexes 1-71, 6-66, 10-62, 14-58, 17-55, 19-53, 21-51, 23-49, 25-47, 27-45, 29-43, and 31-41. The angles for these facets are $44\frac{1}{2}$ to $47\frac{1}{2}°$. The facets should point up at the girdle and at the table facet. In order to do this it may be necessary either to increase or to decrease the angle.

Polish the table facets first, the main facets next, and the girdle facets last.

Transfer the stone to another dop in the V block, place the dopped gem in the facet head with the index at 72 and angle about 72° and align. Cut the large facet, at about 49°, on the pavilion.

Using indexes 40 and 32, cut the facets until they point up at the culet with the first cut, with the proper width of girdle. Cut the remaining facets so that they point up at the culet and leave the same width of girdle using the same indexes as those for the main crown facets. The angles will vary with each stone.

Cut the pavilion girdle facets, using the same indexes as in cutting the crown girdle facets. The angle will vary, usually from 45 to 47°.

Polish the main pavilion facets first, then the girdle facets. When finished with the pavilion, remove the stone from the dop, and polish the girdle on a felt wheel with tin or cerium oxide.

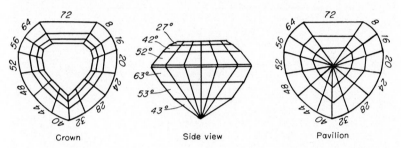

Fig. 221.—Step-cut heart. Numbers designate index positions on a 72 index plate. (*Courtesy M. D. R. Manufacturing Co., Los Angeles, Calif.*)

Step-cut Heart. After cutting and polishing the table in the 45° dop, place in the V block, and check the table to see whether or not it is at right angles to the shank of the dop. If it is not, warm cement, and press the stone against the faceplate while in the V block.

Place the dopped stone in the facet head, and, using a 72 index gear, set on index 72, make a practice cut at 42° (if the material is quartz) to see whether or not the stone is properly oriented. If it is not, loosen the chuck, and correct.

Cut the large top facet on index 72 at 42°, and then cut the remaining 42° facets. Cut them in pairs, each pair being the same width at the table, or the gem will not be symmetrical. Use the following indexes in cutting the facets: 8-64, 16-56, 20-52, 24-48, 28-44 and 32-40.

Change the angle to 27°, and cut another row of facets, using the same indexes as in cutting the 42° facets.

Using a 52° angle, cut a series of facets with the same indexes as in cutting the 42° facets.

Lower the head to 90°, and, using the 72 index, cut to the proper girdle depth.

Fig. 222.—Polishing the girdle of a faceted gem stone with the aid of a girdle grinder attachment which fits the slide base assembly of a Master faceting head. Height adjustment is easily made by moving a knurled screw.
(*Courtesy M. D. R. Manufacturing Co., Los Angeles, Calif.*)

Polish the 27° facets first, next the 42° facets, and then the 52° facets.

Transfer the stone to another dop in the V block, place the redopped stone in the facet head, and align with the 72 index. This is made easy by the previous grinding at 90°.

Cut at 63°, on index 72, a large rear facet; then cut the rest of the pavilion girdle facets in the 63° series, using the same indexes as for the crown girdle facets. Cut the 53° facets and then the 43° facets.

Polish the 43° facets first, then the 53° facets, and the 63° facets last.

Do not facet the girdle. Grind it freehand on the diamond lap after the stone is completely finished. Polish it on a felt wheel with tin or cerium oxide.

If a notch is desired in the stone, rough it out on the corner of a silicon carbide grinding wheel. File it into shape with a three-cornered silicon carbide stick, and sand it with silicon carbide cloth wrapped around the stick. Polish on the corner of a felt wheel. Use extreme caution when putting the notch in a finished stone, as all facets are polished and must not be scratched with the silicon carbide wheel or cloth.

Angles for Facet Cuts

Gem material	Hardness	Refractive index	Main crown facets, degrees	Main pavilion facets, degrees
Diamond............	10	2.42	35	41
Quartz..............	7.0	1.54	42	43
Andalusite..........	7.0–7.5	1.64	43	39
Apatite.............	5.0	1.64	43	39
Benitoite...........	6.0–6.5	1.78	37	42
Beryl..............	7.5–8.0	1.61	42	43
Corundum..........	9.0	1.76	37	42
Epidote............	6.5	1.75	37	42
Andradite garnet......	6.5	1.88–1.89	43	40
Uvarovite garnet......	7.5	1.83	37	42
Almandite garnet.....	7.5	1.83	37	42
Spessartite garnet.....	7.0	1.79–1.81	37	42
Grossularite garnet.....	7.0	1.75	37	42
Pyrope garnet........	7.0	1.75	37	42
Rhodolite garnet.......	7.0	1.76	37	42
Olivine (peridot).......	6.5–7.0	1.68	43	39

Angles for Facet Cuts

Gem material	Hardness	Refractive index	Main crown facets, degrees	Main pavilion facets, degrees
Phenakite.............	7.5–8.0	1.66	43	39
Spinel...............	8.0	1.72	37	42
Spodumene...........	6.0–7.0	1.66	43	39
Topaz...............	8.0	1.61	43	39
Tourmaline..........	7.5	1.63	43	39
Zircon..............	7.5	1.92	43	40
Rutile, synthetic.......	6.5	2.62–2.92	34	41
Rutile..............	6.0–6.5	2.62–2.90	34	41
Feldspar (bytownite)....	6.0	1.52–1.58	42	43
Iolite...............	7.0–7.5	1.55	42	43
Sphalerite...........	3.5–4.0	2.37	35	41
Vesuvianite..........	6.5	1.72	37	42
Rhodonite...........	6.0	1.72	37	42
Jadeite..............	7.0	1.66	43	39
Nephrite.............	6.0	1.63	43	39
Chrysoberyl..........	8.5	1.74	37	42
Chalcedony..........	7.0	1.54	42	43
Cyanite.............	4.0–7.0	1.72	37	42
Diopside.............	5.0–6.0	1.68	43	39
Moldavite...........	5.5	1.50–1.60	42	43
Sepiolite............	2.0–2.5	1.55	42	43
Staurolite...........	7.0–7.5	1.74	37	42
Titanite.............	5.0–5.5	1.90–2.03	43	40
Zoisite..............	6.0–6.5	1.70	43	39
Euclase.............	7.5	1.65	43	39
Axinite.............	6.5	1.68	43	39
Enstatite............	5.0–6.0	1.67–1.70	43	39
Beryllonite..........	5.5–6.0	1.56	42	43
Datolite.............	5.0–5.5	1.65	43	39
Anatase.............	5.5–6.0	2.55–2 49	34	41
Willemite...........	5.0–6.0	1.70	43	39

A summary of the preceding table gives the angles for the main facets as follows:

Refractive index	Main crown, degrees	Main pavilion, degrees
1.50–1.60	42	43
1.61–1.70	43	39
1.71–1.84	37	42
1.88–1.95	43	40
2.41	35	41
2.62–2.90	34	41

Polishing. Facet polishing is done upon flat laps. These laps are usually made of tin, antimony, lead, zinc, cast iron, plastic, copper, bronze, pitch, or mixtures of two or more of the metals.

Various polishing agents are used. These include very fine diamond powder, tin oxide, Linde A powder, cerium oxide, and Damascus ruby powder.

Tin laps are undoubtedly used by more gem cutters than any of the others, but because tin is imported and scarce, the price is high. However, a lap made of tin will give years of service with the proper care, barring accidents.

Metal polishing laps are usually cast into a mold, using the lap plate as a mold or a piece of sheet metal bent to form a circle and clamped down on a flat surface. After the lap is cast, it must be machined or faced so that the surface will be true and smooth, eliminating any wobble. The lap should run within 0.002 inch when turning.

Plastic laps are cut from sheet plastic not thinner than ⅜ inch and machined in the same way as other laps. The cast-iron lap is self-explanatory. Copper or bronze laps may be cast or cut from sheet stock and then machined.

Pitch laps are made by melting polishing pitch as used in lens grinding and pouring it into a metallic lap which has been machined in such a way that it acts as a mold. After the lap has become cool or is just barely warm, it should be machined just like the tin, lead, or other kinds of laps. The pitch lap is the hardest of all to take care of. If the lap is not setting level and is not kept cool in warm weather, the pitch will move and the lap will become uneven. This lap, because of the care it requires and the results obtained by using it, is very disappointing, although many cutters still prefer it.

One will find that in polishing the various gem materials the specific combination of a certain lap with a certain polishing compound will give better results than other combinations.

For stones whose hardness is between 4 and $6\frac{1}{2}$ on Mohs' scale, a tin or tin and type-metal lap, using tin oxide as a polishing agent, will give excellent results.

Stones 7 in hardness work well with a tin lap and tin oxide or with a lucite lap and cerium oxide as the polishing agent. The lucite lap must not be smooth, and it must be run very wet.

Gems $7\frac{1}{2}$ to 8 in hardness polish well on a type-metal lap, using Linde A, Ruby Dix, or Damascus ruby powder as the polishing agent.

Corundum gems (ruby and sapphire)—both natural and synthetic—being 9 on Mohs' scale, are next to the diamond in hardness. There are a great many polishing agents which will polish corundum gems, but with most of these agents one will encounter some facets on the gem which, owing to grain, will be next to impossible to polish in a reasonable time. The synthetics are harder and are more difficult to polish than the natural gems. The method of using diamond to polish corundum is by far the most practical today.

There are a number of diamond grit sizes used in this polishing method—3200 grit to 6400 grit—depending on the speed of the polishing lap. The higher the speed of the lap, the coarser the diamond grit used on the lap. Various laps are used with the diamond powder, such as copper, lucite, cast iron, lead, type metal, tin and type metal, and tin; but the pure tin lap seems to be preferred by the majority of cutters. This preference is due undoubtedly to the hardness and toughness of the tin lap.

There is a certain knack to using 6400 diamond powder on a tin lap for polishing. Do not get too much diamond on the lap, as most persons are likely to do when they start using this combination. Apply most of the diamond near the outer edge of the lap, where most of the semipolishing is done; then move into the inner part of the lap for the final polishing.

There are a number of coolant agents used in polishing with diamond on a tin lap. Among them are water, cleaning solvent, olive oil, kerosene, and mixtures of these, but kerosene works very well for a lap speed up to 650 r.p.m. For speeds above this, a few drops of olive oil will keep the powder on the lap.

Place the diamond in a shallow receptacle such as a cosmetic jar which has a curved bottom or a container without sharp corners. One carat of diamond powder, with a generous supply of kerosene, will polish a great number of stones.

Apply the diamond and kerosene to the lap with a piece of leather belt, a piece of synthetic hard rubber, or the finger. The strip of leather or rubber should be approximately 1 inch wide and 2 inches long.

When diamond is needed on the lap, insert the leather, rubber, or one's finger in the bottom of the receptacle, pick up a little diamond, and put it on the lap. When oil or coolant is needed, this may be taken off the top.

No matter which method is used to apply diamond and coolant, the leather, rubber, or the person's finger should be held at an angle of about 45°, tangent to the center of the lap, in order to keep the polishing compound running back toward the center of the lap. When one builds up a black sludge and is able to keep it in the area on the lap that one is polishing upon, the best results are

Laps and Polishing Agents for Various Gems

Material	Kind of lap	Polishing agent
Quartz	Lucite	Cerium oxide, very wet
	Tin	Tin oxide
	Type metal	Tin oxide
Andalusite	Tin	Tin oxide
Apatite	Type metal	Linde A
Benitoite	Tin	Tin oxide
Beryl	Lucite	Cerium oxide
	Tin	Tin oxide
	Type metal	Tin oxide
Corundum	Tin	6400 diamond
Epidote	Tin	Tin oxide
Garnet	Type metal	Linde A
		Damascus ruby powder
		Ruby Dix powder
Olivine	Type metal	Linde A
		Ruby Dix
		Damascus ruby powder
Phenakite	Lucite	Cerium oxide
	Tin	Tin oxide
Spinel	Type metal	Linde A
		Ruby Dix
		Damascus ruby powder
Spodumene	Tin	Tin oxide
	Type metal	Linde A
		Ruby Dix
		Damascus ruby powder
Topaz	Tin	Damascus ruby powder (nearly dry)
	Type metal	Linde A
		Ruby Dix
		Damascus ruby powder
Tourmaline	Tin	Tin oxide
	Type metal	Linde A
		Ruby Dix
		Damascus ruby powder
Zircon	Tin	Damascus ruby powder
		Ruby Dix
	Type metal	Linde A

obtained. It seems as if the material removed from the gem in itself acts as a polishing agent.

Diamond-charged tin laps are usually serrated with short, shallow knife cuts, but better results will be obtained on any lap if it needs serrating by making short cuts, each cut making approximately a 45° angle with the diameter. Make cuts slanting both to the left and the right.

If a deep cut is made on a straight line to the center of the lap, one will find in polishing small facets that a vibration will be caused by the facet hitting these cuts or ditches and that a flat facet will be hard to obtain. By using the short angle cuts the facet will be supported at all times. The short cuts, made both to the left and the right, form traps for the polishing agent. Some cutters use a kitchen carving knife for these cuts, making them while the lap is in motion.

It is difficult to give any definite speed for the various polishing laps, although 400 to 600 r.p.m. is the usual speed for average material. Some cutters turn their laps at 100 r.p.m., while others run them as high as 1750 r.p.m. Soft gems, under 6 in hardness, will polish on a slow lap, some as low as 10 r.p.m.

CUTTING AND POLISHING TITANIA

Titania (synthetic rutile) was released to the trade in the early part of 1949.

This stone is made in boule form similar to synthetic ruby and sapphire, and it has a refractive index about 20 per cent greater than that of the diamond, its refractive index being 2.62 to 2.92 as compared with 2.42 for the diamond. It is much softer than the diamond, being 6½ on Mohs' scale of hardness, whereas quartz is 7 and the diamond is 10. Titania is, however, very tough. It is heavier than the diamond, being 1⅓ times as heavy. Chemically it is pure titanium oxide.

Each boule of titania generally weighs 60 to 120 carats. It is also available from dealers in sawed sections. Titania is available in clear, amber, and blue.

In sawing titania a very thin blade should be used. Some cutters charge a blade as used in diamond cutting, a bronze disk 0.006 inch in thickness, with 200 diamond grit, and they use this for sawing. Nick the edge of the blade with a millgrain tool, mix the diamond with vaseline, rub the diamond into the nicks, and close the nicks or slots by rolling with a hardened steel roller. One of these blades, so charged, will saw two or three boules before requiring recharging.

The diamond-sintered blade, 0.015 inch thick, is more easily obtained, and it gives excellent results with a minimum of waste.

When titania was first released to the trade, it was recommended that it be cut with the table at right angles to the optic axis. Since then the experience of amateur cutters indicates that it does not seem—to the unaided eye—to make any difference whether the table is at right angles or parallel to the optic axis.

The round standard brilliant-cut gem is the best cut for showing the greatest beauty in the stone.

A greater yield can be had from each boule if the boule is quarter-sectioned, lengthwise, and each quarter then cut into suitable blanks.

Preform the blank in the usual manner, as with any other faceting material.

In dopping, use only enough heat to cement the stone to the dop stick. While excessive heat is not recommended, it does not, in most instances, damage the stone.

If much material is to be ground away, it is suggested that the first grinding be done on a 400 diamond-impregnated copper lap. Finish grinding on an 800 diamond-impregnated copper lap. Polish with Linde A aluminum oxide powder on a tin, tin and type-metal, tin and lead (50-50), or a type-metal lap. Speed is not critical. Use a speed of 400 to 750 r.p.m. Better results are obtained in polishing by using a scored lap.

In the grinding operation some facets will be found that will grind rough or show pits. It is advisable to leave these facets high and to polish them into alignment; otherwise they will have to be overpolished to eliminate the pits.

A very high polish is desirable for maximum brilliance. Because of the double-refracting quality of the stone, one scratch on the pavilion will appear to be three or more scratches when viewed through the table.

Unless it is cut at the proper angles, the finished stone will lack brilliance. After exhaustive experimentation with various angles, the following are recommended to reflect the greatest brilliancy:

Main crown facets .... 34°
Crown table facets .... 20°
Crown girdle facets .... Approximately 39–41°

(This angle may vary 1 or 2°, depending upon the width of the table.)

Pavilion main facets .... 41°
Pavilion girdle facets .... 43°

The table of the stone should be approximately 50 per cent of the girdle diameter. Leave the girdle thick enough to prevent breakage in mounting the stone.

CARE OF EQUIPMENT

Facet cutting is one continual battle against contamination. One diamond or silicon carbide grit embedded in a polishing lap can be very trying when one is polishing a beautiful gem. Sometimes it is possible to remove the grit by scraping the lap with a razor blade, but it is usually best to resurface the lap by turning it in a lathe.

If one is constantly on guard against contamination, one can probably facet for years without trouble. A very good practice is never to put the hands on the surface of a polishing lap, because that is the usual way for the lap to become contaminated. Another good practice is to keep or store the laps when not in use in a folder similar to a phonograph-record folder.

When cabochon cutting is done near the faceting machine, the problem of contamination is greatly increased, especially when the sanding is done on a dry sander. If possible, keep facet cutting away from other cutting operations.

Keep the faceting machine clean at all times. A good practice is to clean the machine each time when through cutting. These machines are precision machines and should be treated as such. Another important factor is to keep the faceting machine well lubricated.

A very neat and compact way to mount the faceting machine is to mount it in a desk-type bench with drawers for the necessary laps and other equipment.

By having the machine set up in such a bench, it is possible to sit down and cut an entire gem without running here and there for different pieces of equipment. This unit can be made very attractive for use in a den or spare bedroom (Fig. 201).

Another advantage of mounting the facet machine on the desk-type bench is that it offers a comfortable way to cut. When a person is comfortable, he has much more patience, and patience is of the utmost importance in facet cutting.

OPTICAL PROPERTIES OF GEMS

The angles for cutting gem materials depend upon the properties of light. Light is a natural force that makes vision possible. White light is made up of the seven colors of the spectrum, violet, indigo, blue, green, yellow, orange, and red, each of which has a different frequency of vibration.

Light travels in the air at approximately 186,000 miles per second. However, light traveling through other mediums has different speeds. If a wave of light is produced at a point in a vacuum, it will be transmitted outward from that point in all directions at the same velocity. At any instant all points equidistant from the point of origin are in the same phase. The locus of these points is called a wave front and is a spherical surface.

A straight line drawn from the point of origin to any point on the wave front is called a ray and represents the direction of the wave itself. The light ray is a convenient method of representing any given direction of the motion of the wave. Light always travels in a straight line when in a medium of a given density. However, in passing from the medium of one density to the medium of another, it will change its direction, by refraction; or, upon striking a polished surface, it will change its direction, through reflection.

Reflection. Reflection is changing the direction of light in the same medium when a light strikes a polished surface. When a beam of light strikes a polished surface at an angle, it is reflected away from that surface at the same angle.

A line perpendicular to the surface at the point where the ray strikes the surface is called the normal. The angle at which the ray strikes the gem is always taken as the angle between the ray and the normal. The angle between the ray approaching the gem and the normal is called the angle of incidence. The angle between the reflected ray, or the ray leaving the surface, and the normal is called the angle of reflection. The angle of incidence and the angle of reflection are always equal.

Refraction. Refraction is the bending of a ray of light when it passes from one medium to another of different density. The refraction, or bending, takes place at the point where the light enters the second medium.

The normal extends inside the gem exactly as on the outside. The angle of refraction is the angle between the normal and the ray on the inside of the gem. The ratio of the sine of the angle of incidence to the sine of the angle of refraction is called the index of refraction, and it is constant for the medium concerned.

Another method of finding the index of refraction of a given substance is to divide the speed of light in air by the speed of light in the given substance. The speed of light in ordinary glass is about 124,000 miles per second. Its index of refraction is found by dividing 186,000 (the speed of light in air) by 124,000 (the speed of light in ordinary glass), which is 1.5.

The light ray entering the gem will always be bent toward the normal. The ray leaving the gem will be bent away from the normal.

Dispersion. Dispersion is the amount of separation of the colors caused by refraction. White light upon entering the gem stone is broken up into its various colors and is bent at a different angle to the normal. The angle of separation may be large or small, depending upon the gem material. A gem material causing a wide separation of the colors has a high dispersion; a gem material causing a small amount of separation has a low dispersion.

Since the beauty of the gem depends upon the number of colors seen as caused by dispersion, dispersion is an important property of the gem.

The path of light traveling through a gem can be traced in Fig. 223. Light ray *AB* strikes the surface *MM'* of the gem at *B*. A portion of the light is reflected along the line *BD,* according to the law of reflection.

The line *EE'* is a perpendicular to the surface *MM'* at the point of contact *B,* and the angle *ABE* between the ray and the perpendicular is the angle of incidence. The angle *DBE,* which is the angle between the reflected ray and the perpendicular, is the angle of reflection. These angles are always equal.

That portion of the ray *BC* that enters the gem does so at a reduced velocity which varies according to the density of the gemstone material. The ray is bent at the point of entry, and its transmission through the stone is in a direction closer to the perpendicular EE'; the angle CBE', formed by the bent ray and the perpendicular, is the angle of refraction.

When light passes from a rarer (air) to a denser medium (gem), this ratio is greater than unity, the angle of refraction is less than the angle of incidence, and the refracted ray is bent toward the perpendicular.

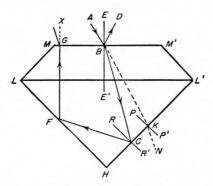

Fig. 223.—Light entering a properly faceted gem stone is reflected back through the crown.

After the light has entered the gem stone, it becomes a problem of reflection to bring the light back to and to release it from the crown of the gem. This is accomplished by the pavilion facets, whose angles are such that the greatest amount of the transmitted light will be reflected back into the gem and toward the crown.

In order to obtain total reflection, it is necessary to know the critical angle of the gem material. As the light ray has entered the gem stone, conditions are now reversed. The ray is traveling in a denser medium (gem), and is trying to pass into a rarer medium (air). Under these conditions the refracted ray would be bent away from the perpendicular, and only light within a certain limited angle of incidence could enter the rarer medium.

In Fig. 223 assume that the refracted ray is BK and that it strikes the surface $L'H$ at the point K. Erect a perpendicular PP' to the surface $L'H$ at the point K. As the ray is entering a less dense medium, its velocity will increase, and it will be bent away from the perpendicular PP'.

The angle $P'KN$, which the refracted ray KN makes with the perpendicular PP' will be the angle of refraction, and the light will enter the air along the line KN.

If the angle of refraction of ray BK should equal $90°$ the light ray would be refracted, enter the air at $90°$ from the perpendicular, and coincide with line $L'H$. The angle of incidence, BKP, would be the critical angle of the gem, and light of any greater angle of incidence could not enter the air.

If the refracted ray is assumed to be BC striking the surface $L'H$ at the point C and a perpendicular RR' is erected to the surface $L'H$ at point C, the angle of incidence BCR is found to be greater than the angle BKP, which is the critical angle of the material. The ray cannot obey the law of refraction, and it must be totally reflected back into the gem along the line CF, at an angle of reflection equal to the angle of incidence; it will strike the surface LH at a point F.

If the angle that the reflected ray CF makes with the perpendicular to LH at the point F is greater than the critical angle of the material, the ray will be totally reflected again along the line FG, striking the surface of the gem MM' at the point G. If a perpendicular is erected to MM' at the point G, it is found that the angle between the reflected ray FG and the perpendicular is much less than the critical angle and that the ray passes through into the rarer medium (air) with a refraction away from the perpendicular GX and with an increased velocity.

Part 4

IDENTIFICATION OF GEM STONES AND GEM MINERALS

SOME 1,200 distinct mineral species are known to science, and of these about 100 are commonly used as gem stones. Many of the opaque and translucent gems of the semiprecious class can be readily identified at a glance, while others present a more difficult problem.

Even with the aid of optical equipment definite determination of a gem is not always a simple matter. Experts often spend hours in the examination of a doubtful species before rendering their opinion. Moreover, it is well to bear in mind that some of the synthetic gems on the market are often very difficult to distinguish from the natural gems, this being especially true of the sapphire and spinel types, which are sold in facet-cut style.

However, there are many simple tests of gem identification within the scope of the amateur. It is the purpose of this chapter to detail a few of the more elementary methods. For more complete information the reader is referred to standard textbooks on optical mineralogy and similar technical works. Determinations involving the use of costly optical equipment are not given in detail here.

In studying a cut gem stone, remember that with very few exceptions every gem stone can be imitated in a form that will readily deceive the layman. It has often been said that the diamond and opal are the only gems of value that cannot be manufactured in a form that will pass easily for the genuine. This is very true of the opal, for the manufactured substitutes are palpable frauds to the eyes of everyone. White zircon, an inexpensive gem, very closely equals the diamond in play of colors, but the great difference in hardness serves to differentiate them immediately. In addition most diamonds present at least small areas of included black carbon, visible under magnifications ranging from low power up to 40 $\times$, or in some instances visible to the unaided eye. Carbon is not found in white zircon.

In recent years a great variety of gem imitations have appeared on the American market, most of this material originating in the foreign gem-cutting centers where labor is cheap. While many of these glass and similar imitations may be attractive in color and general appearance, they have no intrinsic value or interest comparable with that of a natural gem. To the connoisseur and student of gemmology, the fused and similar substitutes hold little fascination—no more than that of any other commercial glass.

METHODS OF TESTING GEMS

There are two general methods by which a gem stone may be determined: first, by a consideration of the physical properties; second by use of data gained by a study of the optical properties. Physical properties give a great deal of valuable information in most instances, but when a doubt arises, it is necessary to resort to a study of the optical properties. In general, it is not wise to use any *single test* as a sole guide in rendering a decision, although special methods are used in some instances.

PHYSICAL PROPERTIES

The physical properties of a gem or gem mineral include color, hardness, specific gravity, luster, cleavage, crystal form, and a number of other features. When rough material is being tested, the problem is generally simplified because less concern is necessary for a possible slight damage to the specimen. Also the crystal form, if present, may offer a valuable clue for identification. Obviously, a cut stone which may prove valuable should be handled with care.

COLOR

Gem stones often depend upon their color for their beauty and charm; yet color alone is an unreliable guide in determining gem stones. Gem stones are known to occur in a wide range of colors and shade even in the same species. For instance, we are most familiar with white diamond; yet this gem is found in black, yellow, brown, and more rarely pink and green shades. Moreover, some gems are subjected to heat-treatment to alter their native color, while some of the semiprecious gems, such as agate and turquoise, can be altered (colored) by various chemical means.

But the color of the gem should be given consideration; lists of colors of gem stones can be found in standard textbooks on the subject. In some gems, such as amethyst and sapphire, the color may not be evenly distributed; it may be seen as patches and layers, with some areas more highly colored than others. This is frequently noted in amethyst, since large-sized crystals of amethyst with the color evenly distributed are seldom found. Hence, a large cut stone of amethyst showing even distribution of color should be viewed with suspicion and subjected to a close scrutiny before it is accepted as a natural gem. Purple-colored fused quartz resembles amethyst, at least in hardness, specific gravity, and color.

HARDNESS

Hardness is a reliable test where the suspected gems vary reasonably in range. However, where the several possibilities of identity are of similar hardness, then this test (by hand) becomes unreliable. It is quite simple to distinguish between two gems where the hardness of one is Mohs' 7 (quartz) and the other 9 (sapphire); but if the hardness of one is 7 and the other $7\frac{1}{4}$ or $7\frac{1}{2}$, distinguishing gems by this means is unreliable. Furthermore, gems of the same species will often vary slightly in hardness, especially on different crystal faces.

Mohs' scale of hardness, used in all standard textbooks on mineralogy and gemmology, fails to indicate properly the actual difference between the various gems. Sapphire is listed on Mohs' scale as 9 and diamond as 10; yet the hardness of the latter is actually several times that of sapphire.

The National Bureau of Standards scale, shown in Fig. 159, enables one to compare the actual hardness of the various minerals as listed on Mohs' scale.

In testing the hardness of gems, care must be exercised to select a place on the stone where, if scratched, the mark will not show when mounted. A steel file or sharp fragments of gem minerals may be used and the test made on the girdle of the stone. A knife blade and glass are both approximately 5.5 in hardness, the steel file generally 6.5. Mounted hardness testing points are available from distributors. The slight dust of abrasion should not be confused with an actual scratch. When in doubt, examine the area with a magnifier.

When accuracy is required in measuring hardness, various instruments are used where the pressure of the scratching tool is under mechanical control and the actual depth of the mark is determined. The gem cutter of experience can usually judge with reasonable accuracy the hardness of the material by the manner in which it is reduced and polished. All standard textbooks on mineralogy and gemmology list tables of hardness for reference purposes. Some gems vary in hardness, but usually not greatly, provided, of course, that the material is pure.

SPECIFIC GRAVITY

The comparison of the weight of a substance with an equal bulk of water is termed its specific gravity, or gravity for short, water being taken as a standard of 1. Most of the gem minerals are nonmetallic in their composition and have gravities of less than 4, the usual range being from 2 to 4.

In one respect, it is unfortunate that gem stones should range so closely in gravity, for this limits the use of this easy and simple method in making determination, unless very accurate balances are available. Further, the gravity of some gems will vary slightly in the same species, thus complicating matters even more. Obviously, the larger the bulk of the substance being tested, the less the factor of error; so less accurate methods can be applied in such instances.

A good habit to acquire in handling loose gem stones is to heft them. If the stones are reasonably large, the practiced hand can gain a good approximate conception of the specific gravity. For example, in handling a zircon and an aquamarine of similar size, bulk for bulk, the zircon will be distinctly heavier since its gravity is nearly twice that of aquamarine. This method is, of course, applicable only to gems of fairly large size or large fragments of the uncut material.

There are two principal methods used for taking the specific gravity of a gem, one involving the use of accurate and sensitive balances, the other the use of liquids of known gravity.

If analytical balances are at your disposal, you can make use of the pycnometer method, which is quite accurate.

The second method of determining specific gravity is to weigh the gem in air by suspending it from the beam of a balance with a fine thread or wire and then to weigh it under water. The difference between the two weighings divided into the weight of the gem in air equals the specific gravity. Thus if a gem weighs 12 carats in air and 9 carats suspended under water, the difference is 3; 12 divided by 3 gives 4, which is the gravity of the gem.

The larger the gem, the smaller will be the percentage of error by this method. A stone weighing 1 carat with an error of 1 per cent in the weighings will give an error of about 0.15 in specific gravity. Hence accurate weighing is important in dealing with small stones or fragments.

SPECIFIC-GRAVITY FLUIDS

For quick work, simplicity, and low cost, the amateur will find specific-gravity fluids very convenient and accurate for use in making gem identifications. Various fluids can be used, but for general work the author prefers the use of Thoulet's solution. This is made by saturating ½ ounce of water with as much potassium iodide and mercuric iodide (red) as the water will dissolve. The solution can be made by any druggist, or you can prepare it yourself. In making this solution, continue to add small portions of each solid to the water until no more will dissolve, taking several hours or longer to complete the saturation. Thoulet's solution, when fully saturated, will at room temperature have a specific gravity of 3.17. It should be kept in a small wide-mouthed glass-stoppered bottle. The stone or fragment to be tested should be dropped in and removed with tweezers, as the solution is somewhat corrosive to the skin. Water readily removes the liquid, which does no harm if permitted to remain on the fingers for only a short while.

With Thoulet's solution one can readily distinguish many gem stones from their imitations. For example, most of the "topaz" of commerce is citrine quartz, usually colored by heat-treatment to give it the lovely topaz shades of color. True topaz has a specific gravity of 3.4 (or slightly greater), while quartz has a specific gravity of not over 2.6. Thus, by dropping the gem in the fluid and noting whether or not it floats, an imitation topaz can be quickly discovered. By diluting this solution with water and using a small fragment of material with a known gravity as a guide, various liquids with lower gravity can be made.

Other "heavy liquids" can be made from various compounds. A saturated aqueous solution of cadmium borotungstate will give a solution with a gravity of 3.28. Thallium malonate formate (in water) will give a gravity of 4.38, and methylene iodide in benzol will give a gravity fluid of 3.32. These solutions are used widely in the field of mineralogy for separating mixtures of minerals, but some of them, being dark in color, have the disadvantage that it is difficult to locate a small gem stone in them.

Do not depend wholly upon this test with gravity fluids in every instance. Some of the glasses that are cut into imitation gem stones have a rather high specific gravity, and the hardness test is therefore a surer test for these, as all glass is relatively soft. Thus, in the test referred to above, if the stone sinks, do not assume it is necessarily topaz without first making additional check tests. In short, in testing any gem stone, do not rely solely upon one single result unless you are certain it is a conclusive one.

EXAMINING FOR FLAWS AND INCLUSIONS

Flaws, inclusions, and structural lines of some gem stones are quite characteristic, and may be taken as criteria in making a determination. For instance, the fine feathers seen in practically all emeralds are characteristic, yet the cheap glass imitations sometimes used are manufactured with similar flaws; hence flaws alone should not be the sole guide. On the other hand, a stone alleged to be emerald and yet free of all feathers should be viewed with suspicion.

As an aid in detecting flaws and blemishes in a cut stone or fragment of rough material, the substance can be placed in a liquid with a refractive index (R.I. or n) similar to that of the gem. Kerosene may be quite effective; a small amount placed in a shallow white porcelain evaporating dish makes a convenient way to view the gem. Assuming the liquid selected has a refractive index very close to that of the stone or mineral, the fragment will become almost invisible, especially if colorless or pale in color. Certain inclusions and flaws present will then stand out in glaring contrast.

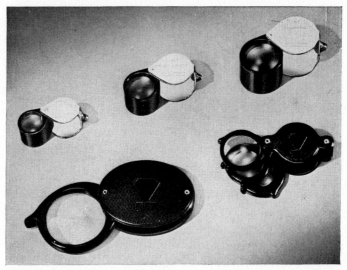

Fig. 224.—Hand lenses used in examining gem stones. (*Photograph courtesy of Bausch & Lomb Optical Co., Rochester, N. Y.*)

Suggested fluids for this purpose include turpentine, oil of cedar, Canada balsam, glycerine, castor oil, and numerous others which are listed with their refractive indices in textbooks on optical mineralogy.

If you have a microscope, the immersion fluids will also be valuable in determining the approximate refractive index of gem minerals by the use of the reaction known as the Becke line. This test is widely used in the determination of all nonopaque substances, including minerals and gems. A very small amount of crushed fragments of the material is used and tested with various fluids of known refractive index. This method is fully within the scope of the amateur and is described in detail in standard works. The method is not easily applicable to a large stone. Fragments crushed to a mesh of 100 to 200 are best used.

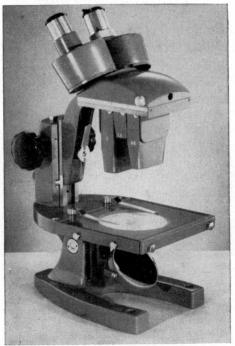

Fig. 225.—The binocular-type microscope, useful in examining gem stones for structural lines, inclusions, flaws and other markings. (*Photograph courtesy of Bausch & Lomb Optical Co., Rochester, N. Y.*)

As an aid in examining flaws, structural lines, inclusions, and other markings found in natural gems and the synthetic types, the binocular-type (Greenough) microscope is very useful. Generally low powers will suffice, ranging from 10 to 40 ✕. The advantage of the binocular magnifier lies in being able to focus up and down and view the various internal as well as external parts of the gem.

The angstrom-unit range of the argon-filled bulb is around 3900, while the Mineralight will give about 50 per cent of its light in the angstrom-unit range of around 2400 and less than 7 per cent as visible light. For this reason, the lights of higher power have a much wider range of usefulness than the argon bulb, since substances that may fail entirely to react under the argon bulb will fluoresce powerfully and beautifully under the higher power lamp.

LUSTER, CHATOYANCY, ASTERISM, FRACTURE, AND CLEAVAGE

The luster of a gem is governed by the reflection of light from its surface; this quality is described variously as adamantine (diamond), metallic (marcasite and pyrite), greasy (jade), waxy (turquoise), and pearly (pearl), and in other terms.

Chatoyancy is used in referring to the silky and changeable luster seen in a few of the gem stones. Moonstone shows this phenomenon.

A few gem stones when cut into steep-sided cabochons will show a four- or six-rayed star, termed asterism, characteristic of the more opaque forms of sapphire. Asterism is also met with in rose quartz, in garnet, and in rare instances in a few other gems (spinel and topaz). Synthetic star sapphires and rubies are now being made commercially.

Imitation stars are generally made of a base of rose quartz with a section of curved blue grass to act as a lens to magnify and bring out the asterism. Obviously, a doublet of this kind can be easily distinguished from a sapphire. The star in any asteriated gem can best be seen by viewing it in a single light, as several sources of light bring out conflicting stars.

Fracture and cleavage are especially valuable in the identification of uncut gem material. Some crystals of gem minerals, such as tourmaline and topaz, present typical cleavages. These crystals often show a flat surface on one or both ends of the crystal, this surface being at right angles to the principal optic axis (C axis) of the crystal. Familiarity with the various crystal forms will enable the gem stonecutter to recognize on sight most of the gem minerals when presented in the natural crystal form.

OPTICAL METHODS

Since all gem minerals, except a few that occur in amorphous form, crystallize in one of the six crystal systems, it would follow that those belonging in different systems would present variations in optical properties. These variations are very important and offer a highly useful means of determining a gem stone. To become expert or even quite proficient in testing gem stones, the gem cutter, jeweler, collector, or hobbyist should have a knowledge of crystallography. Familiarity with the optical properties of crystals (and gems) belonging to the various crystal systems will enable the individual to gain a much better understanding of the optical methods used by experts in determining gem stones. Hence a basic knowledge of crystallography is desirable.

It is not within the scope of this chapter to present the subject of crystallography, but suffice it to say that a great many persons who handle gem stones in a commercial way are handicapped by a lack of knowledge of this subject. An understanding of crystallography, as it applies to gem stones, can be gained from any elementary textbook on the subject.

REFLECTION TEST

By holding the cut gem in a beam of sunlight and casting the light passing through the stone on a white card, it can often be determined whether the gem is of single or double refraction by noting whether the reflections of the facets are separated or together. All gems crystallizing in the isometric (cubical) system are isotropic and give single refraction. Others are anisotropic and may show double refraction to a greater or lesser degree. Where the double refraction is feeble, it will not be possible to observe it by this simple method.

The diamond is isometric in crystallization, while the zircon gives strong double refraction; hence if one is proficient in using this test, diamond and white zircon can be distinguished by this means. Likewise, red garnet shows only single refraction, while ruby shows a good double refraction. Further, all glass imitations show only single refraction, since they are amorphous substances lacking in any crystal form.

USE OF THE DICHROSCOPE

The inexpensive hand instrument known as the dichroscope is one of the most valuable instruments available for determining the optical properties of a gem stone which may give a helpful clue to its identity.

This little instrument consists essentially of a cut prism of calcite (Iceland spar), mounted in a short metal tube. Calcite gives a very strong double refraction and splits up the light entering at one end into two rays, which are seen as small squares at the eyepiece of the instrument.

Not all gems show the phenomenon of dichroism (and pleochroism). To be determined at all by the hand dichroscope, the gem must be colored. The deeper the color, the stronger will be the dichroism. All gems belonging to the isometric crystal system are negative under the dichroscope, as are all amorphous and noncrystalline substances such as glass. The outstanding exceptions to this rule are the fused synthetic types of sapphire and ruby which are actually crystalline. Hence the dichroscope is unreliable in distinguishing between the sapphire and ruby and their synthetics.

In viewing a gem stone for possible dichroism, the stone and instrument are usually held toward the light, and a search is made for twin colors, which would appear, if present, on the two small squares seen in the instrument. Unmounted stones are the most convenient to examine, or a small fragment may be used if the material is in the rough state. The stone should be viewed from different angles, as dichroism is seen only in looking through certain portions of the stone in a particular relation to the various optic axes of the crystal. As the stone is viewed, the instrument is rotated in

Fig. 227—The dichroscope. A calcite prism mounted within the tube of the instrument gives separate views of the twin colors seen in some gems.

the fingers through 90°; the different colored squares will appear and then disappear. In some instances, dichroism will be noted by viewing through the table of the specimen and in others only through the girdle or at some other angle, depending on the manner in which the cutter oriented the material.

Some gem stones, such as sapphire, tourmaline, emerald, quartz, and topaz, show a strong or distinct dichroism in the colored varieties. Textbooks on gemmology list tables of the various gems exhibiting this phenomenon, indicating the twin colors which will appear in the small squares.

By the aid of this simple instrument a great many valuable and helpful clues in making determinations can be obtained. Any gem stone, alleged to be a gem known to show dichroism but which fails to show it, can, of course, be viewed with suspicion. By experimenting with known gem stones and fragments of minerals, you will soon become familiar with the use of this valuable instrument.

POLARISCOPE

An inexpensive substance with the trade name of Polaroid gives excellent polarization of light in various optical instruments. Polaroid is widely utilized in nonglare glasses and inexpensive adapters to convert an ordinary microscope into a polarizing instrument.

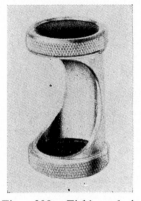

A polariscope made of two 1-inch disks of Polaroid, mounted in a tube open at one side, with the disks separated by about 2 inches of space, makes a useful instrument for the examination of gem stones and fragments of minerals. The material being examined must, of course, be reasonably transparent to permit passage of light. Instruments of this kind can be made or purchased at a cost less than that of the calcite-prism dichroscope, and the polariscope covers an even wider range of usefulness.

Fig. 228.—Field polariscope. Compact pocket size polariscope for viewing gem stones with polarized light. (*Photograph courtesy of Polarizing Instrument Co., Irvington-on-Hudson, N.Y.*)

With a hand polariscope it can be immediately determined whether a substance is isotropic (glass or isometric system) or anisotropic. Thus any and all types of glass used in imitation gem stones can be readily detected. The top section (analyzer) of Polaroid mounted in the instrument is arranged so that it can be rotated, to enable one to view the object under crossed nicols. In short, the polariscope functions on the same principle as a polarizing microscope, except that there is no magnification as the former is not fitted with lenses. Experimenting with various substances will indicate a number of practical uses for the polariscope in gem determination.

REFRACTOMETER

The refractometer is an instrument designed to take a direct reading of the refractive index of a cut gem stone. This instrument is accurate and reliable, but its use is somewhat limited as stones with a very high refractive index, such as diamond, zircon, and garnet, are beyond its range. It is of medium price, costing less than the powerful microscopes and more than the smaller hand instruments.

POLARIZING MICROSCOPE

The polarizing microscope is an entirely different instrument from the ordinary microscope such as is used in biology and bacteriology. The former is equipped with two calcite (nicol) prisms to enable the examination of substances by polarized light, while the ordinary microscope is primarily an instrument for magnification only. Under polarized light the gems belonging to the different crystal systems will present specific phenomena, as will amorphous or noncrystalline substances, thus enabling the operator to make a determination. Experts familiar with a polarizing microscope are generally able to classify every nonopaque mineral known, including the gems.

The use of the polarizing microscope is facilitated where the substance to be examined is available in fragments that can be crushed to a mesh of 100 to 200 fine. Since the instrument is also a microscope, it is obvious that difficulties would be experienced in attempting to examine a cut stone of large size. Crushed fragments are much easier to handle and orient. Aided by this instrument, the operator can quickly determine the crystal system to which the gem mineral belongs, and then, if additional data are required, the index of refraction will serve to identify it definitely. In fact, in some instances this instrument fills a need that can be met in no other way.

With Polaroid the ordinary microscope can be easily converted into a polarizing instrument at a nominal cost. The regular polarizing microscope is fitted with a rotating stage to enable turning the substance and to permit the light to pass through in various directions. Ordinary microscopes have a stationary stage or a mechanical

Fig. 229.—Polarizing microscope with analyzer in tube and rotating stage. Widely used for the determination of gem stones. (*Photograph courtesy of Bausch & Lomb Optical Co., Rochester, N. Y.*)

stage, neither of which permits rotation in a circle. This is a disadvantage, yet for some purposes the revolving stage is not essential, and many determinations can be made readily without its aid, or the specimen can be turned by hand. A special cross-hair eyepiece can be fitted to the ordinary microscope equipped with Polaroid and thus extend its usefulness.

The use of a polarizing microscope involves a working knowledge of crystallography and the optics of light. The reader desiring to take up this work is referred to textbooks on the subject.

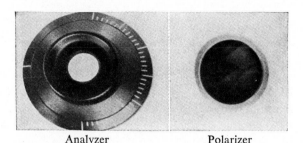

Analyzer   Polarizer

Fig. 230.—Polaroid analyzer and polarizer for converting ordinary micro-scope into a polarizing instrument. (*Photograph courtesy of Polarizing Instrument Co., Irvington-on-Hudson, N. Y.*)

Fig. 231.—Projection lantern. Gem stones and any transparent fragments of gem minerals can be projected on screen with polarized light. Analyzer can be rotated to enable projection with crossed Nicols. (*Photograph courtesy of Polarizing Instrument Co., Irvington-on-Hudson, N. Y.*)

SYNTHETIC GEMS AND ALTERED GEMS

Of the better class of imitation gems, there are two main types of fused substances in common use. One is the sapphire type, a fused aluminum oxide, made in the form of a round pear-shaped boule by permitting the powdered chemical to drop slowly into the intensely hot flame of a blowpipe. The other widely used substitute is the spinel type, of a different composition, but made in the same manner.

In the early years of the manufacture of synthetic sapphire and spinel, the methods in use were relatively crude, with the result that air bubbles and similar defects appeared during fusion. These were readily visible with an ordinary magnifying glass or even with the unaided eye. However, in recent years this manufacturing process has become so highly developed that the boule when cut into a gem stone may defy experts in making a certain diagnosis.

Synthetic ruby (sapphire), for instance, can be made into any shade of red color, with exactly the same chemical composition as the real article, with the same hardness, specific gravity, and refractive index, and even with a crystalline structure. Hence, in order to determine this substitute, it is often necessary to study the gem under high magnification and search for the curving lines of structure or minute air bubbles and similar fusion markings. Natural sapphire (ruby) is always hexagonal in structure, presenting straight and not curving lines.

So difficult is the determination of the synthetic sapphire and spinel that these substitutes have been mixed with a lot of natural stones and sold as such without detection. Likewise, the unwary tourist visiting the native gem-cutting centers of Ceylon and Siam is often sold a "ruby" manufactured in Germany or France, and thinks it genuine. Since these synthetics can be readily manufactured in almost any color or shade, they are widely used as a substitute for gems not even remotely akin to sapphire or spinel.

Bakelite, one of the chief imitations of amber, has a higher specific gravity than amber and can be detected by a simple gravity test. Amber will float in strong salt water, while bakelite with its higher gravity will sink. A strand of suspected bakelite beads can be immersed in a vessel of strong salt water, and if they sink, they certainly are not amber. The cheaper pressed and molded types of true amber will, of course, have approximately the same specific gravity as the untreated fossil resin.

Heat treatment is used to alter and often to enhance the color and value of some gems. Virtually all the blue zircon stones on the market are inferior colored stones which have been subjected to heat treatment. The white zircon is also frequently a heat-treated product.

The deeply colored "topaz" of commerce is a product of heat treatment of smoky, pale, or inferior colored amethyst. The dark varieties are termed "Spanish topaz," and other names are applied to the other shades of color, including citrine (quartz) for the paler shades of yellow and brown. Most of this work of altering gems is carried on in foreign countries, and the methods are looked upon as trade secrets, although some of them are generally known and are being used in the United States.

Turquoise occurring in pale colors can be dyed and the color enhanced. Substitutes for turquoise include the masses of pressed material which are made to resemble rounded and waterworn pebbles of turquoise.

AGATE COLORING

Agate coloring has been carried on in Germany for over 100 years, where the modern methods of color altering were first developed. Agate is also heated in ovens, usually to bring out the deep colors of carnelian and sardonyx.

Various chemicals are used to dye agates. The black colors are produced by soaking the specimen in a sugar solution for a few weeks and then boiling it in sulphuric acid for several hours. The acid carbonizes the absorbed sugar to yield the black color.

Red colors can be had by soaking agate for several weeks in a strong solution of iron nitrate, after which the specimen is heated to a high temperature in an oven for several hours, starting with a gentle heat to prevent fracturing. Agate should be cooled gradually. Repeated applications of the above treatment may be required to attain the desired color.

The apple-green colors are produced by first soaking agate in a solution of nickel nitrate and then heating it in the manner already described. Green colors are obtained by first soaking agate in a saturated solution of potassium bichromate for several weeks, then placing it in a similar solution of ammonium carbonate, followed by the oven treatment.

Various other colors can be had by first soaking agate in the proper chemical, followed either by another chemical or by heat treatment to alter the absorbed substance to an oxide or similar insoluble form. The entire process of coloring agate is merely a matter of elementary chemistry and is no secret.

Although dyed agates may sometimes be desirable, they should be plainly marked as such when placed in museum collections or sold as gem stones. The manner in which agates assume the bands of color when placed in the dye pot is due to the fact that different layers vary in porosity; hence some layers will absorb a dye or chemical, while others lacking in porosity will take on little or no color. The coloring rarely penetrates very deeply into a thick specimen; hence, if such stones are recut, they generally show uncolored material. The crystalline quartz often seen in the central portion of slabs of dyed agate will also show colors which quartz never assumes in nature. Those familiar with agate can easily detect dyed specimens at a glance.

QUALITIES ENHANCING VALUES IN GEMS

In all gems there are certain inherent qualities which tend to increase their value, beauty, and general appearance. The diamond, for example, owes its value mainly to its hardness and brilliance, but it is not a rare gem compared with a stone such as benitoite, which is found in only one locality in the entire world, and there only sparingly. Yet the diamond has a greater value weight for weight.

The delicate color of some gems is taken into consideration in an appraisal of the value. Ruby, for example, is not a brilliant stone; its value is dependent mainly upon its rarity, hardness, and beauty of coloring. Stones of the softer class usually owe their value to color or similar factors.

Rarity of a gem also influences value. For instance, during the days of Queen Elizabeth of England, amethyst, the royal purple of the nobility, was obtained solely from the limited deposits of Siberia, and, carat for carat, it was in a class with diamond in value. Later the enormous deposits discovered in South America reduced the commercial value of amethyst to a point where now a choice amethyst can be purchased at a very reasonable cost. A study of these qualities in gems is of considerable interest, and attention is called here to a few.

Diamond. Diamonds are graded either according to their lack of color or if distinctly colored according to the depth of color, which increases their value. A water-white stone, absolutely free from color, in other words, is very rare. This may not be perceptible to the untrained eye but can be noted when several stones of large size are placed together for comparison. Diamonds showing a distinct green or pink color are classed as fancy stones and bring a substantial premium.

Size is also a factor in determining diamond values and those of numerous other gems. A diamond 1 carat in weight is worth considerably more than twice the value of a ½ carat gem. Small diamonds, emeralds, rubies, amethysts, turquoise, etc., are much more numerous than large choice examples.

Aquamarine. The best quality of aquamarine should present a definite bluish-green color and not a pale blue-white.

Opal. A considerable amount of red showing in an opal increases its commercial value. Stones showing only green, orange, or purple, no matter how attractive, are generally worth less than the "fire" reds.

Experts familiar with opal can usually determine the origin of the specimen at a glance. For instance, the various localities in Australia yield characteristic gems. The Queensland opal is lively, with a strong basic yellow color. The White Cliffs gems are chalky white but full of good fire, while most of the Lightning Ridge material runs from gray to black in matrix. Stuarts Ridge opals are in a dense hard matrix, with a cream-colored background and mainly green and red flashes of fire.

Turquoise. Although some admire the pleasing shades of green in turquoise, the blue colors are the most valuable, particularly the royal blue of a slight translucency. Turquoise should be free of matrix and flaws and should be of a uniform color, but such stones in large sizes are scarce.

Zircons. This gem is often marred by a slight cloudiness, perhaps not noted by the untrained eye, but stones free of this defect are decidedly more brilliant. Practically all the fine blue-green zircon of commerce has been subjected to heat-treatment, but this does not detract from its value since the treatment improves the appearance of the gem.

Garnet. This isotropic gem is often too dark in color; good translucent material is scarce in pieces large enough to cut a stone of substantial size. In the more opaque varieties of garnet the cutter should watch for possible asterism, as this enhances the value. In cutting for the star in garnet, the orientation of the crystal is not important, since it will come at a right angle to any of the three like crystal axes. In orienting sapphire for the star, the steep cabochon surface must be across the principal, or C, axis of the crystal.

Spinel. Rose-tinted shades of spinel are the most attractive and pleasing.

Jade. Jade (or jadeite) should be free of white and gray patches, and, of course, the translucent Imperial jade (green) variety is costly when free of these patches. Jade is not at all a rare gem, being found in quantity in various colors including white, yellow, black, pink, gray, and mixed colors, but the high quality of Imperial jade is indeed rare and commands the market.

Lapis Lazuli. The best lapis lazuli is of a good deep blue color and free of white and gray areas. This type of material is found principally in Russia. Pyrite of iron is often seen on the polished surface of a cut stone.

Amethyst. The deep-colored specimens of amethyst have a much greater value than those showing only a pale purple. Most of the amethyst of commerce comes to us from South America. The deposits of Siberia are said to be nearly exhausted. There is a distinct difference in the shade of color between the amethyst of South America and that of Siberia, and the expert can detect this difference at a glance. Size and uniformity in the distribution of color are also factors affecting value.

DEALERS

The dealers listed below are for the most part current advertisers in magazines devoted to gem cutting and jewelry making. The American Gem and Mineral Suppliers' Association, 145 Pasadena Ave., South Pasadena, California, will furnish a list of their members and supply information as to where materials may be obtained.

Gem-cutting Material and Gem Stones:

Grieger's, 1633 E. Walnut St., Pasadena 4, Calif.

Southern Oregon Mineral Exchange, 411 E. Main St., Medford, Ore.

M. D. R. Manufacturing Co., 4853 W. Jefferson Blvd., Los Angeles 16, Calif.

New England Diamond Corp., 43 West 47th St., New York 19, N. Y. (Precious and semiprecious stones).

Sam Kramer, 29 W. 8th St., New York 11, N. Y.

Ward's Natural Science Establishment, Inc., 3000 Ridge Road East, Rochester 9, N. Y.

A. J. Alessi, 430 S. Highland Ave., Lombard, Ill.

Smith's Agate Shop, 228 S.W. Alder St., Portland 4, Ore.

Stewart's Gem Shop, 2620 Idaho St., Boise, Idaho.

Technicraft Lapidaries Corp., 3560 Broadway, New York 31, N. Y.

Compton Rock Shop, 1409 S. Long Beach Blvd., Compton, Calif.

S-T Gem & Mineral Shop, 7010 Foothill Blvd., Tujunga, Calif.

O'Brien Lapidary Equipment Co., 1116 N. Wilcox Ave., Hollywood 38, Calif.

Eldon E. Soper, 433 S. Central Ave., Glendale 4, Calif.

Mueller's, 1000 E. Camelback Road, Phoenix, Ariz.

Minerals Unlimited, 1724 University Ave., Berkeley 3, Calif.

Tom Robert's Rock Shop, 1006 S. Michigan Ave., Chicago 5, Ill.

International Gem Corp., 15 Maiden Lane, New York 7, N. Y.

Herbert Wm. Lawson, Terrebone, Ore.

El Paso Rock & Lapidary Supply, 2401 Pittsburg St., El Paso, Texas.

Rainbow Gem Co., 546 W. Mission Dr., San Gabriel, Calif.

J. C. Filer & Son, 1344 Highway 99, San Bernardino, Calif.

R. O. Houghtaling, Rt. 1, Bishop, Calif.

Bitner's, Scottsdale, Ariz.

Woodward Ranch, Box 1087, Alpine, Texas.

Murphy's, 210 Angelt Ave., San Antonio, Texas.

Bruce M. Ward, 702 Woodbury St., Miles City, Montana.

Howe Lapidaries, 2834 Carpenter St., Racine, Wis.

Headwaters Agate Shop, Three Forks, Montana.

Minerals and Gems, Box 8072, Albany 3, N. Y.

Stan's Rock Shop, 7952 Lorain Ave., Cleveland, Ohio.

Deming Rock Shop, 420 W. Spruce, Deming, N. M.

Rogmor Lapidary Shop, 106 4th St., Wilmette, Ill.

W. S. Kettering, 14 La Huerta, Pueblo, Colo.

Imperial Jade Ltd., Colt's Neck, N. J.

Lapidabrade, Inc., 2407 Darby Road, Haverton, Pa.

South Bend Rock Shop, 915 S. 32nd St., South Bend 15, Ind.

Dean's Agate Shop, 3427 East Garnsey Lane, Bakersfield, Calif.

The Agate Shop, 704 W. Kimball, Raymondville, Tex.

Olmar Lapidary Supplies, 1645 W. Wolfram St., Chicago 13, Ill.

Gold Pan Rock Shop, 2020 N. Carson St., Carson City, Nevada.

Petersen's Rock Shop, Foley, Minn.

Lapidary Equipment and Supplies:

M. D. R. Manufacturing Co., 4853 W. Jefferson Blvd., Los Angeles 16, Calif.

Covington Lapidary Engineering Co., Redlands, Calif.

Grieger's, 1633 E. Walnut St., Pasadena 4, Calif.

Vreeland Manufacturing Co., 4105 N.E. 68th Ave., Portland 1, Ore.

Lapidary Equipment Company, Inc., 1545 W. 49th St., Seattle 7, Wash.

B & I Manufacturing Co., 461 Washington St., Burlington, Wis.

O'Brien Lapidary Equipment Co., 1116 N. Wilcox Ave., Hollywood 38, Calif.

Minerals Unlimited, 1724 University Ave., Berkeley 3, Calif.

Nelson Lapidary Equipment Co., 520 Mead Bldg., Portland 4, Ore.

Gordon's Gem and Mineral Supplies, 1850 E. Pacific Coast Highway, Long Beach 6, Calif.

Highland Park Lapidary Supply Co., 1009 Mission St., South Pasadena, Calif.

William Dixon, Inc., 36 E. Kinney St., Newark, N. J.

Smith's Agate Shop, 228 S.W. Alder St., Portland 4, Ore.

Young Diamond Saw Co., 3207 N.E. 11th Ave., Portland 12, Ore.

Poly Products, Monrovia, Calif.

Stewart's Gem Shop, 2620 Idaho St., Boise, Idaho.

Technicraft Lapidaries Corp., 3560 Broadway, New York 31, N. Y.

Compton Rock Shop, 1409 S. Long Beach Blvd., Compton, Calif.

Tom Robert's Rock Shop, 1006 S. Michigan Ave., Chicago 5, Ill.

J. C. Filer & Son, 1344 Highway 99, San Bernardino, Calif.

Lapidabrade, Inc., 2407 Darby Road, Haverton, Pa.

Henry B. Graves Co., 3163 N.W. 27th St., Miami 42, Fla.

Highland Park Manufacturing Co., 1009 Mission St., South Pasadena, Calif.

Diamond Powder:

The Diamond Drill Carbon Co., 63 Park Row, New York 7, N. Y.

Arthur A. Crafts & Co., 532 Commonwealth Ave., Boston, Mass.; 30 W. Washington St., Chicago, Ill.; 7310 Woodward Ave., Detroit, Mich.

Standard Diamond Tool Corp., 64 W. 48th St., New York, N. Y.

Gold and Silver:

Anchor Tool & Supply Co., 12 John St., New York 7, N. Y.

Allcraft Tool & Supply Company, Inc., 11 E. 48th St., New York 17, N. Y.

Grieger's, 1633 E. Walnut St., Pasadena 4, Calif.

R & B Art-Craft Co., 11019 S. Vermont Ave., Los Angeles 44, Calif.

J. J. Jewelcraft, 2732 Colorado Blvd., Los Angeles 41, Calif.

Handy & Harmen, 850 Third Avenue, New York 22, N. Y.

Wildberg Bros. Smelting and Refining Co., 635 S. Hill St., Los Angeles 14, Calif.; 742 Market St., San Francisco 2, Calif.

Metalcraft and Jewelry Equipment and Supplies:

Grieger's, 1633 E. Walnut St., Pasadena 4, Calif.

William Dixon, Inc., 36 E. Kenney St., Newark 1, N. J.

R & B Art-Craft Co., 11019 S. Vermont Ave., Los Angeles 44, Calif.

J. J. Jewelcraft, 2732 Colorado Blvd., Los Angeles 41, Calif.

Metal Craft Supply Co., Providence, R. I.

Craft Service, 337 University Ave., Rochester 7, N. Y.

American Handicrafts Company, Inc., 45 S. Harrison St., East Orange, N. J.; 915 S. Grand Ave., Los Angeles 15, Calif.

Anchor Tool & Supply Co., Inc., 12 John St., New York 7, N. Y.

M. D. R. Manufacturing Co., 4853 W. Jefferson Blvd., Los Angeles 16, Calif.

Technicraft Lapidaries Corp., 3560 Broadway, New York 31, N. Y.

Allcraft Tool & Supply Company, Inc., 11 E. 48th St., New York 17, N. Y.

Flexible Shaft Motor Tools:

Foredom Electric Company, 27 Park Place, New York 7, N. Y.

The Dumore Company, Fourteenth and Racine St., Racine, Wis.

Hand Motor Tools:

The Chicago Wheel and Manufacturing Co., 1101 W. Monroe St., Chicago 7, Ill.

The Dremel Manufacturing Co., Racine, Wis.

Centrifugal Casting Equipment and Supplies:

Kerr Manufacturing Co., 6081 Twelfth Street, Detroit 8, Mich.

Torit Manufacturing Co., Walnut and Exchange Sts., Saint Paul 2, Minn.

Alexander Saunders & Co., 95 Bedford St., New York 14, N. Y.

Grieger's, 1633 E. Walnut St., Pasadena 4, Calif.

Gem-testing Instruments:

Bausch & Lomb Optical Co., 195 Bausch St., Rochester, N. Y.

Polarizing Instrument Co., Irvington-on-Hudson, N. Y.

Harry Ross, 68 W. Broadway, New York 7, N. Y.

Ultra-Violet Products, Inc., San Gabriel, Calif.

MAGAZINES DEVOTED TO
MINERALOGY AND
GEM CUTTING

The Lapidary Journal, Del Mar, Calif.
The Desert Magazine, Palm Desert, Calif.
Rocks and Minerals, Peekskill, N. Y.
The Mineralogist, Mentone, Calif.
Gems and Minerals, Mentone, Calif.

BOOKS OF INTEREST

Borin: "Jewelry Making," Forest Hills, L. I., N. Y., 1952.

Dake, Fleener, and Wilson: "Quartz Family Minerals," McGraw-Hill Book Company, Inc., New York, 1938.

Davidson: "Educational Metalcraft," Longmans, Green & Co., Inc., New York, 1932.

English: "Getting Acquainted with Minerals," McGraw-Hill Book Company, Inc., New York, 1934.

Howard: "Revised Lapidary Handbook," Greenville, S. C., 1946.

Kraus and Slawson: "Gems and Gem Materials," McGraw-Hill Book Company, Inc., New York, 1947.

Kronquist: "Art Metalwork," McGraw-Hill Book Company, Inc., New York, 1942.

Kronquist: "Metalcraft and Jewelry," Manual Arts Press, Peoria, Ill., 1926.

Linick: "Jewelers' Workshop Practices," Henry Paulson & Company, Chicago, Ill., 1948.

Pack: "Jewelry and Enameling," D. Van Nostrand Company, Inc., New York, 1941.

Payne: "Art Metalwork," Manual Arts Press, Peora, Ill., 1929.

Pough: "A Field Guide to Rocks and Minerals," Houghton Mifflin Company, Boston, 1954.

Rose: "Copper Work," Metal Crafts Publishing Co., Providence, R. I., 1931.

Rose and Cirino: "Jewelry Making and Design," The Davis Press., Worcester, Mass., 1946.

Sperisen: "The Art of the Lapidary," The Bruce Publishing Co., Milwaukee, Wis., 1950.

Whitlock: "The Story of the Gems," Lee Furman, Inc., Publisher, New York, 1936.

Whitlock and Ehrmann: "The Story of Jade," Sheridan House, New York, 1949.

Wiener: "Hand Made Jewelry," D. Van Nostrand Company, Inc., New York, 1948.

Willems: "Gem Cutting," The Manual Arts Press, Peoria, Ill., 1948.

Winebrenner: "Jewelry Making," International Textbook Company, Scranton, Pa., 1953.

INDEX